TAKING YOUR TENNIS

ON TOUR

The Business, Science, and Reality of
GOING PRO

Bonita L. Marks, PhD

Racquet Tech Publishing
Vista, California, USA

Racquet Tech Publishing
(An imprint of the USRSA)
330 Main Street
Vista, California 92084
760-536-1177
www.racquettech.com

Library of Congress Control Number: 2005938185

Cover and interior design by Kristine Thom

Printed in the United States of America

ISBN-13: 978-0-9722759-6-5
ISBN-10: 0-9722759-6-7

This book is dedicated to the men's tennis sub-culture, the fierce competitors who are rarely seen on television, battling their way out of the tennis dungeons with hopes of making it into the pro arena. These guys are the gladiators of the tennis world.

Table of Contents

Table of Contents

Table of Contents

Acknowledgements

There have been so many people without whom this book would not have been possible. If it weren't for two of my former students, Elizabeth Galleher and Tripp Phillips, this endeavor would not have been a thought, much less a book. To them I owe my gratitude for opening up to me this tennis odyssey. I am indebted to the more than 50 former and current players plus coaches who graciously participated in personal interviews, completed surveys, and underwent fitness evaluations. Some even became email pen pals. Among them, a special thanks goes to the following individuals for enduring my stream of questions: Thomas Blake, Dave Borelli, Jack Brasington, David Cheatwood, Scott Draper, Mardy Fish, Joan Jimenez-Guerra, Jose Hanza, Bobby Hession, Don Johnson, Ivo Karlovic, Cedric Kauffmann, Alex Kim, Ben Kronk, Peter Luczak, Nicolas Mahut, Eric Mauszewski, Mark Merklein, Huntley Montgomery, Frank Moser, Ogidi Obi, Tom Oliver, Donny Opici, Jon Pastel, Sam Paul, Andres Pedroso, Doug Root, Marc Schwartz, Marc Silva, Marcio Torres, Eric Taino, Matthew Rutherford, Brian Vahaly, Johnny Valenti, Louis Vosloo, Jack Waite, Rogier Wassen, and Glenn Weiner.

I must also thank the "anonymous" players who answered my queries but preferred to remain unsung heroes, as well as the college tennis teams (and their coaches) who tolerated my poking and prodding in the spirit of furthering tennis science. Mikiko Senga was invaluable with her valiant attempts to collect some of the pro's questionnaires. A heart-felt thanks is extended to Andrew Parker, the administrative assistant at the UNC Tennis Program, for his never-ending assistance as I plowed through this creative endeavor. Although I amused myself with my digital camera throughout the tournaments (and inadvertently annoyed a few persnickety players as well), some of the action shots contained in this book were obtained from the professional collection of Rocky Mount photographer, Harry G. Fish, III, and www.propix.com photographers Jeff and Manuela Davies.

Of course much of the research for this book would not have been possible without the cooperation from three major professional tennis organizations—the International Tennis Federation (ITF), the Association of Tennis Professionals (ATP), and the United States Tennis Association (USTA). I am indebted to the ITF for providing some of the funding which enabled me to conduct my studies. Appreciation is extended to the ATP governing board, especially Dr. Gary Windler and Paul Settles, for taking time out during their meetings at Wimbledon to approve my request to gather data at the Newport Miller Lite Hall of Fame Championship event. Without the assistance of Danielle Tin-Aung at the USTA, my journeys to Elkin, NC,

Acknowledgements

Futures and Rocky Mount, NC, Challenger events would not have materialized. Keith Crossland, the USTA tournament supervisor at both sites, was a fair, organized, no-nonsense type of guy who not only kept the players happy and in line, but also permitted me to interact freely with the players and refs. A warm thank you is also extended to the on-site tournament hosts, Jim Cornelius in Elkin and Albie Brice in Rocky Mount, who were very accommodating in facilitating player access and discussing what it takes to put on a tournament. A personal thanks must be extended to Wayne Howell, PT, ATC (the USTA trainer), for permitting me to warm myself in the players' lounge during those Rocky Mount spring rains and for the great tape job he did on my abused aging ankle. All of the refs were incredibly supportive, but I must single out one in particular—Gabe Pace, the ex-NASA engineer. He taught me that there's more to tennis than watching the bouncing ball—such as determining if Newton's Law of Gravity is defied in Blowing Rock, NC.

A special thanks goes to my editor Crawford Lindsey, copy-editor Greg Raven, and designer Kristine Thom for their patient editing and creativity. Without them, this book would have rivaled the *Lord of the Rings* trilogy in terms of number of pages.

My acknowledgements would not be complete without a word to the www.stevegtennis.com message board participants—Crazy Diamond, Ex-Satie, Fiona, Dave (the Canadian), Marcus, Seb, Euge, and Fredde, plus all the other chat board participants who posted the witty (and absurd) tidbits about competitive tennis life on and off the court. And a big hug goes to the guy named Hervé who, in much detail (but in French) told me where and when to buy my French Open tickets once in Paris at Roland Garros rather than prepurchasing over the net, saving me about three hundred bucks. Merci!

Last, but certainly not least, I must thank my husband, Larry Katz, for his unending support and patience during all of my tennis travels, trials, and tantrums.

"The Gladiator"

*"It is not the critic who counts; not the man who points out
how the strong man stumbles, or where the doer of deeds
could have done better. The credit belongs to the man who is
actually in the arena, whose face is marred by dust and
sweat and blood, who strives valiantly; who errs and comes
short again and again because there is no effort without
error and shortcomings; but who does actually strive to do
the deed; who knows the great enthusiasm, the great devo-
tion, who spends himself in worthy cause, who at the best
knows in the end the triumph of high achievement and who
at the worst, if he fails, at least he fails while daring greatly.
So that his place shall never be with those cold and timid
souls who know neither victory nor defeat."*

—Teddy Roosevelt, April 23, 1910

PART 1
The Road
to the Pros

"Getting ahead in a difficult profession requires avid faith in yourself, that is why some people with mediocre talent, but with great inner drive, go much further than people with vastly superior talent."
— Sophia Loren, Actor

1

Chapter 1
The College Route to the Pros

"Imagination is more important than knowledge."
—Albert Einstein, Mathematician

This book is not about the famous, or infamous, pros. This book is not about how to improve your tennis skills. This book is not even about how to improve your on-court strategies. This book is about the tennis pro subculture and whether you have the non-tennis weapons necessary to fight your way up the ATP ladder to join the recognized pros. Are you really prepared to turn your pro dream into a successful reality? The way you handle the business of being a tennis pro can make or break you, physically, mentally, and financially. This book will shed some light on the behind-the-scenes actions necessary to propel your tennis career into a successful business endeavor if you're not an Agassi, Sampras, McEnroe, or Roddick, with sponsors salivating after you. This book is for the 1,500 plus others who come and go, trying the college route in hopes to strengthen their game before turning pro. All too many are oblivious to the business aspects, which often wind up blind-siding them into tremendous debt. Scores of talented, hopeful college players have crashed and burned in the early stages of the pro circuit. But that's not to say it can't be done. It has been. But it takes time, patience, and lots of money.

After being unexpectedly drawn into tennis due to two exercise science students of mine, Elizabeth Galleher (in search of a research honors thesis project) and Tripp Phillips (willing to be a research subject), I found myself delving deeper and deeper into the trials and tribulations college players experience once they embark upon the pro tour. Much of the information I was seeking seemed to be passed on almost as if by tribal ritual via word of mouth, chat boards, and locker room discussions. Occasionally a website, tennis book, or tennis magazine article would

Tripp Phillips, Rocky Mount Challenger, NC, 2002.

pop up with tidbits of information. But the player still had to figure out how to pull it all together in the brief amount of time he had between college graduation and seriously competing on the pro circuit. Although this book is written from a male college tennis perspective, the information is equally valuable for the college female or junior player contemplating the pros as all will face similar challenges.

As with most pros, Tripp had been playing tennis since he was four years old. He finished seventh in the nation as a junior, and in college he maintained a consistent 70 to 80 percent win record. Tripp earned annual bids into the National Collegiate Athletic Association (NCAA) Division I Singles Championships each year he played, advancing as high as the quarterfinals. Tripp finished his collegiate career ranked 12th in the U.S. by the Intercollegiate Tennis Association (ITA), earning First-Team All-American honors. He received the Southern Regional John Van Nostrand Award in Tennis. His college major honored him by including him in its "21st Century Club Wall of Distinction"—a tribute to athletes who excel in their academic major, exercise and sport science. And finally, his alma mater, the University of North Carolina at Chapel Hill (UNC), awarded him the Patterson Medal, the highest honor the university could bestow upon an athlete for athleticism, sportsmanship, scholarship, and character.

But would this be enough to ensure success on the pro tour? Due to a shoulder injury, Tripp was red-shirted for a year, which delayed his graduation. So at the relatively old age of 23, he joined the USTA pro tennis circuit full time to compete against a gambit of players—younger collegians, others with no college but tons of talent, some with talent and money, and those who should have hung up their racquets several seasons ago.

Within a year, Tripp was well on his way to breaking into the top 500 in singles and top 250 in doubles. But it's well known that as one creeps up the ATP ladder, the points are harder to come by. Despite his early Satellite Tour successes, he was unable to win enough points to replace those that "fell off" as time went on. As Tripp approached his two-year mark, he was again battling in Futures competitions overseas in an attempt to reverse the downward slide of his ranking.

Tripp dropped back down to 639 in singles and 389 in doubles. As far as rankings go, it was as if time had stood still. True, he had doubled his earnings within two years, but he was far from actually making any money. His two-year earnings totaled only $12,000, he still bummed living arrangements off his friends, and his expenses were twice his income. As with most players at this level, financial backing was thin.

Over the course of 22 months, he played in over 90 matches across the globe, went to a tennis training camp in Spain, tried out numerous doubles partners, received guidance from several coaches, and suffered through a variety of aches and pains. Then the unthinkable happened. While Tripp was playing in a tournament in California, a close personal friend was killed in the 9/11 terrorist attacks on the World Trade Center in New York City. Tripp had to learn how to maintain an even keel focus, while striving to break into the major tournaments.

Tripp Phillips' story is by no means unique, nor is it typical. Others of Phillips' contemporaries had their own experiences with personal twists. But it in all cases one fact looms paramount—it takes money to survive and succeed on tour.

Brian Vahaly, one of Tripp's friends and graduate of the University of Virginia (UVA), was another very talented college player. He had left the USTA Junior Development Program to attend UVA. As Tripp was struggling, Vahaly was defying everyone's predictions about his pro potential. He moved up the ranks quickly, and after only eight months on the tour, broke into the top 250 in singles. Since joining the tour full time after graduating in 2001, Vahaly has earned over $585,000 and achieved career-high rankings of 64 in singles and 94 in doubles.

UVA alum Brian Vahaly playing on Center Court, Newport, RI, 2002.

And then there's the case of another UNC tennis player alum, Don Johnson. Don was an average college player with no collegiate distinctions or All-American honors, yet he won back-to-back Wimbledon championships: Mixed doubles with Kimberly Po in 2000 and gentlemen's doubles in 2001 with Jared Palmer (a Stanford graduate). Don reached the number one position in world doubles competition after 12 years on the tour, with over half of that time devoted exclusively to doubles. By age 34, he won over two million dollars in prize money and had been selected for the 2003 Davis Cup

Don Johnson shows off his 2001 Wimbledon Gentlemen's Doubles Trophy.

Jack Brasington, Rocky Mount Challenger, 2002.

Alex Kim, Rocky Mount Challenger, 2002.

Team. In 2006, Don was inducted into the North Carolina Tennis Hall of Fame and he is currently the assistant men's tennis coach at UNC.

There are other recent success stories for college graduates, such as Paul Goldstein (Stanford), Alex Kim (Stanford), and Jack Brasington (UT). Each achieved a measure of success on the pro tour after completing four years of college, attaining rankings in the top 200 in only two years. Alex and Jack have since retired, Alex into banking and Jack into college coaching.

Then there is the college dropout route—the most famous recent example being James Blake, who spent two years at Harvard before joining the pro tour at age 20. Blake, ranked as high as 8, has hit the big time, earning over $2.8 million since 1999. He joined the U.S. Davis Cup Team, has lucrative sponsorship deals, and has a modeling career of sorts.

Robert Kendrick (Pepperdine dropout) is no slouch either, although

James and Thomas Blake, Doubles Trouble. Newport Miller Lite Hall of Fame Championships, 2002.

Robert Kendrick lost in the first round at the Rocky Mount Challenger, NC, 2002.

Mardy Fish, Miller Lite International Tennis Championship, Newport, RI, 2002.

not nearly as successful as Blake. He has wavered back and forth in the 100-ranking range for singles (as high as 90 in doubles) and since 2000 has earned over $360,000.

In Blake's and Kendrick's cases, a little bit of college went a long way.

And what about the college "no-gos"—players such as Andy Roddick, Mardy Fish, Taylor Dent, and Robby Ginepri? These are players, along with Blake, who are touted as America's tennis future.

Taylor Dent prepares to serve at the Newport Miller Lite Hall of Fame Championship, 2002.

Robby Ginepri, Rocky Mount Challenger, NC, 2002.

It would appear that less is more when it comes to college attendance and pro success. But appearances can be deceiving, and it would behoove you not to rely too heavily on them when it comes to making that first big decision for most hopeful future stars—whether or not to go to college. The answer to this question is crucial, yet simple. The bottom line is this: If you have any hope at all in making it early in pro tennis, the chances are that the USTA has hand-picked you for its junior development and high performance programs and already tried to talk you out of college. If they haven't, then it's a no-brainer—go to college and get more preparation.

There is much to say for going to college versus hitting the tour circuit immediately after (or even during) high school. Playing college tennis, you get free coaching, ready-made practice partners, organized tournaments, sports-medicine professionals at your disposal, tennis clothing, shoes, and racquets. You'll have a chance to grow up, perfect you game, and gain confidence in yourself. According to head coach Sam Paul at the University of North Carolina at Chapel Hill, "Playing college tennis gives the player a chance

UNC Men's Tennis Coach, Sam Paul.

to improve his game, learn a few new things, and mature, all at the college's expense, not his own. Once he's out on the pro tour, there are too many other things he has to deal with." Furthermore, say the advocates for the college route, graduates will have a degree on which to fall back if professional tennis doesn't pan out as expected—an education is never wasted.

Of course, there are intangibles, too. Duke singles star, Andres Pedroso (USA) said, "College made me more mature mentally on and off the court. I learned how to bounce back from losses." This valuable lesson may be easier to learn when the stakes aren't so high.

Another ex-"Dookie," Marko Cerenko (USA/Croatia) said: "College matured me and gave me a sense of organization and

Newly graduated Andres Pedroso winning the Elkin Futures Singles title in 2002.

a sense of team play. I was able to play a lot of matches, something that might not happen on the tour if you lose early in the qualifying and then you have to wait the whole week to play another competitive match." Marko lasted about a year on the pro tennis circuit, so he is probably thanking his lucky stars he did finish college.

Similarly, Duke singles standout Doug Root (USA) advises, "Go to college, because it is extremely tough out here. At the very least, have a back-up plan. There are no guarantees you will make it." After touring professionally for two years following college graduation, Root accepted a job at Prince Sports.

Bobby Hession (USA), who toured from 1991–94, said this about his college tennis days: "It provided discipline and the ability to play at a competitive level...it also gave me confidence to try the circuit out, realizing I had a degree to fall back on."

Jack Brasington (USA) offered this bit of wisdom he learned from his college years: "College made me a more rounded person. I learned how to handle adversity better and understand team aspects and

Doug Root delivers one of his last USTA Pro-Circuit serves at Rocky Mount, 2002.

its importance in life. Socializing and communication skills are important."

Peter Luczak (AUS), who didn't finish college due to running out of tennis eligibility, advised: "If you are not one of the top juniors, you should definitely go to college first to work on your game a while."

Mark Merklein (BAH), who has been competing since 1994, stated, "College made me into a real person.

Peter Luczak (AUS) at the Rocky Mount, NC Challenger, 2002.

Mark Merklein competing at the Rocky Mount Challenger, NC, 2002.

I wasn't just an athlete when I decided to play pro tennis!" Mark still has hopes of completing his college education someday—in elementary education.

On the other hand, Eric Taino (USA) did not have a favorable opinion of college. He dropped out of college to pursue the professional life: "I left college to play professional tennis as I felt it was holding me back." While not as successful as James Blake, Taino has earned a respectable tennis ranking, and has played in well over 20 ATP pro events, making the main draw numerous times.

Eric Taino battling it out at the Rocky Mount Challenger, 2002.

Finally, Rogier Wassen (NED), who did not go to college, had these words of advice: "Finish school first!"

Surviving College

"Consider the postage stamp…it secures success through its ability to stick to one thing till it gets there."

— Josh Billings, Author, Humorist

If you go to college first, if you are good, you won't lose much—on the contrary, you may have much more to gain. Just remember, when you venture onto the pro circuits between semester breaks to gain some experience, NCAA rules are that you can't take the prize money, or else you will forfeit your amateur status, lose your athletic scholarship, and be dropped from your college team. You also can't accept "gifts" of any kind. To be safe, make sure you discuss your circuit plans and opportunities with your college coach and the school's NCAA compliance officer.

Taking the college route won't be easy, though. You have to find some way to pay for your four years (or get a scholarship), select a major (hopefully one that will do you some good in the future), do well academically, and still have the time and energy to play tennis.

The key to achieving all this as a student athlete is to develop a good relationship with your academic advisor. Sometimes he will be good, sometimes not. You will find this out quickly enough if he screws up your academic schedule. The first time your advisor messes up, you can be forgiving, and maybe it was an honest mistake. The second time he messes up you need to take action. If you stick with him and he screws up a third time, you may be screwed out of graduating "on time"—so try not to let that third time happen.

Your coach may not be of much help either. He has other players to worry about, future players to recruit, and a conference to win, all while dealing with the university administration. But, it doesn't hurt to ask, as he may know other members of the faculty who happen to be tennis enthusiasts. Also, check your university's website for a listing of faculty names and contact numbers. Make it a point to meet faculty who teach courses of interest to you. Get to know them. Let them know what you want to do, what you want to learn. Simply be yourself and state your interests. If you put forth a reasonable effort in class and demonstrate interest, the instructor will most likely take an interest in you.

It's also important to try your best. You may not earn an A, nor even a B, but do try. Your instructor will usually be sympathetic if he feels you tried your best. You don't want to get into a situation where the instructor does not care about you because he knows you have the ability and feels you are just being lazy. If you have the time, volunteer to attend a special lecture or an event relevant to the course material. Make sure your instructor knows about the extra effort you've extended.

If you see one of your instructors outside the classroom, say hello. You don't need to engage him in a deep conversation, but a sincere greeting is usually appreciated, and the extra little effort you make may serve you well later. Use your time in college to work on your socialization skills. That includes interacting with authority figures. When you get onto the pro circuit, you will have plenty of opportunities to interact with authority figures from the USTA, ATP, and ITF in the form of referees, tournament organizers, and the like. Think of it as practice for that time when you really want a wild card. Your success in getting one may depend on whom you know and who knows you. Social lessons learned in school will serve you well with the tennis politics.

You will have lots of options available for peer socializing, but don't forget your tennis team can become your social network. Socializing mostly with your teammates will keep you focused and bonded, although it may be somewhat limiting. If you choose to join a fraternity, make sure it is one that will respect your need to be absent from functions due to training and academic responsibilities. And definitely, avoid the "animal house" fraternity, no matter how much you liked the movie.

Whatever you do, don't blow off classes routinely. Even in large classes professors notice empty seats. Things do come up, but not every Friday. I don't care if your class is 8:00 a.m. on Friday morning and you were up until 3:00 a.m. broadening your social horizons the night before. Brush your teeth, splash some water on your face, grab your class materials and get to class—on time. You can gulp some orange juice on the way to give yourself a sugar rush to help get you through class.

Even if you're not totally "with it" during class, you need to tap into presence power. Getting there is half the battle. Something as easy as being in attendance may make or break your grade. You may zone out now and again once you're there, but it is important to be physically present—as long as you don't appear to be sleeping, or worse yet, snoring, in the back of the room. Your instructors were once college students, and most will understand, up to a point. But their job is to educate you, and your job is to learn. Attendance is expected.

Now if you are really exhausted because you had a particularly grueling match the night before, were studying for an exam in another course, or you were sick, communicate this to your instructor. Depending upon the circumstances, an instructor may be sympathetic and helpful.

But don't be totally naïve. There are a few professors out there who simply hate athletes and fraternities. Interacting with those curmudgeons will take a great deal of finesse. Find out who they are and put your best foot forward. Be prepared to prove that you're not just another "dumb jock." Like it or not, this is simply the reality for many student-athletes.

Last but certainly not least, study and keep up with your coursework. If you find yourself falling behind or bewildered, contact your instructor(s) immediately. If he has a teaching assistant, contact him. If there are study groups, join one; if not, create one. Inform your instructors in advance of your travel schedule, especially if missing classes will impact your grade or cause you to miss required items, like homework assignments, labs, or exams. You are ensuring yourself a future when your tennis career ends, whether that happens as soon as you graduate or after you win a few grand slams.

After four years of the college scene and traveling with your team, traveling the world by yourself should be much more manageable. You should have acquired enough discipline to keep yourself focused on your ultimate goal—to win as many matches as possible so you can get out of the Futures quickly and move up into the Challengers and beyond.

Does An Outstanding College Tennis Career Predict Your Pro Future?

But even if you do take the college route, and even if you are wildly successful in your collegiate tennis career, there is still no guarantee that your pro career will be equally successful. This is evidenced by looking at the lack luster accomplishments of some former collegiate standouts.

At the end of each college season the ITA names the "player to watch" for future success. This list has included Sam Warburg (Stanford, 2004), Bobby Reynolds (Vanderbilt, 2003), Romain Ambert (Mississippi State,

2002), Shaun Madden (Texas A&M, 2000), and Jeff Morrison (University of Florida, 1999). It's nothing more than an educated guess and does not predict a college graduation. From this list, you can see that the big winning prediction was for Jeff Morrison, who achieved top 100 rankings in both singles and doubles by 2004. He has made over $500,000 since dropping out of college and turning pro in 2000. On the other hand, both Ambert and Madden have disappeared from the ATP scene after rather short performances on the pro circuit.

Another measure of an outstanding college career is being awarded the national Van Nostrand Award. This coveted award (approximately $2200) not only acknowledges one's college tennis accomplishments but also helps ease the financial strain when first starting out on the pro tour. The winners do not necessarily graduate college, and they may not even have been on the ITA's "player to watch list." Review the winner's roster of the past five years and draw your own conclusions (Table 1.1).

2004 Van Nostrand Award winnier Nick Monroe with UNC Assistant Coach Don Johnson.

Table 1.1
National Van Nostrand Award Winners, 2000-2004

Recipient	Career-High ATP Rankings, S/D	ATP Earnings (Through 2005)
Nick Monroe (UNC, 2004)	477 / 251	$ 21,819
John Paul Futerro (California, 2003)	183 / 405	$ 66,817
Peter Handoyo, (Tennessee, 2002)	520 / 351	$ 15,420
Peter Luczak (Fresno State, 2001)	110 / 129	$ 380,330
Ryan Sachire (Notre Dame, 2000)	391 / 184	$ 49,284

S = Singles; D = Doubles

Life after College and Tennis

Fast-forward a couple of years to when you decide to retire from the pro tennis circuit. You'll have options based on the degree you earned, but with your tennis talents, you may want to pursue a tennis-related career, such as coaching. The base salary for an assistant college tennis coach is often 20 to 30 grand, before taxes. If you become a head coach with a couple years of assistant coaching under your belt, expect about 55 grand, give or take a couple thousand, depending upon winning seasons and, of course, location. Some tennis programs, as with other nonrevenue sports, have better endowments than others. Depending on the division, it's not likely that you will get a job as a college coach without a degree. You need to have that college experience, and some success on the pro tour wouldn't hurt.

You can supplement your income by working at camps, holding private lessons, and signing endorsement deals. Having paid for tennis lessons for years, you are already familiar with what tennis lessons cost. Don't forget that if you are being paid as a subcontractor for giving lessons, you probably won't get to keep the total amount that each student pays. A percentage of your fee is often required by the tennis facility out of which you operate.

An increasing number of touring players are coaching other touring players, and most of the female players have male coaches. As a traveling coach, you can get a base salary, per diem, a percentage of the purse (if any), and, if you're good enough, a share of product endorsements.

In any teaching or coaching position, you need to have good communication skills. In an interview with *Tennis Week,* Tommy Haas' coach David "Red" Ayme said, "Not to take anything away from a former player coaching on the tour, but the fact of the matter is that coaching remains communication. That's the key to coaching, I'm not sure you have to have been a player to communicate Xs and Os better."

PART 2
The Science of Going Pro

"If you train hard, you'll not only be hard, you'll be hard to beat."

—Herschel Walker, Football Player

These next three chapters on physical, nutritional, and mental toughness are not meant to be comprehensive guides for "how to train for success in tennis." With the library, bookstores, and on-line sources, there are literally hundreds of training books out there each proclaiming to have "the" answer on how to improve your game. The USTA has published its own very good player development series. Several well-known tennis camps have similar materials. And of course, every tennis magazine has regular features on these topics. The intent of this section is to serve as a primer of sorts, to start you off on the right foot by providing you with accurate information from sports science research and pointing you in the right direction so you can continue your self-education. Be sure to check out the references listed for each chapter at the end of the book, so you can get more information on the topics touched upon in this section.

Chapter 2
Physical Toughness

Sports Success: Born or Bred?

"I owe a lot to my parents, especially my mother and father."

—Greg Norman, Golfer

E ach of us brings to the tennis court the natural skills we inherited from our parents. What you do with their personal gifts is up to you— you can train to improve upon on your natural gifts or you can try to develop new skills. What you become depends on your willingness to push yourself, the ability of your body to handle the physical stress of training, and the limit of your financial resources. Take for instance Ramsey Smith, one of Duke's star athletes. Many had assumed that as the son of tennis legend Stan Smith, Ramsey would excel in the pros. However, he exited quickly from the pro circuit due to injuries and is now an assistant coach for Duke's Men's tennis team.

Research has shown that your genes have a huge effect on your height, arm length, muscle size and strength, joint flexibility, heart and lung size, resting heart rate, and aerobic fitness. Moderately influenced by your genetics are factors such as blood pressure, lung function, your speed of movement, and your explosive power ability. Your genes will have a small to moderate effect on your ability to utilize enzymes necessary for energy production, reaction time, waist circumference, weight, and agility. Your DNA will only exert a small effect on your balance ability and the number of aerobic cells (mitochondria) you have.

While all of these factors are generally important for various types of sports participation, tennis researchers agree that the characteristics of your aerobic and anaerobic energy systems are critical for excellence in tennis.

Anaerobic energy is the ability to generate power quickly so that you can move like Hewitt or serve like Roddick. However, you need aerobic energy, or stamina, to stay on court for three-plus hours of tennis in the heat of day. You are not doomed if you were not born with the "right stuff." You can compensate to some degree by training appropriately and not sabotaging yourself with destructive behaviors. For instance, if you were born slim with some athleticism but do nothing all day except play video games and eat Cheetos, you will probably not realize your potential athletic ability. Conversely, if you inherited the so-called "fat gene," you will most likely

Ivo Karlovic with practice partner, Rocky Mount, NC, 2002.

always be fighting to keep that gene "turned off." Obesity is not only caused by a genetic predisposition, but it is also caused by succumbing to the environmental cues of "supersizing" everything you eat.

On the other hand, short of trying to stretch yourself on a hanging rack or wearing platform shoes, you have no control over how tall you will be. If you are short, you will have to develop some effective tennis weapons to overcome your height disadvantage when you find yourself facing an opponent such as Ivo Karlovic, the 6-foot 10-inch Croatian.

Being a great athlete is not just reserved for the genetically endowed, it can be created with a good training ethic. Put these two factors together, a good training ethic and sensitivity to your environment, even without special genes, can spell "athletic success." It's the "Cinderella story" in the sports world. You need to train your body in such a way that you will be able to optimize your tactics and techniques. This is where a good coach is needed. He can devise training programs to optimize your natural endowments, help to refine your skills, and be an external source of motivation to help keep you fired up. But if you don't have and can't afford a personal coach, you will have to learn how to do many of these things for yourself. Either way, to become a successful tennis player, you will need to be motivated and disciplined in your training and controlled in your competition.

Conditioning: You Really Must "Just Do It"

"The will to win is important, but the will to prepare is vital."
— Joe Paterno, Football Coach

There are lots of training programs available, including some endorsed by star athletes. No one program fits all, which is why a personal trainer can be so important.

How to Hire a Personal Trainer

Having a personal trainer is ideal, but you will need to pay $35 to $60 per session for this service. If you have the money, hire a trainer who minimally has an undergraduate college degree in exercise science. Remember that not everyone who calls himself a personal trainer is actually a training expert. An exercise science degree at least tells you that the trainer sat through human physiology, anatomy, exercise physiology and biomechanics courses. It doesn't tell you if he actually learned or passed anything.

For that extra bit of assurance, look for one of these three certifying credentials after their name: NASM-PES, NSCA-CSCS, or ACSM-HFI. NASM stands for the National Academy of Sports Medicine; the PES represents their best certification, Performance Enhancement Specialist. NSCA stands for the National Strength and Conditioning Association; the CSCS represents their top of the line certification, the Certified Strength and Conditioning Specialist. ACSM stands for the American College of Sports Medicine; the HFI represents Health Fitness Instructor certification, which is one of their starter certifications. Each requires a bachelor's degree in the exercise/allied-health sciences. These certifications guarantee that the trainer has at least an average working knowledge of the exercise science behind the training experience.

Personal trainers who really know and have experience with athletes will have NASM or NSCA certifications. These are heavily sports-oriented certifications, whereas the ACSM certifications are more general in nature and apply to a range of clients. However, ACSM certifications above the HFI level (CES, Certified Exercise Specialist, or RCEP, Registered Clinical Exercise Physiologist) are the only fitness certifications that require proof of experience in the field. These latter two certifications are more intensive in their science and clinical background, and while professionals with these certifications theoretically can train anybody, they tend to gravitate toward populations found in wellness centers. However, it is entirely possible that they have had experience with athletes as well. The ACSM-CES certification has been around the longest, since the late 1970s, when there were no other choices for certification to prove they had what it takes to train people, so some "older" professionals will just have that certification. Each of these certifications also enables the trainer to test your physical performance with simple field tests or with more elaborate processes that require more expensive equipment and time.

Be wary of an obviously self-proclaimed and self-educated fitness guru without appropriate credentials. Be cautious with any trainer who only has the initials CPT (certified personal trainer) after his name, especially if he has no college degree in exercise science. Fitness organizations sell the CPT certification under the guise of "tightening up the industry standards," but for many the real goal is simply to sell as many fitness-training certifications as possible. In order to do this, the criteria tend to be loose. Hence, the only requirements for a CPT are being 18 years of age, having the bucks to pay for the certification (about $200), and taking some type of written exam. Every certifying organization sells exam prep courses and has a list of materials the wannabe trainer can purchase. No real hands-on training experience is required. No previous internship-type training is needed to make sure that the CPT actually knows how to put into practice the book knowledge—although the ACSM tries to qualify its CPTs by saying that once certified, they are only able to practice under the supervision of a higher-level certified person. To be a CPT, one only need have a GED (general education diploma). Having a trainer with only a CPT without a college degree in exercise science or the allied health field, and potentially without actual sports training experience, puts you in a very precarious situation—you are being trained by someone who might have just enough knowledge to be dangerous. In fact, you could probably pass the same exam after reading a couple of the conditioning books listed at the end of this chapter. Then you, too, could earn a couple extra bucks on the side as a CPT.

Once you sign up with a personal trainer, pay very close attention, as you may be able to afford only a few sessions, and you will need a lifetime of training.

You might be required to join a club to work with a trainer, so strike a good deal. Most health clubs are like car dealerships: There are always deals that can be struck. Fitness facilities may even be willing to work out a deal with you to use their equipment/trainer in return for marketing purposes. Club members like to think they train where the pros train. If you have friends who are members of a club, see if they will let you use guest passes and trial offers which will get you in for free.

When you do plunk down your money, be certain that you get a receipt. Verify that the trainer charged you the amount promised for a certain number of sessions. If you change your mind about the deal (or the club membership) before you embark upon your first session, you have 72 hours to cancel and get all of your money back. Never enter into a contract on a Friday—you won't have enough time to cancel before your 72-hour grace period is up. Weekends are busy for everyone and are often the hardest time to find any management-type person in a club who can actually cancel your contract. And your new trainer may be unreachable on weekends, after all, he has a life too.

Paying by a charge card is the safest, easiest, quickest way to cancel this transaction. Don't ever pay in advance by cash or check. Cash is the hardest to get back, and stopping a check will cost you money. Canceling a charge transaction is as quick as calling your credit-card company. Plus, you will get a written statement in the mail, so you won't have to worry if you lose the receipt. This can be a tax write-off as a work-related expense.

Be certain to read the contract carefully. If it says no refunds for any reason whatsoever, find another trainer. If it says that you must have your training sessions within a certain period of time or forfeit your money, be 99.9 percent certain you will actually be in town to get your money's worth. Naturally, you can't foresee problems that might negate your ability to train (such as an injury), therefore you need to discuss this with your trainer before signing. He may be able to write in a few exceptions, within reason. Write down whatever alternate agreements your trainer agrees to. There is also usually a statement about missing appointments or being late. If you blow off an appointment, you'll be charged anyway. If you are late, you will still have your session, but only for whatever time is remaining. So instead of an hour at $50, you get a half-hour for $50. Not bad for the trainer, but very bad for you.

Make certain the trainer checks your medical history to take into account any health risks you might have. You don't want the training to aggravate an existing medical condition. Then your trainer should do a battery of pretests in order to design a training plan based upon your test results and stated goals. All of this is confidential information by law, so you should be asked to sign some type of printed form advising you of your rights and assuring you that all information collected about you will not be made available to anyone else without your written consent. If the trainer doesn't take the time to evaluate you, get your money back and walk away. He is only going to give you a cookie-cutter workout plan, which you can do far cheaper by following a good training book. You are hiring him for individualized attention to your specific needs as well as for motivation. Finally, get a copy of your test results and training records before your last paid-up session. You've paid for it, and you deserve a copy for your own records. Make certain you understand the tests, the results, and how he has been devising your training so that each workout is beneficial. You'll need this information if your money runs out or for when you are out on the road training yourself.

Your Energy Systems

If you hire a trainer, he should know the basic exercise science of your energy systems. You should be familiar with this too so that you can better communicate with your trainer. It will also help you evaluate your trainer's competence. This information will help you design a better training program for yourself. As a consumer of exercise, you don't need to be a biochemist or know all the details in order to develop a program that works for you. You just need to have some understanding of a few basic principles and, more importantly, know which types of training to use for your specific conditioning needs.

First, let's better define the aerobic and anaerobic energy generating systems. The difference between the two depends on whether or not oxygen is needed or used to create energy (ATP, adenosine triphosphate). The classic definitions are *aerobic,* meaning "with oxygen," and *anaerobic,* meaning "without oxygen." Given that tennis is a sport that relies heavily on anaerobic metabolism (those short, all-out bursts of rallies, serving, sprinting, jumping), while also requiring a foundation of aerobic conditioning in order for you to sustain 3 to 5 hours of match play, these terms must be well understood.

When you sprint full speed up to the net from the baseline, you are using anaerobic energy, but you aren't really running without oxygen. However, it takes time for the oxygen you breathe in to be transported throughout your bloodstream for use by your cells. Your body is able to get immediate energy for this brief period of time without that oxygen. Hence, the term anaerobic really means that your cells can create energy immediately without the need of oxygen being directly involved.

Immediate Energy System

Anaerobic work occurs in relatively brief spurts when your oxygen supply cannot meet your energy demands. This always happens at the beginning of any exercise and can persist up to four or five minutes. That's why you feel sluggish or even lousy when you first start to workout. The more aerobically trained or fit you are, the less time you spend in this somewhat uncomfortable anaerobic stage. An aerobically fit person only endures about two minutes of anaerobic start-up time because oxygen is delivered to and used by his cells faster. During the first 10 to 30 seconds of playing tennis or working out, you are tapping into stored energy in your cells known as phosphocreatine (also known as creatine phosphate or PCr). This anaerobic stage is called the ATP-PCr stage (or the "immediate" energy system). This stage occurs so quickly that the body doesn't even produce lactic acid. Everybody goes through this initial start-up stage. Some activities, such as short distance sprinting or performing a long jump don't go beyond this stage. The plyometric drills you practice, such as jumping, hopping, and skipping, concentrate on training this energy system. PCr contributes most heavily to energy production during the first ten seconds of exercise, then slowly diminishes. Your body makes this substance naturally, but anaerobically trained athletes have about 60 percent more PCr and 35 percent more muscle creatine than the anaerobically untrained. This is why it is important to devote some of your training time to anaerobic drills. Still, trained or not, you have a very limited supply of PCr in your muscles. You can boost your muscle creatine stores with supplementation—the pros and cons of that will be discussed later.

Short-Term Energy System

As your PCr supply dwindles, another anaerobic process known as glycolysis starts to kick in. For this short-term energy system, enzymes break down glucose (blood sugar). Your body relies on this process to create energy for the next one to two minutes. Glucose comes from carbohydrates—veggies, cereals, fruits, and even beverages. This is the only nutrient that can be converted to use for energy during anaerobic work. Fat and protein require oxygen (and a lot of time) in order to release energy, carbohydrates do not. At this point, you have two anaerobic processes running at the same time, with glycolysis becoming the dominant energy provider and the ATP-PCr system gradually fading. This is also when lactic acid starts to form. If you continue at a near all-out pace, you will build up lactic acid in your blood stream and fatigue will set in. But, if you pace yourself correctly and don't put out too much too soon, your lactic acid production will be minimal and you will cross over into the more comfortable aerobic stage.

Long-Term Energy System

Over the next two minutes, the anaerobic demand for energy gradually diminishes. You attain a nice comfortable training or hitting pace as you transition into aerobic metabolism (the long-term energy system). Oxygen has not only been transported through your body but can actually now be used. This is called steady state, when you are not short of breath. You have enough oxygen meeting your cell's energy needs. If you are jogging, this is when you can jog and chat with your running partner without difficulty. If you are playing tennis, this is when you are hitting at an easy to moderate pace, perhaps even carrying on some banter with your coach or hitting partner. You can easily stay in this zone for 20 minutes or more if you are aerobically trained. Aerobic training gives you twice as many mitochondria than when you are untrained. The increase in mitochondrial number is important because that's where all the aerobic action takes place.

For any activity to be classified as aerobic, it must meet the following conditions: (1) the activity must be sustained for at least 15 continuous minutes, (2) the activity must be rhythmic and repetitive in nature, and (3) the activity must utilize about two-thirds or more of your total body muscle mass. These activities include running, cycling, swimming, and tennis. Meeting these three conditions ensures that the body has enough time to provide oxygen as the main source of energy to your working muscles.

Exercising aerobically does not mean that anaerobic energy sources (i.e., PCr and glucose) are not being used. It just means that for aerobic work, your body won't need to tap into your anaerobic energy stores much. You will be able to use your fat stores for energy, and fats provide lots of energy. But it takes about 15 minutes from the start of your exercise for the fat-burning energy process to get into full swing because fats must go through a lot of pre-processing. As long as you keep your match or practice at a steady-state intensity, most of your energy will continue to come from your fat stores. This level of intensity is also called your "fat burning zone" for weight loss.

At this point, protein still isn't really a factor for providing energy. It, too, takes a lot of preprocessing effort and isn't a great energy-giver. What it is good for is assisting with regulating your sugar stores, helping you to hold some back for later when you are in desperate need for extra energy. So early on in your match or practice, nibble on a protein energy bar in order to realize its energy benefit later on.

During all of this, your anaerobic system is quietly humming along in the background, providing just enough energy to get the food you consumed ready to supply your energy aerobically. It is almost in standby mode, ready to kick in when you have to make a mad dash for a shot. At that demanding moment, your body instantly switches from aerobic to anaerobic energy production. You then revert back to the aerobic state, and so it goes, until you are in the fifth set and your body is struggling. At this point you go back to relying heavily on your anaerobic energy stores to complete the match from carbohydrates.

This time, however, the carbohydrates are coming not only from the glucose circulating in your bloodstream from whatever you have been consuming during your rest periods (such as a banana or sports drink), but your body is also tapping into your muscle carbohydrate storage reserves, called glycogen. These are any carbohydrates you consumed hours before your match, which were then packed away into your muscle cells, waiting to be called into action when you desperately need them. These are also the carbohydrates that your protein-laced energy bar hopefully helped to conserve. You might even be calling a little bit of that protein into action, but like fats, protein won't be your primary energy source as it just takes too long to process to be of much good in an instant-need situation.

When you are trained anaerobically, you have the advantage of a boosted glycogen storage capacity (as much as 40 percent). You may even tolerate more lactic acid than the untrained person. The player who can better call up his energy reserve power and manage this near-energy-depleted state will ultimately win, assuming skill and experience levels are equal. As you can see, nutrition plays a huge role in your ability to train and play well, but so does how you train your energy systems.

Training Specificity
Dynamic Warm-up and Cool-down

Let's turn our attention to specific training techniques for your energy systems. Every training session, whether it is for aerobic or anaerobic training, must begin with a brief 10 to 30 minute dynamic warm-up period. Your warm-up should be designed to get your muscles warm, blood flowing, and joints lubricated. The warm-up should ready you for a heavier workout (the stimulus conditioning phase) and it should be specific to the muscles you plan to use.

The current recommendation is to not go beyond basic static stretches during the warm-up. A few light stretches are okay, but save the intense stretching for cool-downs and off-court flexibility maintenance routines. This avoids injuries to cold muscles and prevents tiring out the neural circuits in your muscles before you even begin your match. Research is showing that 30 minutes of static stretching (those slow, holding stretches) before competition actually fatigue the muscles cells and reduce explosive power for about an hour. Even if you don't feel tired, your muscle circuitry may in fact have become fatigued.

I recommend slow dynamic stretching as part of your cool-down, as well as a couple of times a week if you tend to have tightness in your range of motion for any joint area. Research has shown that stretching for 30 minutes twice a week can improve your flexibility in about a month. Note though, that I am not recommending ballistic (bouncing) stretches, as these do tend to overstress your muscles and tendons too quickly, resulting in decreased strength performance as well as an increased probability of acute injury. Research has also shown that light pre-match stretching during warm-up will not hurt the power or precision of your strokes, specifically your serve (where you typically try to develop the most power). So if light, slow static stretching makes you feel a bit better, go for it—just do it *after* you've hit a bit during your warm-up so that your joints are lubricated and your stretching won't accidentally cause an injury. Only stretch like this for about five minutes.

One final comment about stretching: The impression that stretching during warm-up reduces muscle injury is wrong. There have been several scientific studies refuting the belief that warm-up stretching reduces the risk of injury during play. Stretching is good to help maintain or increase slightly your flexibility, which is genetically determined. It may even feel good to help relieve muscle soreness momentarily following an unusually hard workout (as will a sports massage) rather than resorting to pain relievers. However, your muscles will heal on their own in a couple of days from a hard off-court training session, with or without stretching, massages, or pain pills.

Easy plyometric hopping demo by personal trainer, Stacy, at Bollittieri's Training Camp.

This is what a training buddy is all about.

Dynamic warm-ups do not include bouncing. Bouncing your way through the initial phases of your warm-up can cause injuries by tearing cold muscles and ligaments. Before tennis practice and matches, you should team up with a partner and hit for a bit, practice your serves, volleys, and overheads, then incorporate some light plyometric drills such as hopping, skipping, and jumping. Conclude with only a few briefly held (5- to 10-second) static stretches if you really feel the need. A proper warm-up also prepares your brain for action, and gets you focused.

For off-court aerobic conditioning (e.g., running), start out fairly light and then build up to the pace you want to maintain. If you are going to run at 6 mph, start off by walking at about 3-4 mph for a couple of minutes, increase to a 5 mph jog for a couple of minutes, and then settle in at your 6 mph pace. If you don't know how fast you walk, jog, or run, test yourself on a treadmill to get the feel for each of these speeds. You'll be able to replicate it outdoors.

A dynamic warm-up is not only for aerobic conditioning. It also applies to weight lifting. If you are going to be lifting, you can do a dynamic range of motion warm-up (DROM) on the cycle ergometer and rowing machines with no or low resistance.

You must also spend 5 to 10 minutes cooling down your muscles after you've finished running or playing tennis. This helps your body return to a less stressed-out state, gets your breathing back to normal, lowers your body temperature, and gets some of the exercise-induced metabolic by-products (such as lactic acid) out of your blood stream a little bit faster. This is also the part of the workout that is most likely to be skipped, especially if you are pressed for time. But be forewarned, without cooling down, you will not recover from your match or workout as quickly. Instead of feeling recovered in about 30 minutes, it may take well over an hour.

Lactic acid is a metabolic by-product produced inside the muscles during the anaerobic component of your training. When it builds up in your bloodstream, it causes fatigue by reducing energy production. The resultant lowered blood ph level even stimulates pain receptors in your brain. You'll feel lousy and want to stop playing (or exercising). Lactic acid is removed from your system within an hour after stopping exercise. A lower intensity cool-down removes lactic acid much faster and even recycles it into useable energy. A low-intensity cool down is one in which your intensity is about 25 percent of what you are able to do maximally. This will not develop more lactic acid. A more intense cool-down will be counterproductive, so make sure the intensity of your cool down is sufficiently low.

If you work out harder than your body can handle, it will take you longer to feel recovered—you could feel overly tired for up to three hours afterward and possibly have some stiff muscles for the next few days as well. At this point, you are not feeling the effects of lactic acid build-up; you are experiencing delayed onset muscle soreness (DOMS). DOMS is the pain you feel 24-48 hours after an excessively hard workout. It is reflecting your body's natural inflammatory healing process due to repairing the microtears in your muscle tissue.

Therefore, besides including proper warm-up and cool-down techniques, you want to avoid overtraining. Overload your muscles just enough to stimulate the adaptive response to get stronger, but not so much so that after practice all you can manage is a vegetative state in front of the TV. A good sports medicine or exercise physiology book will give you more of the biochemistry behind this, if you are interested.

If you do over-exert yourself to the point where you get DOMS, a massage or warm bath/Jacuzzi might make you feel better

This easy-to-pack 18-inch plastic wand is rolled over your muscles for a massage-like effect.

temporarily, and an ibuprofen-type product (NSAIDS, non-steroidal anti-inflammatories) can help reduce the symptoms. But in general, DOMS will resolve on its own within two to three days, so just be patient. There has been some research to suggest that huge doses of Vitamin C (ascorbic acid) might prevent DOMS from occurring if you take it for at least three weeks prior to anticipating overtraining, but the side effect is stomach pain from too much acid. It's better to prevent DOMS by not overtraining. Overtraining on a regular basis can also result in other problems such as colds, depression, injuries, and poorer performance. By the way, training until you throw up is just stupid. Train smart.

Aerobic Power Conditioning

Aerobic power conditioning is a training plan designed to improve the efficiency of oxygen transport and utilization in your body. Think of oxygen as your number one "free" fuel. It is your energy source and you need lots of it to stay competitive during a long match. Your body has to be able to get the oxygen to your cells via your bloodstream, and your cells must also allow the oxygen to enter and be utilized. The purpose of aerobic training is to perfect this oxygen delivery and use system. When aerobically adapted, or trained, you will prevent (or at least delay) fatigue.

The training goal is for the first few aerobic sessions to feel difficult but not impossible or overly draining. For the next few sessions, the routines won't feel as difficult, and eventually your sessions should feel a bit easy (but not too easy). This adaptation should take one to two weeks if you are running three days a week. If you are doing more, you will improve quicker. When your aerobic training begins to feel easy, crank up the intensity by 5 to 10 percent. If you were really deconditioned, only increase your intensity by two percent.

Your heart rate training zone. To increase the intensity of your workouts, increase one of the following factors during the training session: your duration (either time or distance covered), your speed, your program level (if you use indoor equipment with different computerized programs), or the number of drills you do (agility drills or cardio tennis).

The easiest way to check intensity is by monitoring your heart rate. For aerobic training, you want your heart rate to be in a range that will strengthen your heart. That is called your heart rate training zone, and it is generally 70 to 85 percent of your maximum heart rate. For de-conditioned people, that range can start as low as 55 percent—but you are a young healthy athlete, presumably in fairly good shape. You can estimate your maximum heart rate by subtracting your age from 220. This isn't exact, but it gets you into the ballpark. For a precise measurement, you need to undergo a max fitness test. A university exercise science lab is probably your best bet for getting this test done inexpensively.

To ensure that you are training in your heart rate zone, monitor your heart rate response periodically by taking your pulse. Find your radial pulse on the underside of your wrist (palm up, same side as your thumb). Use your other hand's index and middle fingers and lightly press on the artery there. You should feel a pulsation.

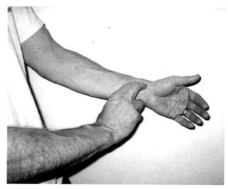

Taking a radial pulse rate.

Count those pulses for 10 seconds and then multiply the number of pulses you counted by 6. If you're math phobic, you can do an even quicker (but less accurate) estimate by counting the pulse beats for six seconds and then adding a "zero" to that pulse count number. Of course, if you are not in a rush, you can count your pulse for the entire minute and that will be your heart rate in one minute (called beats per minute, or bpm).

The best (and easiest) way to determine your heart rate is to wear a heart rate watch. Reliable units range from $50 to $300, but for a simple pulse check, the $50 model will work just fine. You can find these at all discount stores as well as sporting good stores.

When your workout gets too easy, your heart rate drops below the recommended 70 percent range. When it is too hard, your heart rate rises above the 85 percent range, and you are not training aerobically. Any training where your heart rate exceeds 90 percent is anaerobic training and nobody can keep up that intensity for long. The range between 85 and 90 percent is a challenging transition zone. For aerobic training it is okay to fluctuate briefly somewhat above and below your heart rate training zone, as long as your average heart rate remains within your training zone. See Table 2.1 and record your estimated max heart rate and aerobic training zones. Do not estimate your max heart rate if you were able to get a max fitness test. Use the highest heart rate you attained from that test. Just make sure it was a true max test—that is, that you didn't hold back, that you weren't sick or tired when you took it, and that your testers knew what they were doing. Included are calculations for lactate threshold training too. Its utility is discussed in the description of the training methods coming up shortly.

What you don't want to do is change too many factors during one training session—for instance, don't increase your pace and your distance on

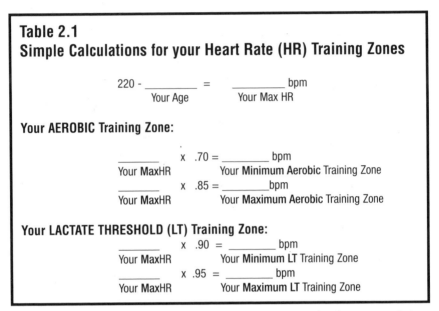

Table 2.1
Simple Calculations for your Heart Rate (HR) Training Zones

220 - _____ = _____ bpm
Your Age   Your Max HR

Your AEROBIC Training Zone:

_____ x .70 = _____ bpm
Your MaxHR   Your **Minimum Aerobic** Training Zone
_____ x .85 = _____ bpm
Your MaxHR   Your **Maximum Aerobic** Training Zone

Your LACTATE THRESHOLD (LT) Training Zone:
_____ x .90 = _____ bpm
Your MaxHR   Your **Minimum LT** Training Zone
_____ x .95 = _____ bpm
Your MaxHR   Your **Maximum LT** Training Zone

the same day. Too many increases in one session can lead to overtraining. You can always step up your workout again tomorrow if the workout is still too easy. Your aerobic training regimen is a never-ending cycle until you get to your predetermined ultimate goal, whatever that might be.

Cross-training. Utilizing different types of off-court training is known as cross-training. Basically, anything that isn't tennis can be considered a type of cross-training, even those agility drills you do. If you just want to relax and have fun, any sport or training exercise will do. If you want to kill two birds with one stone, try swimming to improve your upper body flexibility while training your aerobic system. When you engage in an activity that you aren't "trained" in, you naturally have to participate in it gradually. The last thing you want to do is pull a groin muscle lunging for a wild Frisbee throw! At the end of this chapter I have a sample listing of activities plus a couple sample programs to give you an idea of how cross-training can be incorporated into your training plan. The list obviously is not all-inclusive, but it should get you thinking about what cross-training is and how to use it.

I primarily use running as the training example because it involves the same large lower body muscles as tennis. Specificity of exercise is important to keep in mind for improving your specific sport focus. The best choices would be running on dirt trails, cushioned outdoor tracks, or a sandy beach. All will improve your aerobics as well as your agility, since you may need to dodge obstacles in your path. These outdoor running surfaces will also be more forgiving than a concrete road, especially if you have a back, knee, hip, or ankle joint problem. If the weather is bad, move indoors to a treadmill, indoor track, or gym. You don't play tennis on wet courts, so there's no need to practice running in similar conditions. Doing so will only put you at risk for a preventable injury.

Energy Systems Training. Throughout your years of tennis practice, you most likely have been exposed to each of these energy-system training methods: long-slow distance training (also known as LSD, the nonpsychedelic type), fartlek training ("fartlek" is a Swedish word meaning "speed play"), high intensity continuous (HIC) training, and interval training. There is some debate now about how much time you should actually devote to each of these training styles given the type of competitive tennis being played today. Up to this point, tennis conditioning has been adapted from these training regimens rather than developing conditioning plans more in tune to the specific demands of tennis, so classical tennis conditioning involves lots of aerobic foundation building.

True, tennis requires you to be able to play a match that may last five hours, but within that time span, you have bursts of play and periods of rest. It is not "continuous" effort—it is intermittent, or interval-like. It has been reported that for every second of tennis play there are actually two or three seconds of rest. That comes out to a 1:2 or 1:3 work:rest ratio. In college tennis, an average rally might last 10 to 15 seconds. Playing style and court surface have also been shown to influence the length of playing time in a match. Baseliners tend to keep the ball in play longer than serve-volleyers; hard court play is faster and quicker than clay court play. There are on average about 20 seconds of rest between each point, and you have 90 seconds to rest between changeovers.

Compare this to current professional tennis performances. In 2003 at the Men's U.S. Open Singles Final (where Andy Roddick defeated Juan Carlos Ferrero 6-3, 7-6(2), 6-3), the average point duration was a mere six seconds with about 15 seconds of rest between points (that's about a 1:2.5 work:rest ratio). Almost eight more seconds of rest were added each time a player served up a fault. There were only 30 seconds of rest between games without a court changeover, but almost 2 minutes of rest between games with a court changeover. The match lasted a bit more than 1.5 hours. Although their work:rest ratio within each game was 1:2.67, the overall match work:rest ratio was 1:4.73. So all told, with basically a 1:5 work:rest ratio for the entire match, these guys were in actual play only 20 percent of the time, while 80 percent of their time was spent resting. Knowing all this, it would be prudent for you to spend a bit more time on anaerobic interval training rather than focusing too heavily on aerobic intervals. That's not to say you can simply ditch your aerobic training. Rather, you may need to alter your training priorities and place a bit more emphasis on anaerobic training than what has been traditionally done in the past. Specificity of training is key.

Long Slow Distance (LSD) Training. Running lots of miles at a slow, easy pace is what LSD training is all about. This is usually the first type of aerobic training athletes embark upon to "get fit" or to build a solid aerobic foundation. It's good to get you started, clear your mind, and reduce stress. It will get you ready to cover the singles court. But too much of this type of training gets boring and can induce overtraining injuries. And more important, it is not really tennis-specific. So only use it occasionally after you have built up your aerobic "base." You'll know you have built up your aerobic base when you can run or cycle at a steady comfortable pace at about 70 to 80 percent of your max heart rate, maintain that pace for 30 to 60 minutes, and accomplish this by off-court training at least 3 times a week for four to six weeks. Once you reach this level, do a nice comfortable running or cycling workout only twice a week, just enough to maintain your general aerobic fitness.

Fartlek Training. Fartlek training is different from LSD training in that you speed up and slow down while running or cycling, pretty much at whim. I caution against adding agility and flexibility drills into this type of training unless you are on a track. Running backwards, sideways, hopping, and flailing your arms about can distract you from irregularities in the road surface or road traffic conditions, both of which can result in personal injury to you.

High Intensity Continuous (HIC) Training. This is the demonic alternative to LSD training once you are in great condition. HIC requires 25 minutes of training at 90 percent of your maximum heart rate. It is supposed to help prevent overtraining injuries that are due to too much distance work and accomplishes more work in less time. HIC training is grueling, so you might not overtrain, but you can overstrain and possibly get hurt, so do use with caution. Plus, it is really not specific to tennis. How many times can you recall needing to run all out at maximum speed for even 10 minutes?

The training purpose of HIC is to train at or near your *lactate threshold*—when blood lactic acid levels accumulate in your system dramatically—so you really learn how to put out a maximum effort under uncomfortable circumstances. The problem is that lactic acid doesn't accumulate to a critical level during tennis matches. It can, however, do so during certain intense tennis suicide-type drills. While fast, hard drills with little recovery time will increase your lactic acid production dramatically, they can also cause you to shortchange your stroke mechanics during practice, so be careful. Now, if you are trying to get in shape for a cardio tennis fitness program, then HIC training would probably be helpful. There are, however, somewhat less vicious lactate threshold training programs built into interval training programs that will more than adequately accomplish what you need for tennis.

Interval Training. Interval training is highly structured with very specific time allotments for the working phase (such as sprinting or playing) and the resting phase (recovery). This type of training is ideally suited for tennis because it is a work-rest type of sport. The structure of this training is what determines which energy system is being trained. As with HIC training, interval training is demanding and requires you to have a solid aerobic base so you can endure the friendly abuse. You start this type of training once you feel as if you can complete at least a few sprint repetitions in a somewhat respectable fashion. Sprint repetitions (reps) are a specific number of sprints you plan to run. This is your work phase.

Coaches most often use this method during the preseason. You run all-out down the court, rest briefly, and then run again, while being timed. Heart rate monitoring makes the intervals a little more individualized.

To coach your own sprint drills, all you need is a stopwatch, a place to run short distances, and motivation. *Aerobic interval training* assumes your sprint takes longer than a minute. *Anaerobic interval training* requires your interval sprint to take less than a minute. The more time you allow for rest between sprints, the more time your body has to recover. When a point is played out in the pros, on average it will take 15 seconds or less. That requires immediate energy system training. The most you are allowed for rest between changeovers is 90 seconds. Therefore, you should be focusing on completing a series of maximum speed sprints under 50 yards (or meters). Each 15 second sprint should be followed by a 45 second rest period (1:3 ratio). That would allow for complete recovery with basically little carry-over fatigue into the next sprint. A beginner plan would have you completing between 5 to 10 sprints. When you find completing 10 sprints has become easy, you can add another set of 5 to 10 sprints. When you add a second sprint set, just as in tennis between sets, you should allow for 90 seconds of recovery between the sets. One set will require less than seven minutes to complete. Add a second set and you're looking at 15 minutes. Do this training at the end of your practice, but before cooling down. If you do it at the beginning of practice, you stand a good chance of being too fatigued to put in a good practice.

You could also devise a more elaborate scheme and use it as one of your cross-training days. See the sample interval training programs in Table 2.2—there's one easy, one moderate, and one hard program. Mark Kovacs, the Director of the IFPA Tennis and Fitness Academy in Tampa Florida, and an NSCA certified strength and conditioning coach developed the hard program. He was also the winner of the NCAA doubles championships in 2002. I modified his "moderate" program, and the "easy" program I devised based on his moderate program in order to give you a full training progression with a range of time commitments. As you review these programs, you will note that even the longest sprint takes less than a minute. The shorter sprints will focus on your immediate energy system; longer sprints will help train your short-term anaerobic system. Each of these programs will also improve your long-term aerobic energy system by virtue of the length of the training interval session—as the entire program will take you from 30 minutes (easy) to an hour (hard) to complete.

Kovacs was also adamant about not trying to turn your interval energy system training into an agility session in an effort to kill two birds with one stone. If you do, you just short-change the intent of each training method. Even though your agility drills are timed and seem to fit within the time span for training your short-term (glycolytic) system, recovery time usually used for interval sprint training is insufficient for agility training. With agility training, you need to allow more rest between trials for complete recovery and no carry-over effect between trials. Otherwise you can get sloppy in performing your drill. Bad footwork spells disaster; disaster spells injury. So if you are pressed for time and need to get creative with how to fit everything into your two-hour practice session, put some agility drill training in at the beginning of practice, right after your warm-up, complete your practice, do an interval sprint drill, and then cool down.

Interval Heart Rates. For interval training, your average heart rate response, taking into account the high values during the sprint plus the lower values during rest, will probably be at the high end of your aerobic heart rate training zone. For the sample programs above, with the incremental nature of the sprint time, combined with the decreased rest time between sets, you will be training to tolerate lactic acid build-up.

If you were interval training with your team, taking your pulse can individualize your training. This requires checking your heart rate after each sprint repetition. Before beginning your next sprint rep, your heart rate should be 100 to 120 bpm. This will be down quite a bit from your sprinting heart rate, which should be at or near your maximal heart rate. It is best to use a heart rate watch because trying to take your pulse rate when you're jazzed up from sprinting is difficult. When you have finished your intervals and you are totally recovered, your resting heart rate should be

Table 2.2
Sample Interval Training Programs

Program 1: Easy Interval Training Session (1:4 work:rest ratio)

Work (seconds)	Rest	Reps	Sets	Rest Between Sets	Time to Complete (24.6 minutes total)
5	20	10	2	90 seconds	590 seconds or 9.8 minutes
10	40	8	2	90 seconds	890 seconds or 14.8 minutes

Program 2: Moderate Interval Training Session (1:4 work:rest ratio)

Work (seconds)	Rest	Reps	Sets	Rest Between Sets	Time to Complete (39.2 minutes total)
5	20	10	2	90 seconds	590 seconds or 9.8 minutes
10	40	8	2	90 seconds	890 seconds or 14.8 minutes
15	60	5	1	----	375 seconds or 6.3 minutes
20	80	5	1	----	500 seconds or 8.3 minutes

Program 3: Hard Interval Training Session (1:4 to 1:3 work:rest ratio)

Work (seconds)	Rest	Reps	Sets	Rest Between Sets	Time to Complete (58.4 minutes total)
5	20	10	2	90 seconds	590 seconds or 9.8 minutes
10	40	8	2	90 seconds	890 seconds or 14.8 minutes
15	60	5	2	30 seconds	780 seconds or 13 minutes
20	80	5	2	30 seconds	1030 seconds or 17.2 minutes
30	90	2	1	0 seconds	240 seconds or 4 minutes
45	135	2	1	0 seconds	360 seconds or 6 minutes

Modified from: M. Kovacs, *Strength and Conditioning Journal*, Volume 26, Number 5, October 2004, pp 12

between 50 and 70 beats per minute when you are relaxing. The lower your resting heart rate, the more aerobically fit you are. This is because your heart doesn't have to beat as fast to get oxygen to your cells. Instead, your heart is stronger and able to pump out more blood (oxygen) with each beat.

Strength Conditioning

At this point you have spent a lot of time learning about how to train your energy systems. Now it's time to learn about training your skeletal muscle system. Competitive tennis today seems to consist of a series of one, two, or three shots—not long intensive rallies. You need to focus on strength training that will enable you to persevere.

The basic principles of weight training remain the same across sports. What differentiates the tennis player from the football player is how you tweak these basic principles. You can train your entire body two to three times a week, or you can train almost daily if you alternate the muscle groups you are training. Use proper lifting techniques. That means be able to execute a lift without undue straining, without incorrect postures, or without recruitment of assisting (but incorrect) muscle groups for any given lift attempt. If you are using machines rather than free weights, simply follow the lifting instructions/diagrams imprinted on each machine. This is also how you can determine if that piece of equipment will benefit your tennis. Does the diagram highlight muscles that you use during tennis? If yes, do it; if not, move on to another piece of equipment. If you are using free weights, the onus is on you and your training partner to help each other perform the lift maneuver correctly. Training with free weights requires a spotting partner to assist you with heavier weights and/or correct your lifting technique. Allow your muscles 24 to 48 hours between training sessions to repair and rebuild.

In an ideal world, you should get an estimation of your *one rep max* (1RM) for each a piece of equipment you plan to use for training. It's better to estimate your max because actually conducting a max test on yourself could inadvertently cause an injury. The basic goal, after you have estimated your max, would be to plan on lifting approximately 70 percent of that on a routine basis. The best weight lifting book for tennis I have found is also available on-line as an e-book training for tennis. Just go to www.sportsworkout.com and click on the "Tennis" link. From there you will be able to design your own tennis-specific weight-training program. There is a hard-copy book version too, if you prefer to have something to hold in your hands.

Cross-cable machine.

Here's an executive summary: First, for any given weight-training station, be sure you can lift the weight stack 8 to 15 times (with correct execution) but no more. If you can lift more than 15 reps, the weight load is too low; if you can't lift eight reps consecutively, your weight load is too high. You should strive to complete two to three sets, allowing about three minutes of recovery (rest) between sets. This intensity of training (70 percent 1RM, 8 to 15 reps, two to three sets) will build endurance as well as strength. If you only lift "near maximal" for six or fewer reps, then all you are training for is sheer power—important for your first serve attempt perhaps, but only training for power won't facilitate your repeated ability to perform well. For that your muscles must be trained to put out more consistent, but perhaps slightly less powerful, efforts. Remember, you need to be able to harness your power for accurate shot placement. Once a week you can satisfy your power urges, but twice a week go for the strength-endurance approach. This will result in strength training three days a week.

When you are executing your lifts, pay attention to the speed of your lifting movement. Recent reports have suggested that lifting too slowly actually may limit your ability to overload your muscles, whereas moderate to fast movements are needed for increasing your power. Even if you are lifting "fast," the movements must still be performed in a controlled manner. A "slow" lift takes 10 seconds during the concentric (muscle shortening or positive) phase of the lift and 5 to 10 seconds for the eccentric (muscle lengthening, or negative) phase of the lift. In plain speak that means taking 10 seconds to lift the weight stack, and 5 to 10 seconds to return that weight stack to the starting position. For tennis power training, *lift fast!* Take two seconds to lift the weight stack (concentric phase) and four seconds to return the weight stack to the starting position (eccentric phase).

Start with variable resistance machines. They load your muscles through the full range of motion and are much easier to control than free weights. Plus, you don't need a partner/spotter. For core stabilization and isolating smaller muscles, such as the forearm and shoulder, free weights would be advantageous. Start light and build gradually. Do you need big bulky muscles? Just look at the successful pros for your answer. They are muscular, but not huge. Muscle size doesn't really matter here, but strength for muscular endurance as well as power does matter, and being able to control that power is critical. If you are sketchy about how to start, look up the conditioning resource options I've listed for this chapter.

Through all of this, bear in mind that the less fit you are, the greater results you will see when you first begin any sort of training program. That's because you have more room to improve. The closer you get to your peak condition, the changes will be small and perhaps even subtle, but nevertheless important and worthwhile.

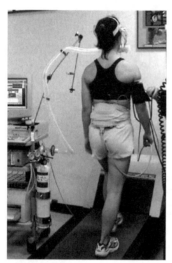

VO$_2$ max test

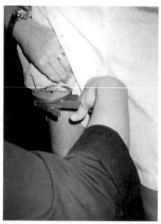

Measuring the fatfold on a player's thigh.

How Do You Measure Up?

The USTA has spent a lot of time and effort researching what makes a good tennis player a champion tennis player and developed an entire program around their findings—High Performance Tennis. What can you do to determine if you "have the right stuff"? First, get a personal trainer to give you an aerobic fitness test as well as a body fat analysis. You should strive for an aerobic fitness "score" of greater than 50 ml/kg/min. This is the amount of oxygen your cells use maximally per kilogram of your body weight per minute (VO$_2$max). Values below this indicate you need more aerobic training. Some elite players have a VO$_2$max as high as 65 ml/kg/min.

The average percent body fat for male college and pro tennis players is 8.2%, but they range from as low as 4% to as high as 18%. Why worry about your body fat? It's not just to look good. Lugging extra weight around on the court slows you down and interferes with your body's ability to regulate its heat production. On the other hand, being underweight can be equally dangerous. Heat regulation is also a problem if you have too little fat, plus your heart and brain don't appreciate being starved either. So pay attention to your body fat composition. Don't do anything crazy, but maintain a healthy weight and body fat for your energy needs. See a certified sport dietitian or nutritionist who is knowledgeable about tennis energy demands.

Besides aerobic fitness and body composition testing, the USTA includes several other tests that reveal how ready you are to join the tour. These tests include: sprinting, jumping, sit-ups, push-ups, medicine ball throws, and lower back/hamstring flexibility (sit-and reach test).

You and your hitting partner can test each other—while one is performing the test, the other is timing, counting, and providing motivation. I've summarized the testing highlights below. You can obtain more details from the USTA's book *Complete Conditioning for Tennis.*

20-Yard Sprint (18.3 meters)

During intense competition, an average point will last 5 to 10 seconds, hence, you need good very short-term anaerobic ability. There are many sprint/agility tests, but the simplest test is a 20-yard sprint. Mark off 20 yards on a tennis court with a cone or ball pyramid. You should have enough distance to run through the 20 yards, so you don't slam into a wall or fence. A "good" sprint score for this short 20-yard distance is 3.3 seconds or faster. If you prefer testing an even shorter distance, sprint 5 meters (about 16 feet). Your sprint time should be under 1.6 seconds. You see it's not that much time at all—almost a blink of an eye—so make sure your timing buddy pays attention and has good reaction time so as to be able to accurately time you!

Touch cone.

Vertical Jump

You need to be able to explode quickly off your feet to get to shots. For this, lower body strengthening is needed—a favored type of training for that is plyometrics—e.g., the kangaroo, or box jumps, and such. The vertical jump test measures your leg power. In the lab we have a piece of fancy equipment, called the Vertex. It's just a pole with a bunch of movable metal flags at the top. The athlete jumps up and attempts to tap a flag out of alignment. This makes it easy to see your jumping height—for a cost of several hundred dollars. But a simple wall will also work—and it's free. Secure a tape measure on the wall in a room with a high ceiling. Coat your fingers with some colored chalk dust that will show up on the wall. Stand against the tape measure with your side to the wall, and extend your arm above your head. Note the distance where you fingertips reach. That's your standing reach height. Simply crouch a bit and jump, reaching as high as you can, and tap the wall with your chalked finger. Your jump height is your jumping reach measurement minus your standing reach measurement. To be considered "good," your jumping score needs to be at least 16 inches.

Low-tech vertical jump.

Muscular Endurance

According to the USTA, the velocity of your serves, forehands, and back-hands can be dramatically improved by strengthening your upper body and abdominals because they are contracting with every swing you take. You can train these muscles with medicine ball throws, resistance bands, weights, and a variety of abdominal exercises.

The simplest way to test your strength/endurance for the upper body and abs is with the sit-up and push-up tests that each of us has known since grade school P.E. These tests are based on how many reps you can perform correctly in one minute. I emphasize correctly so that you don't injure yourself or get sloppy by trying to use muscles that you aren't supposed to be using in an effort to squeeze in a few more reps.

Sit-Ups

Your sit-ups are done in the bent-knee position for back safety. Hook your feet under your sofa (or some other heavy piece of furniture) or have a partner hold them against the floor. Cross your hands across your chest. A correctly executed sit-up will consist of your elbows just touching your thighs. When you return to the start position, you should uncurl so that your back, but not your shoulders, touches the floor. Your goal for a "good" rating is a minimum of 40 sit-ups.

Push-Ups

The push-up test position is your standard "military" style, the palms of

Medicine ball throws.

your hands placed shoulder-width apart on the floor, your legs stretched out behind you, with weight on your toes, feet together. No bent-knee push-ups here. You want to get into the "good" range, which means you need to be able to execute at least 34 push-ups in a minute.

Medicine Ball Throws

You may also have your upper body power determined by how far you can throw a medicine ball in various directions.

These tests are best conducted with your coach/trainer as you need a specific ball weight, the floor must be measured off in order to determine how far you've thrown it. If you are prone to shoulder, arm, or elbow injuries, this test could aggravate your condition, so proceed with caution if at all.

Sit-and-Reach

Your hamstring/lower back flexibility can be tested using the sit-and-reach test. Sit on the floor with your legs outstretched, feet flat against a measurement box, arms stretched out in front of you, sliding your hands along the measurement stick (see photo). You should strive to get a score in the "good" range (four to six inches beyond your toes). An "average" score would be if you reached two to four inches beyond your toes. If you don't have access to this box, you can simply use your toe-touching ability as your guide—position yourself in the same manner as shown in the photo and note how far beyond your toes your fingertips extend. Because back problems are prevalent in tennis, this is an area upon which each player should strive to improve by performing flexibility exercises at least twice a week.

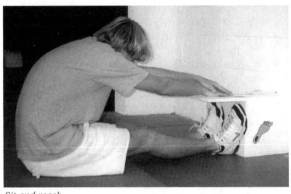
Sit and reach.

These test results help point the way to what you need to emphasize in off-court conditioning sessions. If you don't score in the good range on each of these tests, you need to target those issues in your conditioning routine.

You must be diligent and committed to your off-court training program. Because when it comes down to it, when you are matched against an equally talented and smart player, it will be what you bring to the court that makes the difference.

Tables 2.3–2.7 contain some extra tips and information that you might find helpful in designing your training program.

Table 2.3
Books & Websites Worth a Look

Books
- *Cross-Training for Sports.* Gary T. Moran and George H. McGlynn. Human Kinetics 1994.
- *Complete Conditioning for Tennis.* USTA. Human Kinetics 1998.
- *Handbook of Sports Medicine and Science: Tennis.* Edited by Per A.F.H. Renstrom. Blackwell Science Publishers. IOC Medical Commission Sub-Commission on Publication in the Sports Sciences, 2002
- *The Ultimate Guide to Weight Training for Tennis.* Robert G. Price. Sportsworkout.com. Third Edition, 2003.
- *From Breakpoint to Advantage.* Babette Pluim, MD, PhD and Marc Safran, MD, Racquet Tech Publishing, 2004.

Websites
- www.ovphysio.com/stretchg/tennis/tennis.htm: stretching photo examples
- www.donchu.com/articles: Core conditioning exercises
- www.fitfortennis.com: General conditioning for tennis
- www.ucsdtritons.com/ViewArticle.dbml?DB_OEM_ID=5800&KEY=&ATCLID=188321: nutrition for the athlete

Table 2.4
Anatomy of a Cross-Training Plan

Warm-Up and Cool-Down: *Preparing the body for more action; that period of time beyond rest but before your main training stimulus; done with every workout*

> Good: light jogging on a treadmill, rowing machine, cross-country ski machine, stepping, jumping rope, jumping jacks
>
> Best: dynamic stretching (warm-up), on-court jogging, light stationary cycling, focused breathing, static stretching (cool-down)

Flexibility: *Range of motion around a joint; done 3x/week to daily*

> Good: swimming
>
> Best: sport-specific stretching—see website listing in Table 2.3

Aerobic Conditioning: *Cardiovascular endurance, staying power; done 2-3x/wk*

> Good: swimming, treadmill running, cross-country ski machine, bicycling, stepping, aerobic dance-type classes, rollerblading, jumping rope, aqua-jog
>
> Best: outdoor running, indoor cycle training (aka spinning)

Anaerobic Conditioning: *Power training, tolerating the lactic acid buildup; done 2-3x/wk*

> Good: treadmill sprinting, fast rowing, racquetball, basketball, arm ergometer, jumping rope, agility drills, plyometrics
>
> Best: sprint cycling, sprint running, versaclimber

Agility and Balance: *Ability to move quickly in multidirectional fashion; ability to remain upright under normal or stressed condition; equal strength between antagonistic muscle groups; done 1-2x/wk*

> Good: aerobic dance-type programs, rollerblading, jumping rope, racquetball, basketball
>
> Best: specific agility exercises like ladder runs, figure eights, zigzag running, obstacle running, ball balancing.

Muscular Endurance: *Ability of a muscle to sustain repeated contractions over a period of time; the number of reps you can perform with a given workload or weight; done 2-3x/wk*

> Good: arm ergometer rowing, plyometrics (dynamic explosive power training)
>
> Best: endurance resistance training (resistance bands, free weights, machines)

Muscular Strength and Power: *Total amount of force, or power, a muscle is able to generate in one repetition; done 2-3x/wk*

> Good: plyometrics
>
> Best: power-resistance training

Table 2.5
Training Guide

	AEROBICS	ANAEROBICS
FREQUENCY	3x/wk	2-3x/wk, alternate days
DURATION	30-60 min	10-30 minutes
INTENSITY	70-85% Max HR*	70% of estimated 1RM,**
		8-15 reps, 2-3 sets

PROGRESSION: Increase intensity or duration (not both on same day) every 1-2 weeks or when the workout feels "easy"', whichever comes first. How much to increase intensity? About 2-10% above last easy workout. Start slow and progress slowly to avoid over-use injuries.

* MAX HR = 220 - your current age
** estimated 1RM = the estimated maximum amount of weight you can lift once correctly (in good form, no assisting muscles).

Table 2.6
Injury Management
Prevention Tips
> Be well rested
> Be well hydrated
> Maintain flexibility
> Maintain general conditioning
> Strengthen wrist & elbow muscles
> Don't rush your strokes
> Don't train when overly tired
> Eat nutritiously
> Avoid overtraining
> Develop a training program based on you, not someone else!

Treatment Tips
> See your doctor and your trainer A.S.A.P. Key: Follow their advice!
> Remember RICE: Rest Ice Compression Elevation
> Begin sports rehab as soon as possible

Table 2.7
Terminology for the Anatomy-Challenged

Tennis Movement	Anatomical Term	For The Anatomy-Challenged
Forehand	anterior deltoid, pectorals, Internal rotator cuff, elbow flexors, serratus anterior	front part of upper arm, chest, shoulder, biceps, upper front ribcage
Backhand, single	rhomboids, middle trapezius, posterior deltoid, middle deltoid, external rotator cuff, triceps, serratus anterior	upper back, back of neck, lower and upper shoulder, front and back upper arm upper front ribcage
Backhand, double	all of the above for single plus pectorals, anterior deltoid, internal rotator cuff	just add the forehand muscle list from above
Serve, Overhead	pectorals, internal rotator cuff, latissimus, triceps	chest, shoulder, back, back of upper arm
Trunk Rotation (aka 'coiling')	internal and external obliques, spinal erectors	side muscles/waist backbone region
Push-Off	soleus, gastrocnemius, quadriceps, gluteals	center and sides of calf, front of thigh, buttocks
Knee, Hip Extension	quadriceps, gluteals	front of thigh, buttocks
Wrist Flexion	wrist flexors	wrist
Lunges	adductor longus, biceps femoris	groin and hamstring (back of thigh)

Chapter 3
Nutritional Toughness

"If you don't do what's best for your body, you're the one who comes up on the short end."

— Julius Irving, Basketball

You Are What You Eat
"Food is an important part of a balanced diet."

—Fran Lebowitz, Food Writer

So much of what we eat can be classified as a non-food, with no nutrient value whatsoever. A study conducted in 2001 by Jacobson, looking at dietary intake of Division IA athletes, found that almost two-thirds of the athletes surveyed were not sure of the amount of carbohydrates they needed to eat for sports participation. As you know from Chapter 2, carbs are the critical nutrient for providing on-court energy needs. They also had misinformation regarding the need for protein and grossly underestimated the amount of fat they should be eating. Shifflett and his group of researchers followed up in 2002 with a study on athletes' perception of their nutrition knowledge. As you might suspect, the athletes felt they were much better informed than what they actually were. When they took a basic nutrition test, their average score was equivalent to a "D." Unfortunately, their coaches didn't fare any better; they nearly failed as well, but they admitted before the test that they didn't know much about nutrition. Despite the coaches' admitted lack of nutrition knowledge, most did not utilize a sport dietitian in their athletic programs. They appeared to rely on their athletic trainers for nutrition direction. How did the athletic trainers score on this nutrition knowledge exam? They got a "C," which represents only "average" knowledge.

What Should You Eat?
"You better cut the pizza in four pieces because I'm not hungry enough to eat six."

— Yogi Berra, NY Yankee Baseball Manager

How often have you fooled yourself into believing that you are eating the right stuff in the right amounts? In an attempt to answer this question, I gave 50 players a five-page in-depth nutrition survey.

Their ATP rankings ranged from "not yet ranked" to top 50 in the world. The full report can be seen at www.itftennis.com/technical and www.bonitamarks .com, but the main points will be covered in this chapter.

Food content is divided into two categories: macronutrients and micronutrients. Macronutrients are the major categories into which you are used to seeing dietary advice divided—carbohydrates, proteins, fats, and total calorie intake. The micronutrient content is everything else—vitamins, minerals, fiber content, and so on. Keep in mind that a competitive athlete's high-energy needs are very different from those of the average person, the person needing to lose weight, or the active person who is not competing; one diet plan doesn't fit everyone. So what your best buddy eats in a day may not be what you should be eating. It depends upon your actual energy output, body composition, training goals, where you are in your season (competing heavily, just practicing, vacationing, etc.), your food likes and dislikes, and metabolism. Nevertheless, there are some generic guidelines, which you can tweak accordingly.

The quickest, easiest formula I have found for estimating your (daily) athletic caloric needs is as follows: multiply your body weight (in pounds) by 20. If you are 170 pounds, your approximate daily caloric intake should be around 3,400 calories. If for some reason you cut back on your tennis competition and reduce your activity level, you need to reduce that multiplication factor of 20 to 17, or 2,890 calories. If you become a total slug, you use a factor of 14, which gives you 2,380 calories. While more complicated formulas are available, this simple one at least gets you in the ballpark and on the right track. These formulas appear in Table 3.1 so you can calculate your approximate caloric needs.

Table 3.1
How Many Calories Do You Need?

Sedentary Slug:	_____pounds x 14 = _____	calories needed
	(Your weight)	
Moderately Moving:	_____pounds x 17 = _____	calories needed
	(Your weight)	
Awesome Athlete:	_____pounds x 20 = _____	calories needed
	(Your weight)	

(Reprinted with permission from: Tennis Pro magazine)

If you want a more accurate estimate, go to the University of California at San Diego's website for athletic nutrition. It has an on-line calculator to determine an athlete's caloric needs based upon age, weight, and estimated intensity of exercise. From there you will be a click away from suggested meal plans:

http://www.ucsdtritons.com/ViewArticle.dbml?DB_OEM_ID = 5800&KEY = &ATCLID = 188321

All Fats are Not Created Equal

Let's start with fat intake, as that is the most universally recognized recommendation regardless of your goals. For good heart health, less than 30 percent of your dietary intake should consist of fats. To qualify that recommendation even further, the type of fat is very important. Less than 30 percent of your fat intake should be saturated or trans fat. That means you don't want to eat much of the fats that will clog your arteries and potentially lead to an increased risk for heart disease (e.g., stroke or heart attack). This fat is typically solid at room temperature, can be molded into shapes (such as sticks of butter or margarine), or when you fry up something and let it cool, you see a whitish substance coating the pan or your food. It's also the type of fat found in processed foods, junk foods, and rich, creamy foods. You can eat small amounts of this stuff, as it does taste good (ice cream, for instance), but don't gorge until you drop. Likewise, potato chips, while a great source of salt, are also loaded with saturated fat. Almost 50 percent of the calories in regular-style chips are due to the fat content, so you shouldn't eat these as a dietary staple. If you are a chip-oholic, a simple solution is to switch to baked chips. You cut down on the fat but still get the salt which may help replenish your electrolyte stores. It is not recommended that you totally eliminate fat from your diet. Fat makes the foods you eat taste good, and it provides a ton of energy, which is needed for endurance-type exercise. One way of checking the fat in your food is to look at the food label and see how much dietary cholesterol is listed. You want the item to be well under 300 milligrams (mg), as that is the maximum daily allowance currently suggested by the American Heart Association for maintaining heart health. For every gram of fat you eat, you get 9 calories, which is double the amount you get from carbohydrates or protein. Fat does have its place in your world, but don't let it take center stage.

Just as there are bad fats, there are also good fats. The good fats are unsaturated or polyunsaturated. This type of fat actually helps keep your arteries clear of clog, much like drain opener cleans your kitchen pipes. These good fats are found in olives and fish. Some fish are better than others based upon the amount and type of fat they have. But don't fret over the type of fish you should eat, just try to increase your intake of broiled or grilled fish. Be picky and request that your fish (or chicken or steak) be grilled or blackened, but not fried. If you have a choice between butter and olive oil for your fresh bread, go for the olive oil. It's tasty and much healthier, as long as it's not mixed with drawn butter. Usually herbs and spices are added to the olive oil to make it even more flavorful. Don't worry about the calorie content (olives have a lot of calories), because being a competitive athlete, you probably need the extra calories, unless body composition and performance testing indicate that you are over-fat and it is hampering your ability to play well.

The results from my diet questionnaires suggest that if we look at averages for all of the pros combined (from Futures on up to seasoned ATP players), players consumed about 32 percent of their calories in fat, which isn't too far off from the recommended value (under 30 percent), but still on the high side. However, the range of fat intake based on total food intake told a different story. It went from a low of 18 percent up to a whopping 52 percent, with the higher fat intakes being among the least experienced touring players.

When I compared their fat intake values (32%) to some reported in the literature for young junior players (36%), I realized that these touring players' intakes hadn't changed much from puberty to adulthood, even though most had been through college and presumably had the benefits of coaches and athletic trainers for advice. The juniors' fat intake was closer to the average sedentary American diet, which of course helps to explain the rising obesity rate in youth in the U.S. When I asked players why they thought their fat intake was so high, most were basically clueless and said they didn't realize it. They were just eating what was provided at the competition sites, going for the protein in lunchmeats, and eating at places that were convenient and within their limited budgets. Others just didn't know, or care, how to choose their foods wisely. Not all lunchmeats are taboo. Lean lunchmeats are available, but those are more expensive. Unless marketed as such (highlighted on the menu as having lower fat), the lunchmeats are most likely the high-fat kind. Furthermore, most players didn't understand the impact food intake could have on their performance.

The Protein Story

Many players and coaches mistakenly believe that the latest popular diet recommendations apply to them, that the self-declared diet guru at the gym really knows what he is talking about, and the so-called nutrition expert at the nutrition supply store is actually formally trained in nutrition. The protein recommendations for athletes have changed dramatically over the past 10 years and continue to evolve. What I say today may be modified next year. For that reason, you, or whomever is responsible for your general diet plan, need to keep abreast of the latest scientific findings published about athletic and gender-based nutritional needs. Note I said scientific, not what was published in *Good Housekeeping, Men's Health,* or touted on a TV-news talk show. Go directly to the science source for accurate information.

You don't need, nor will your performance benefit from, a diet that severely limits your carbohydrate intake and is focused on protein. Protein's main role is not to provide you with energy, although it can, and does, do that eventually. Supplying energy via protein metabolism is not quick. It takes much more time to metabolize protein as an energy source than it does to use your carbs (your quick energy source). But, if all you have on board is protein, your body will be forced to burn your stored fat—which is great for an obese person with tons of fat to burn. The down side is, because you now won't have a carb source for instant energy, you can wind up feeling tired. Furthermore, the average competitive tennis player, at 8% body fat, does not have huge fat reserves. So a high protein diet that limits your carb intake will result in a quicker onset of fatigue. In five-setters, your protein stores will finally assist in providing you some energy, but it is certainly not the preferred fuel choice. More importantly, protein will definitely be a key factor in muscle recovery after you are done playing. Protein's primary role is its anabolic, or muscle rebuilding, properties. Protein resynthesizes your muscle tissues, enabling them to recover and get stronger from your last workout. The harder you work out, the more tissue reconstruction necessary, thus the more protein required to do this job.

There is a limit to how much protein is enough, and how much is actually too much, even for the competitive tennis player. Dr. Jack Groppel, honorary chair of the USTA Sports Science Committee, suggested that the protein dietary intake for tennis athletes in the USTA's High Performance program should range between 15 to 25 percent of their total caloric intake. The reason you sometimes get such vague recommendations is because there is a lot of disagreement among strength and conditioning experts versed in nutrition and the various scientific boards that publish the dietary recommendations.

A more refined way to determine if your protein intake is adequate is to determine the amount you need per gram in relation to your body weight. For instance, my study suggests that the average protein intake for touring tennis pros is 1.6 grams for every kilogram of their body weight (abbreviated g/kgBW). For sports that combine endurance and power, such as tennis, it has been suggested that you need at least 1.7 g/kgBW of protein, but no more than 2.0 g/kgBW. That translates into 6.8 to 8 calories of protein for every 2 pounds of your body weight. So if you weigh 170 pounds, you would minimally need 578 calories of protein daily (6.8 x 85 pounds).

A quick way to see if you are eating too much protein is to take a urine test—called a urinalysis. It can measure the amount of nitrogen in your urine, thereby letting you know if you are taking in too much protein.

A real issue with protein supplementation is adequate hydration. Higher amounts of protein intake promote diuresis (that is, frequent urination), and this in turn increases the risk for dehydration, which is a bad thing for tennis players. Therefore, players taking protein supplements need to drink more, and they need to drink more often. This means drinking fluids that won't promote more urination, so alcoholic and caffeinated beverages don't cut it.

There is a way for you to determine your protein needs in terms of calories rather than percentage of total food intake or grams of intake. If you know how many calories an item has, you will know how much of that item you should eat, based upon your current body weight. Because of the body-weight factor, when you lose weight, your protein needs will be different than if you gain 10 pounds. In order to determine your individual protein needs, you first must know how to convert the weight of the protein from grams into calories. Also, the formulas require your weight to be in kilograms, not pounds. You will need to do a couple metric conversions, but it's really not that difficult if you have the conversion factors, a calculator, and a notepad.

Here are simplified worksheets for you to use, plus an example log of how to determine your actual daily protein intake (Tables 3.2 and 3.3). Just write down in a small notebook whatever you eat and the amounts. Later you can go online and look up the food's protein content (www.become-healthynow.com/article/proteins/567), or if you eat at home, look at the nutrient label on the package or container. You can also go to the bookstore and simply buy one of the many diet books that list calorie tables—make sure they give you nutrient breakdowns in grams.

Table 3.2
Determining Your Protein Needs

A. Change food weight from U.S. System to Metric System:
 _____ pounds x 454 = _____grams.

B. Change grams of protein into calories:
 _____ grams x 4 = _____calories

C. Calculate your DAILY protein needs:
   a. Metric System: 1.7–2 g /kgBW (more accurate)
   b. U.S. System: 6.8–8 calories for every 2 pounds of your body weight. (Note: US System = less accurate, but close enough; Start at the lowest recommended dose and adjust upwards as needed.)

D. EXAMPLE: 170 lb. person = 77.3 kg person (just divide lb. by 2.2)
   a. Metric System: 1.7 x 77.3 = 131 grams x 4 = 526 calories of protein;
   b. U.S. System: 6.8 calories for every 2 pounds of body weight
     6.8 x 85 = 578 calories of protein.

E. YOUR daily protein needs:
   a. Metric: _____ grams x _____kg x 4 = _____protein calories
     b. U.S. System: _____calories x _____lbs = _____protein calories

---

Table 3.3
Tracking Your Daily Protein Intake
(For this you need to have a calorie chart with protein content information)

Food Item	Amount	Grams	Multiplied by	=	Calories
Sirloin burger (8 grams protein per ounce .25 lb = 4 oz. 8 x 4 = 32 grams)	.25 lb.	32	x 4	=	128
Protein Powder	1 scoop	20	x 4	=	80
Non-Fat Milk	8 oz	8	x 4	=	32
TOTAL PROTEIN INTAKE:					**240 calories**

Write your protein intake here:

YOUR TOTAL PROTEIN INTAKE: _____ **CALORIES**

If you take protein powders, don't believe the amount they tell you to use on the package. It's usually three to four times higher than what is really needed. You will save money by determining how much protein you really need.

The Low-Down on Carbs

The purpose of this section is to de-villainize the much-maligned carbohydrate as well as to explain what the Glycemic Index (GI) and net carb index ratings are all about. Understand that all carbs are not created equal.

Carbs are the staff of life for the tennis player. You'll find carbs (sugar, fiber, starch) in veggies such as potatoes, squash, corn, broccoli, lettuce, and peppers (the green, yellow, orange, red, and purple foods). Your cereals, pancakes, waffles, even parts of the blintz or crepe, are all carbs.

As stated in Chapter 2, carbs provide you with instant energy. They are the only fuel source that can provide energy anaerobically, thereby allowing you quick energy access within a few seconds. That cannot be said for protein or fat. Carbs continue to be a primary source of energy until you hit the 10 to 15 minute mark, then fats begin to kick in. After that threshold, if your intensity remains easy to moderate, your body burns your fat reserves for fuel instead of your carbs. But, if for any reason you need to rev up your engine and make a mad dash for a ball, or if you want to blow out your opponent with power serves and returns, your body will automatically switch to carbs and/or your PCr stores for that energy. So you'd better have some in your system. If you've been eating a low carb diet, chances are you will have used up your carb stores fairly early on in your match. The result? You won't have much left in you to pull out any type of power shot or quick sprint late in a long, difficult match. In other words, you will fatigue quickly and either not make it to the final set or your final set will be over quickly, probably with you losing.

It has been proven that an endurance athlete needs his total caloric intake to consist of at least 60 percent carbs during training and competition. This will provide enough carbs for excellent performance as well as replenishing the athlete's glycogen stores. This is especially crucial for successive days of competition. Because tennis taxes both the anaerobic and aerobic systems, adequate carb intake is essential for immediate energy as well as endurance for those longer matches. The explosive repetitive movements common to tennis use up your glycogen stores quickly and don't permit sufficient time to tap into your fat stores for the extra energy needed. Not only are carbs important for providing energy to your muscles, carbs are also important for fueling your brain. Tennis is not just a grunt and run sport—you have to be clear-headed and think about your shot placement. So you need to make sure you have enough carbs to see you through all aspects of your match. That means, if you eat 3,000 calories a day, about 1,800 of those calories should be from carbs.

To precisely determine how much you need, calculate your carb requirement similarly to how you figured out your protein needs. It is recommended that an athlete in a game-type sport (with anaerobic and aerobic needs) consume 5 to 7 grams of carbs per kilogram of his body weight (g/kgBW). Carbohydrate provides four calories of energy per gram, and one kilogram (kg) is equal to 2.2 pounds. Another way to look at this is that you need 20 to 28 calories of carbohydrate for every two pounds of your body weight. If you weigh 170 pounds, you need to eat at least 1,700 calories in carbohydrate form (20 calories x 85 pounds). That's why you may need meal supplement shakes—it's easier to drink a liquid high calorie meal than to sit down to five plates of spaghetti. When you are trying to refuel for your sec-

ond match of the day, which might be only a couple hours away, liquid supplements are digested far faster than solid foods. Generally, liquid supplements are a carb-protein-fat combo, so they are nutritionally sound for
competition. The extra hydration is an added benefit. A more in-depth look
at supplements comes a bit later.

Tables 3.4 and 3.5 allow you to figure out your carb needs and log your
intake. Here's a web link if you want to look up carb grams online:
www.ntwrks.com/~mikev/. The list is arranged from zero carb content to
highest carb content, so it might take you a bit of time to find your foods,
but it's a free listing.

Table 3.4
Determining Your Carb Needs

A.   Your weight converson factors:
    Metric System: _____ kg x 2.2 = _____lbs.
    U.S. System: _____ lbs. ÷ 2.2 = _____kg

B.   To convert grams of carbs into calories:
    _____ grams x 4 = _____calories
(Note: this is the same average value as for protein!)

C.   Calculate your daily carb needs:
    a. Metric System: 5-7 grams/ kgBW
    b. U.S. System: 20-28 carb calories for every 2 pounds of your weight

D.   EXAMPLE: 170 lb. person = 77.3 kg person (just divide lb. by 2.2)
    a. Metric System: 5 x 77.3 = 387 grams x 4 = 1546 calories of carbs;
    b. U.S. System: 20 calories for every 2 pounds of body weight
       20 x 85 = 1700 calories of carbs.

E.   YOUR daily carb needs:
    a. Metric: _____ grams x _____kg x 4 = _____ carb calories
    b. U.S. System: _____calories x _____lbs = _____carb calories

(Note: U.S. System tends to overestimate a bit in conversion from metric)

Table 3.5
Tracking Your Daily Carb Intake
(For this you need to have a calorie chart with carb content info)

Food Item	Amount	Grams	Multiplied by	=	Calories
McDonald's Fries	large	34	4	=	136
Coke, small	8 oz	25	4	=	100
Burger King Garden Salad (no dressing)	1 serving	7	4	=	28
TOTAL CARB INTAKE:					**264 calories**

Write your carb intake here:

TOTAL CARB INTAKE:	_____	**CALORIES**

Your Basic Competition Meal Plan

News Reporter: "What do you eat before a match?"
Andy Roddick: "Food. You?"

As you might suspect, just as there are guidelines for how you should eat on a daily basis, there are also guidelines for how to eat immediately before, during, and after competition. The goal is to maximize your energy stores so you have enough of the right stuff at the right time. Given this, it is important to eat in accordance with your food preferences and your psychological mind set. But, you must also pay attention to the digestibility of the foods you are selecting in relation to your match time. Generally speaking, proteins and fats are hardest to digest. They take the longest to breakdown to use as fuel sources, but, as explained earlier, fats will eventually yield a lot of energy once the body can get to them. Even some carbs can be hard to digest if they have a lot of fiber.

First, let's discuss "net carbs." "Net carb" advertising is grossly misleading to the public, similar to the "low fat" ad craze, because it doesn't tell you the whole story. Low carb diet promoters state that net carbs are the total number of carb grams you get in a "low carb" food minus those carbs that supposedly cause little (or no) elevation in your blood glucose (sugar) level. This would be great for the tennis player—to be able to eat right before a match and not feel like dying 15 minutes into your first set. According to the net carb concept, the carbs that are subtracted out as inconsequential (i.e., not counted) are the dense fiber-carbs, the carbs that create bulk and help with your digestive system (bran, indigestible cellulose, etc.). These high fiber (low net) carbs could also be categorized as "low GI" carbs, but we'll get to that in a minute.

The basic idea of the "net carb" advantage is to avoid sugar highs (and the corresponding rebound lows) as well as avoiding the insulin-related storage of dietary carbs as fats. But this doesn't work if you have a metabolic disorder such as diabetes, or if you are unable to metabolize the sweeteners used. The way these new low-carb snacks are sweetened is with sugar alcohols (note they all end in the suffix "ol"): erythritol, glycerine (AKA glycerol), lacitol, maltitol, and sorbitol (you've probably seen these in sugar free gum). Consider this, malitol, a primary sweetener in many of these products, has three calories per gram, whereas regular sugar has four calories per gram. The lowest-calorie sweetener is erythritol, at one calorie per gram. So you may not have avoided many calories.

Furthermore, if the whole idea is not to spike your blood sugar level, which is the net carb claim, these sweeteners fall short, as they have been scientifically proven to do so in many people, only it takes about an hour longer. And what goes up, must come down (via insulin response), so these products are not really reducing the insulin response either. As a result, people with metabolic disorders, such as diabetics, or those whose systems do not metabolically respond to sugar alcohols, could run into trouble believing they have permission to eat more carbs.

Your competition dietary plan comes down to timing, types of food, and quantities—what to eat and when. When your body is trying to breakdown your meal for energy, the blood flow to your gut is increased. If you go out to play right when your body is trying to digest your food, a significant portion of that blood has to be diverted from your stomach to your working muscles, which need more oxygen. This slows down the digestive process and can make you feel quite uncomfortable. The time it takes to absorb your meal depends on the size of the meal as well.

Pre-Match Nutrition
It can be especially difficult to consume the food you need prior to an early

morning match or between matches that are only hours apart. First, eat breakfast. If you are not a breakfast person, start conditioning yourself to become one. Begin by drinking some juice or a liquid meal such as Ensure or SlimFast. These are readily available in grocery stores and convenience marts. You can then add a bit of toast with jam or peanut butter, a cereal bar, or even a Pop Tart (go easy on the ones with icing). A bagel, cheese stick, cup of yogurt, or banana are easy to eat as you walk around the house trying to wake up or on the way to practice. There are even yogurt sticks that don't require utensils.

Once you get used to this, you will begin to feel hungry in the morning, and the thought of eating a real sit-down breakfast will not be so awful. Most of the items mentioned above, in addition to cereal and waffles, are usually available at Futures and Challenger events' player hotels, either at their restaurant or complimentary breakfast bar. This way, you don't change what you are used to eating, thereby reducing the chance of getting sick from eating something different.

Nutrition gurus suggest the pre-match meal ideally should be consumed three to four hours before your match, but if that's too difficult (say if you have a 9:00 a.m. match and you don't particularly feel like waking up at the crack of dawn), shoot to eat no later than 90 minutes before your match. As for how much, the guidelines say the meal should be anywhere from three to five grams of carbs per kilogram of your body weight. This means you should eat 12 to 20 calories of carbs for every two pounds of your body weight (multiply grams by 4 to get calorie count). Admittedly, that's a lot to eat for breakfast. If you are 170 pounds, this works out to between 1,020 and 1,700 calories. The goal is to make certain you have enough stored carbs in your muscles to get you through the most arduous match. You can eat this much a lot easier if you go for pancakes, cheese omelets, and toss in a slice of bacon or two. Other gurus recommend 600 to 1,200 calorie breakfasts. You will need to determine what works best for you by keeping tabs on your performance results. If you read the nutrition labels on your food products, you'll see the calories can add up quickly. The key is, the more you eat, the longer you need to digest your food. So if you get up at 7:00 a.m. for your 9:00 a.m. match, you'll be forced to go lighter. Have a calorie-dense liquid shake before 7:30 a.m., and make sure you bring lots of easy-to-eat (and easy-to-digest) snacks for change-overs because you won't have a lot of pre-match energy reserves. You can help negate the lighter meal by making sure you ate enough the night before to restock your energy supply. You will also need to refuel adequately afterward to make certain you continue to keep your muscles stocked with energy.

As the clock ticks down to match time, eat 100 to 300 more calories. Then you might snack again about 15 minutes beforehand. This is where that Glycemic Index (GI) rating becomes helpful in determining what to eat and what to avoid. The GI rating lets you know how quickly foods are changed into glucose (sugar). When your blood sugar is elevated (as it is after eating), insulin is released to bring it back down to normal. For instance, when you eat a candy bar, or drink a sugary drink, you will immediately spike your sugar level and feel very energetic for about 10 to 15 minutes. Then when insulin rushes in to counter this sugar high, your energy level will drop—hence the feeling of sudden tiredness or even nausea and/or dizziness. If that happens, you have just experienced a sudden onset of hypoglycemia (low blood sugar level). It's a rebound effect for correcting the high blood sugar level. This is something you want to avoid, especially when you are out on the court.

There are a couple different GI rating scales available, but I will be using the original one, based on the glucose-oriented GI rating scale, which ranges from 1 to 100. The faster the food is converted to blood sugar (glucose), the higher the rating. Thus, with glucose as the anchor, if you had a glucose IV drip into a vein, the rating would be 100. The speed at which your food is converted to glucose is not determined by whether it is a "simple" or "complex" starch; rather, it is determined by how much fiber, protein, or fat it has. These three nutrients (fiber, protein, and fat) each slow down the digestive conversion process. Therefore, foods containing higher quantities of fiber, protein, or fat will all have a lower GI rating. That's probably the best way to remember which foods to eat when, rather than trying to learn actual ratings, as there are just too many, though Table 3.6 lists some of the more common foods. There is not much distinction in timing for consuming the "moderate" versus "high" GI foods, but it is imperative not to confuse when to have LO GI foods versus Moderate to Hi GI foods. Choose the Moderate to HI GI foods based upon availability and absorption rate and whether you need the energy relatively fast (moderate), or "right now" (HI). Visit the following website to see a more comprehensive GI rating list: http://www.mendosa.com/gi.htm

Unless you are diabetic, don't get yourself confused with the health-alert recommendations. Your athletic needs are much different, and you absolutely require high GI foods at certain times. Read the tables only for your food listings. From there, you'll need to experiment during practice sessions and see how you feel after consuming whatever product(s) you're considering having with you at match time.

With this in mind, if you are a little hungry at 2:15 and your match is set to start at 2:30, a handful of peanuts will be better than a handful of raisins. If you're thirsty, a cup of water will be better than a cup of Gatorade. Water, by the way, has no GI rating if it has no supplements added. Consider it a "neutral" fluid. The peanuts have fiber, protein, fat, and salt and will

Table 3.6
Sample of Common Foods: GI Listing per Match Timing

LO GI FOODS (30-60 min pre) (slowest digestion)	MODERATE GI FOODS (3-4 hours pre, during, & post)	HI GI FOODS (3-4 hours pre, during, & post) (fastest digestion)
Liquids		
Fructose	Sucrose	Glucose
Dairy	Orange Juice	Gatorade
	Apple Juice	Pedialyte
		Honey
Breads/Grains		
Barley	Pasta	Bagel
Power Bar	Bran Muffin	Cheerios
	Pumpernickel Bread	White Bread
	Popcorn	Cornflakes
	Potato Chips	Shredded Wheat
	Oatmeal	Instant Oatmeal
	All-Bran Cereal	Graham Crackers
		Pretzels
Fruits		
Apples	Oranges	Watermelon
Apricots		Raisins
Under-Ripe Banana		Ripe Banana
Grapefruit		
Pear		
Veggies/Legumes		
Most Beans	Peas	Baked Potato
Chickpeas	Corn	Carrots
Peanuts	Sweet Potato	Beets

give you feeling of fullness, stop those stomach pains, and give you some electrolytes. Plain water hydrates and gives you a sense of fullness, but won't cause that hypoglycemic rebound right as you are starting your first set. On the other hand, raisins and Gatorade are highly recommended during match play because they are almost total sugar with low to no fiber content. They provide "instant" energy.

In-Match Nutrition

Eating and drinking during competition (or practice) is simple: You need instant energy, and you need energy to last you at least two hours, so it doesn't really matter what you eat as long as it sits well in your stomach and digests quickly. For this reason, moderate to high GI foods and drinks are usually recommended. This is when you go for your bananas and sport drinks (as long as they are only five to eight percent sugar, anything higher slows down absorption), raisins, pretzels, and energy bars (in small bites). The key is to eat and drink something at every change over to keep your sugar level high and avoid that hypoglycemic rebound effect.

Bryan brothers fuel up at break—Miller Lite International Tennis Championship, Newport, RI, 2002.

Post-Match Nutrition

After your match, your post-match nutrition becomes critical for recovering from your energy depletion. You need to start this within 30 minutes of stopping play, beginning with a recovery sports drink as you walk off the court. Recovery sport drinks are generally heavier in carbs and electrolytes, contain more antioxidants and vitamins, and add protein to the mix (e.g., Endurox, Accelerade). You want to continue replenishing your stores over the next two hours—this will prepare you for your second match of the day, or for tomorrow's. Again, because you need to restock your muscles with glycogen, you need to carb-load with foods considered to have moderate to high GI ratings. The caloric count should be about 500 grams, or 2,000 calories before you hit the sack (about 7 to 10 grams per kilogram of body weight, which translates to 28 to 40 calories for every two pounds of your body weight).

Red Flag: The Dehydration Road to Cramping

"The water was not fit to drink. To make it palatable, we had to add whiskey. By diligent effort, I learned to like it."

—Sir Winston Churchill, Statesman

When your body water content becomes too low due to not drinking enough of the right stuff, you become dehydrated. To avoid dehydration, you should drink beverages that are caffeine- and alcohol-free, because caffeine and alcohol cause you to urinate more. If the fluid level in your body gets too low, your blood will get thick. This makes it more difficult to circulate, thereby requiring your heart to work that much harder to pump the blood through your body and deliver the nutrients needed to your muscles. If you couple dehydration with exercising in the heat, a frequent situation tennis players encounter, you have a double whammy.

When you get hot, your body manages its heat by sweating. The evaporation of your sweat is what cools you off. But if you are low on fluids, you won't be able to sweat much, so your natural cooling mechanism (sweating) will be impaired. Now you have two problems—an overworked heart and a limited ability to sweat. This will set you up for nasty heat-related illnesses, such as heat cramps and heat exhaustion. It is therefore vital to maintain the amount of liquid that is available to the body. The more you sweat, the more you need to replace the lost liquid in order to maintain your body's ability to regulate its temperature.

Players and refs alike take shelter from the mid-day heat under umbrellas at an unusually hot spring day in Elkin, NC.

If you are an athlete preparing your body for competition, alcohol will definitely mess you up. If you are accustomed to having a glass of red wine with your dinner, then you should not experience much of a problem. In fact, red wine is actually good for you—it aids in digestion and helps to prevent heart disease. However, aside from the sociological implications of alcohol abuse and its consequences, and the fact that it dehydrates, alcohol interferes with your energy systems. When you need that energy most during a crucial moment in your match, you simply won't have it.

Alcohol is a carbohydrate and a very non-nutritious source of calories. In fact, it is not even changed into glucose as are other carbs. Rather, it is metabolized as a fatty acid and most likely will be stored as fat. It has nearly as many calories as fat too, seven calories per gram (fat has 9, regular carbs have only 4). So unless you are drinking low-carb beers, the average 12-ounce beer serves up around 146 calories while one "chaser" shot (1.5

oz) of hard liquor (gin, whiskey, etc.) contains about 125 calories. So you can pack on the pounds with partying hearty. Even though you urinate out the fluid, the calories remain.

Calories aside (hopefully you are training enough to offset the occasional beer or two), remember that alcohol is a central nervous system depressant. That means it will negatively affect your balance, coordination, reaction time, judgment, strength, power, and aerobic endurance if you try to practice or play a match with alcohol in your body waiting to be metabolized. Depending upon individual metabolic differences, it can take anywhere from 24-48 hours to fully process just one drink out of your system. This means that if you went to a party and drank heavily on Thursday night and had a Saturday afternoon match, the alcohol could still be in your system impacting your game. You may find yourself "slightly off" in shot placement, late getting to the ball, or just not able to think clearly.

As for dehydration, more often than not, that cramping can be traced back to inadequate hydration—not the day of the match but, rather, the days leading up to the match. It's not just what you do the day of the match that counts, although that is important. It's what you do that entire week before. Once your body gets dehydrated, for any reason, it takes some time to get fully rehydrated.

If you've had successive days of not replenishing your fluids adequately, no amount of what you drink on court on match day will prevent the cramping episode. It's going to happen. At that point, all you can do is treat the cramp and then try to prevent it in the future. Standard treatments for cramps include stretching and massaging the muscle and rehydrating with electrolyte sports drinks containing glucose. If you don't trust the commercial sports drinks, you can easily create your own sport drink from water, salt, and sugar. The recipe calls for three grams of salt (equivalent to a half teaspoon or 1-2 small picnic packs) and 60-80 grams of sugar (or 15-20 sugar cubes/packets) dissolved in one liter (64 oz) of water. It isn't as flavorful as the commercial brands, but it will do the job—namely rehydrate with needed carbs and the most important electrolyte, salt.

Hydration!

Other hydration fluids that some athletes have said worked for them include V-8 juice, tomato juice, pickle juice, and canned chicken broth. Why do these perhaps work? It could be a placebo effect—that is, it works because they believe it will. But there is some scientific logic behind these drinks. They each have high sodium (i.e., salt) content. However, the palatability and digestibility of some of these fluids are questionable, especially if you plan on going back onto the court anytime soon. Tonic water with quinine doesn't really work well in a tennis-cramping situation. It is carbonated which slows down stomach absorption and the quinine content isn't really enough to work—it just makes the drink taste bitter. Another anecdotal remedy that some trainers claim to work is Alka-Seltzer. Their theory is that the high sodium content aided with water retention and the bicarbonate content helped neutralize the low pH (higher acid level) in the blood that might be contributing to the cramp. This is a questionable practice for a couple of reasons. First, Alka-Seltzer contains a good dose of aspirin; the trainer has to know ahead of time if the athlete is allergic to aspirin (many people are) or if the athlete has a stomach disorder (like a pre-ulcer condition) as aspirin can aggravate stomach problems. How many trainers have asked you about your drug allergies or stomach problems recently? Second, you can't multiple dose—that is, the player thinks he's getting a cramp late in the first set and takes a dose, then he pops another dose in the third set because he is cramping. Overdosing on sodium bicarbonate preparations can cause nausea and vomiting. Third, Alka-Seltzer also contains more than 500 mg of citric acid. This is Vitamin C and doses that high have been shown to cause stomach pain in some people. Lastly, if the trainer accidentally used the cold-formula Alka-Seltzer rather than the "regular" formula, then you'd also get some pseudoephedrine into your system. While pseudoephedrine is no longer on the 2005 World Anti-Doping Agency (WADA) banned substances list, it is being monitored (as is caffeine). This means they are watching the dosing of the athletes for the time being. Substances such as this tend to have an on-and-off again history of being banned. In short, it's best to be wary if somebody offers you a magic pill to cure your pain. The cure could be worse than the cramp.

The Gatorade Sports Science Institute (www.gssiweb.com) also has resources on-line, including a fluid intake calculator and a short video. All you do is plug in your current weight and exercise information. Table 3.7 summarizes the major hydration guidelines, and Table 3.8 is a simplified weight-hydration tracking score sheet. After a while you won't need to write this stuff down, you'll know what to do.

It's difficult to keep up with the different sport drinks available these days, to say nothing of those other drinks that claim to be healthy for you. First off, water is good for you, just don't over do it. It's a great choice

Table 3.7
Hydration Guidelines

Dehyration Warning Signs:
1. Your urine is dark yellow or even brownish—and very strong smelling.
2. You suddenly get very tired out on the court and it's not due to lack of rest.
3. You feel weak, dizzy, or shaky and it's not flu season.
4. You have a pounding headache and it's not due to vision problems or not eating.
5. You have a little twinge in your leg that can progress to a full-blown leg cramp.

Hyponatremia:
1. Definition: Water intoxication!
2. Cause: Drinking too much plain water during long matches, especially in the heat. High sweat rates with high sodium losses are coupled with not replenishing the sodium losses.
3. Symptoms: Mild cases look similar to dehydration warning signs—fatigue, nausea, headache. This is why some players mistake it for dehydration and drink even more water. Severe cases progress to cramping, seizures, and coma resulting in hospitalization.
4. Prevention: Don't over consume plain water; DO drink electrolyte-laced sport drinks.

Avoiding Dehydration:
1. Hydrate off as well as on the court. Avoid or limit alcohol and caffeinated drinks, especially leading up to and during tournaments.
2. During practice/matches, drink 1-2 cups of fluid every 15-20 minutes even if you don't feel thirsty. If you feel thirsty, you're already getting dehydrated.
3. Remember the Drinking on Court Rule: 4-8 large gulps at every changeover.
4. After the match/practice, rehydrate based upon how much body weight you lost. So remember to weigh yourself before and after your match/practice.
5. Remember the Rehydration Rule: Drink 2 cups for every pound lost.
6. If your practice, work-out, or match takes longer than 30 minutes, make sure your fluid choice has electrolytes in it (especially sodium, about 100 mg). Sodium (i.e., salt) helps your body retain the fluids in your muscles. Carbs (sugar, 5-8%) also help to retain fluids and gives you an added energy boost benefit without stomach upset.
7. Do Not limit your dietary salt intake unless you have a medical problem.
8. Do Not Overdrink—yes, this is possible. If you GAINED weight during your practice or match, you drank TOO much! Next time, cut back a little.
9. Do Not Overdrink Plain Water! This too is very possible. If you are playing for a long time in a hot environment and drinking just plain water, you can dilute your electrolyte balance and promote cramping due to loss of sodium.
10. Do Not try to shed extra pounds by sweating it out or not drinking enough—this is very dangerous and provides no lasting benefit.

Table 3.8
Weight—Hydration Tracker

Directions: Weigh yourself before practice, ideally in the nude. Record this value. After practice, before you void (go to the bathroom), re-weigh yourself in the nude, or in DRY underwear/shorts (if you pre-weighed yourself in your shorts). The amount of weight you lost during practice (or a match) should be doubled to determine how much fluid, measured in cups, you need to rehydrate and quicken your recovery.

To get started, just use a notebook to record as shown below.

Notes: To convert kilograms to pounds, multiply by 2.2
To convert ounces to milliliters, multiply by 29.57.
1 Cup = 8 ounces. Most sports drinks bottles contain at least 12 ounces.
Four LARGE gulps is close to a cup.

Date	Weigh-in - (pounds)	Weigh-out (pounds)	= Weight Difference x 2 (pounds)	= Fluid Needed (in cups)
Example:				
Tues, 8/10	175	170	5	10

Notes: 10 cups x 8 ounces = 80 ounces x 29.57 = 2365 ml / 1000 = 2.4 L. In Gatorade-sized bottle terms, I need to drink the HUGE 64 ounce container, Plus one 16-ounce bottle. Or at least get close to this. And do it over the course of the evening, don't chug it all at one time.

---

because there are no aftertastes, so it's usually not aversive to anyone (especially if you get bottled water). It is good if you are exercising moderately in a moderate temperature/environment for about 30 minutes. If, however, you practice longer than 30 minutes at a pretty high intensity level, chances are you are sweating much more and probably losing electrolytes in your sweat. If you have white stains or white patches on your clothing where your sweat dried, try a taste test. It will be salty. That's a tip that your sport drink should have some sodium in it. If you lose focus during your practice or matches and feel fuzzy headed and weak, then your carb stores are also probably low. So you need something quick to boost your energy that won't feel heavy on your stomach. Remember, you still have to think out there on the court—sometimes brainpower is what is needed to defeat your opponent. Carbs fuel your brain as well as your muscles. That's the point of adding carbohydrates (sugar) to your drink. This is not marketing hype, as many players seem to think. These are real sports medicine science facts. Some companies are just better at capitalizing on these facts than others.

Drink a sports drink that has a slight to moderate amount of carbs and electrolytes. That means, sugar in the form of glucose, maybe a dab of fructose, and sodium (salt) plus a bit of potassium. The label will tell you what each drink contains. But not only do these items need to be in there, they need to be in there in the right amounts, otherwise, they will be ineffective, and can cause stomach distress. Hypotonic and isotonic drinks are "less heavy" in terms of their carbohydrate and sodium content. On the other hand, too much carbohydrate or sodium during practice or competition is actually bad, as either will delay fluid from emptying out of your stomach, thereby causing nausea and stomach cramps. So watch out for the *hyper*tonic drinks.

Sports research has proven that the best fluids to consume during exercise are ones that taste good (so that you will drink it), replenish your carb and electrolyte stores, and don't make you sick to your stomach. The most effective drinks that fit this bill have a carbohydrate solution that is between 5-8 percent and the sodium content is about 100 mg. Less is not effective and more has been shown to cause stomach distress during competition. These three guidelines—time, carb amount, and sodium content—are the guiding factors you should use in choosing your on-court drinks. Sodas and fruit juices are eliminated as both are higher in sugar, 9-12 percent. Many popular well-marketed sport drinks are also ruled out because they are too low in sodium and too high in sugar. If you find yourself with products that are less than desirable, you can water down the sugar and electrolyte content. Hence always have water with you—its usefulness goes far beyond drinking straight up or pouring over your head! Also always have with you little packets of salt. You can easily spike any drink with extra salt.

Some products add protein to the formula. These drinks are better suited for recovery fuels as they tend to be a bit heavier and sit longer in the stomach. Used as a recovery fuel, these heavier drinks really do help to replenish your used up glycogen stores faster—and the sooner you start drinking the stuff after your match is over, the better off you will be, especially if you have two matches a day or matches several days in a row. You don't have much time to refuel, so every minute counts.

Supplements: Help, Hype, or Horror?

"I dunno. I never smoked any Astroturf."

—Tug McGraw, Baseball, when asked if he preferred grass or Astroturf.

These days anytime anyone does anything spectacular, the "doping" question pops up. I will address this issue by asking five questions: (1) What is an ergogenic aid? (2) What works? (3) What doesn't work? (4) What is legal? (5) What should you avoid?

What Is an "Ergogenic Aid"?

In its purest form, an ergogenic aid is anything the athlete does or takes to improve his performance. With that broad of a definition, an ergogenic aid could be anything from a new warm-up routine or hypnosis to popping pills of various sorts. More commonly, an ergogenic aid is any exogenous substance taken that gives one an unfair performance advantage in sports. This includes anything you eat or drink or inject into your body to help your performance. The "unfair" part comes in to play when that substance you took was not equally available for use by everyone competing.

What Works?

Safe and approved nutritional supplements such as sport drinks are available in several categories, ranging from pre-, during-, and post-hydration periods for on-court energy, speeding recovery, or glycogen boosting. We know that certain foods and nutrition bar snacks are better at certain times—these can each be considered an ergogenic aid if it helps keep you oriented, gives you energy, or prevents or delays fatigue. All legal. All safe. All easily obtainable.

Protein supplementation is used to help resynthesize muscle tissue and for weight gain. According to the nutrition research, the powdered protein supplements haven't been shown to be any more effective than simply eating more protein from natural sources—but it may certainly be more convenient. Research suggests arginine or lysine supplements may stimulate human growth hormone (HGH) to promote muscle growth, but even so, HGH doesn't appear to help improve strength in strength-trained individuals. Your muscles get larger but not necessarily stronger, so these types of supplements won't help you blast a 150 mph serve. But they could make you look better with your shirt off.

Caffeine has in fact been demonstrated to improve a variety of factors relating to athletic performance, ranging from increasing your ability to generate short bursts of power to facilitating fat use for more energy. It keeps you awake, alert, and oriented. But there are a couple of problems with caffeine as an ergogenic aid. First, it takes a ton of it to get the beneficial effects, so much so that the side effects of the jitters, lack of precision, and heart palpations overshadow the small performance benefits that have been reported. Furthermore, it doesn't work consistently—you build up a tolerance to it, so that the amount which worked for you before may not be enough once you grow accustomed to it. In addition, if you are "used to" caffeine, that is, you regularly consume it with your meals, snacks, and so on, then it would take even more before you find it useful for helping your game. Of course, more caffeine means more jitters too.

Creatine does work and it's still legal. The purpose behind this supplement—either in liquid drops or powder form—is to increase phosphocreatine stores in your muscles. It works for short-term (under 10 minutes), high intensity (near max), exhaustive exercise or short explosive power bursts. However, it doesn't work for everyone, specific dosing techniques must be followed carefully, and caffeine use seems to negate creatine's effects. In terms of strength gains, use of creatine, because of its ability to enhance power production, has enabled athletes to train harder and lift more so that strength gains are maximized. However, it is not clear if the weight gain attributed to creatine use is muscle, simply excess water bloating, or a little of both. Therefore, you might put on added pounds that could actually hurt your running ability on the court—you may feel sluggish or slow, or not as agile. While this is relatively unimportant for a weight lifter, it is a big deal for tennis players. It could cause a significant problem in getting to difficult shots. Maybe you'll be able to explode on your serve, but what if your opponent is equally adept at returning that serve to the far corner of the court away from you? There have also been reports of stomach upset, muscle cramping, and dehydration—some of which is related to not boosting your fluid intake when taking this supplement, taking too much of the supplement, or just being sensitive to the supplement itself. The good news is that short-term studies have not shown organ damage to the kidneys as originally feared. In fact, some researchers liken the use of creatine supplementation to carbohydrate supplementation for use to enhance recovery. However, it is still not known if there are any long-term side-effects.

What Doesn't Work?

Any of those "strength enhancing" supplements whose name ends in the suffix "ine"—you know the ones, the amino acid complexes and such—don't live up to their claims. Suffice it to say that despite their purported benefits, valid scientific studies have yet to show that any of them actually do what they claim to do regarding enhancing your athletic abilities. The same goes for those vitamin complexes, triglyceride or fatty acid products, or herbal products claiming to increase testosterone-human growth hormone precursors. So next time you're in a health-food store, save your money for your real touring needs. Pick up a couple nutrition bars, some Accelerade, a Myoplex extra-meal drink, but don't go for the pills or protein powders. Eat more healthfully. If you seriously don't know how to do this, get a consult from a registered licensed sports dietitian. By doing this you will spare yourself the very real potential agony of getting caught with traces of illegal compounds in your urine.

What Is Legal?

The World Anti-Doping Agency (WADA) updates its banned list annually. This is important because what was legal last year may not be legal this year, or the allowable limits may have been changed. A few substances may even have been removed—such as caffeine (although that has an on-off history of being banned or restricted, so keep current). If your favorite dietary supplement doesn't contain any of the banned items listed, and if it doesn't metabolize into one of those items, then you're probably okay to use it. But that last part is tricky unless you are a biochemist. Furthermore, because of the loose, or almost zero, regulation of the dietary supplement industry, the labels on your product don't always tell you the whole story. As long as the manufacturer doesn't make true physiological claims (that is, they can suggest things may work in a certain way, but then buffer their statements by saying this has not been empirically proven, not approved by the FDA, etc.), then they aren't held to the same strict regulations as the pharmaceutical industry. However, some of that is hopefully going to change due to high profile anti-doping cases.

Your best approach is to not take supplements that don't guarantee a safe, standardized, clean lab for the production of their products. If you want more information about doping rules and regulations, go to the WADA anti-doping site (www.wada-ama.org). Australia has its own classification guidelines (www.ais.org.au/nutrition). Likewise, the ATP has an anti-doping guideline booklet posted on its website (www.atptennis.com).

If you want more detailed consumer information about the supplement industry problems, go to www.consumerlabs.com. For about $25 you can become a member and get more detailed information about which labs label products accurately. A final word of caution: Be extremely careful when anyone offers you any substance to take for any purpose (whether it's to help for cramps, speed up recovery, or get some sleep). Unless you are 100 percent certain that the product they are about to give you is 100 percent safe and approved for competition, don't take it. Some trainers, coaches, parents, and friends are well meaning but may be ill informed. The ATP has begun to address this problem as well. They have joined forces with the pharmaceutical giant GlaxoSmithKline in an attempt to provide uncontaminated vitamin supplements to players. Hopefully this will reduce the non-intentional doping infractions. Remember, ultimately, it's your butt on the line, not theirs.

What Should You Avoid?

If it is on the "banned" list and it is not being used for medical purposes to correct a disease/illness/injury process and you have not obtained official approval for its use, then you absolutely, positively, at all times, must not take it. Don't experiment with it even once. The amount required to catch you is often times miniscule. The anti-doping rules state you can be spot-tested at anytime, whether you are in competition or not. Once you are labeled a cheater, it will stick with you, and the cost can be very heavy—from public distrust to loss of income to being banned from your sport for life.

Chapter 4
Mental Toughness

"Whether you think that you can or that you can't, you are usually right."

—Henry Ford, Automobile Magnate

Brian Vahaly and Don Johnson believed in themselves when almost no one else did. And you should too, because at some point, you may be your only fan. Throughout all the mental trials and tribulations described in this chapter that will challenge you, there are three basic rules that you must follow religiously. First, believe in yourself at all times. And I do mean at all times, as there will be times when you will wonder why you are "wasting" your time. Occasionally your friends, parents, and even your coach might question the pursuit of your dream. You must remember that a dream will remain a dream if you don't doggedly pursue it. Second, push yourself hard most of the time. I say most of the time as you will need some strategically placed blow-off time to recoup mentally and physically. This does not give you license to party at will. This acknowledges that there is a time to work and a time to play. Third, don't give up!

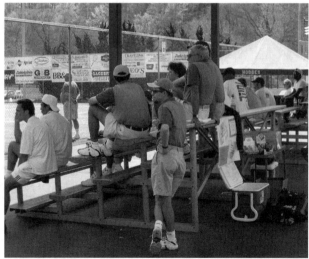

Sparce crowds to cheer on players during the early rounds at Futures and Challenger tournaments.

So You Were a College Super-Star: Now What?

"I really lack the words to compliment myself today."
—Alberto Tomba, Olympic Skier

In tennis, you are only as good as your last performance, and as you know, the matches keep rolling on. You can't expect to win them all, but you should strive to have a good, consistent won/lost average. Eventually you will need to be winning at least as many as you are losing. None of that should surprise you, it's not much different from college expectations. But if you realistically plan to make a go of professional tennis, you'll need to do just as well, if not better, than in college—or at least make sure your wins are from the higher paying tournaments.

Let's assume that you were a good and consistent college player, with a win record around 70 percent or better (remember, you were a college super-star, or had the potential to be one). Of course there will be a transition period between college and the pros. When you first take the tour plunge, you may be losing more than you are winning. This might feel very foreign to you. You might even see others having a stroke of beginner's luck. Don't despair. Remind yourself that you had a good college career, and with some hard work, you will have a good pro career. After you've been on the road a while, you should be able to get into your groove and become a consistently good pro player. You need to remember how you motivated yourself in college. If you don't have access to a coach, you need to be able to "hear" your best coaches in your mind. Filter out negative, unconstructive comments—in fact don't even listen to them lest you start believing them instead of believing in yourself. If you allow yourself to partake in negativity, your tour life will be short. Remember the saying, "misery loves company"? Avoid or limit contact with those people. They may be more than just players who are mad at the world; they could be the refs, fans, or even well-meaning relatives who "know it all" or are simply "concerned for you."

Try to surround yourself with upbeat, positive people both on and off the tour. This includes your coach. Your coach should be correcting whatever problems you may be having with your game. That might mean making some difficult comments to you when your game is in trouble or being "tough" with you if you are misbehaving or slacking off. In any event, he should still inspire confidence in your ability to succeed in your goals or assist you to realistically rethink your short-term goals so that they are achievable. However, ultimately, you must be the keeper of your goals. Becoming a successful pro is going to take a lot of hard knocks, and it probably won't happen in a year. But if you keep striving for attainable short-term goals (such as continued improvement in shots, etc.) and re-evaluating your play every three or four months, eventually your long-term goal of making it in the pros will be realized, without you needing to spend every waking hour worrying about it. Your success must be internally driven.

Keep that carrot dangling in front of you, close enough to almost touch, but far enough away to keep you working hard.

Brasington loses.

But losing happens. Deal with it with confidence, not arrogance. Confidence means that you retain the "I can do this" mentality regardless of the loss, no matter how big or small the loss was. The trick to this is to have a very selective memory. You need to cultivate the ability to forget about your loss (or losses) and remember that you can (and do) win. Every match is a fresh new opportunity. Confidence means that even when you are down 1-4, you believe you can fight back to win 6-4. Confidence means that you realize your abilities and you accept compliments gracefully. Confidence means that you discuss your wins matter-of-factly, acknowledging your own hard work as well as that of your opponent. Exuding confidence is appealing. Exuding arrogance is nauseating. What is arrogance? It is projecting an obnoxious air of self-importance or superficial superiority, conceit mixed with selfishness, willful boasting about your own accomplishments. Recall the self-proclamation, "I am the greatest"? Suffice it to say, if you use those words, you better be the greatest.

None of the nasty traits we see on court, such as being a prima donna, acting out, or trash-talking your opponents is likeable, and none will win you any accolades. Remember, the way the sport of tennis stays in business is by financial support—commercial sponsorships and fans' hard-earned dollars to watch you play. Maybe you'll be able to get away with being a jerk when you become a super-star, but on your way up, it would behoove you to reign in your behavior.

To find out how you present yourself, have an honest chat with a person whom you respect and trust to be honest. If that doesn't work, then once you have some spare change, hire an image consultant. If you persist in having trouble projecting a good public image, visit a shrink to work through your personal and professional demons. It will be an investment in your future. The ATP actually has classes for up-and-coming pros about image projection and how to handle the media tactfully. Obviously, some players (and their entourages) failed these classes, but you don't need to join them.

Cultivating Discipline:
The Making of a (Successful) Tennis Pro

"Don't stay in bed unless you can make money in bed."

—George Burns, Comedian

Irst you need to define for yourself the word "success"—what does that mean to you? Does it mean that you get to travel all over the world and meet some cool people before getting a "real" job? Does it mean that you just win a couple of matches on the pro circuit? Does it mean that after expenses, you will be able to live comfortably on your prize earnings? These are important questions for you to answer, as they will determine how far you are willing to push yourself in this pro arena. You need to give 100 percent during practice, during your matches, and during your off-court training. No slacking off, no laziness.

You have to behave responsibly and be accountable. Unlike college, you probably won't have your coach around to talk some sense into you. If you sleep through your alarm and arrive late to your match, you lose. If you miscalculated the time it would take to get from your hotel room to the court and you arrive late, you lose. And if you're having a bad day as a result of partying, pre-match anxiety resulting in insomnia, or for no earthly reason whatsoever, no one is going to tolerate tantrums if you get frustrated when playing poorly. Tantrums will only tick off your partners, refs, and organizers, plus embarrass friends and family. The spectators may initially be amused and laugh at you (not with you), but even they will tire of bratty antics. You will get a dubious reputation. If your meltdown is televised, brace yourself for the verbal abuse from the commentators when you watch the taped version later.

Contested moment during the French Open, 2003, Kim vs Philippousis.

The refs have a system for this. They assign any player with a reputation for being difficult to the toughest, no-nonsense, no-sympathy refs. While refs try to be fair and unbiased regardless of player personalities, they are, after all, only human. Picture your father sitting up there in the ref's chair. How would you like it if some young 20-something began mouthing off telling your father that he is a blind, senile, stupid idiot not capable to judge a line call? Even if you think you are the next McEnroe, contain yourself. You're not going to get very far on the pro circuit without a lot of discipline both on and off the court. Times have changed from the bad-boy tennis days. There's a lot of talent out there and less tolerance. Don't waste everybody's time. Don't just talk the talk—live it. Get a grip. The next section will give you tips on how to do this.

Handling Match Stress: Learning from Losing

"How can I lose to such an idiot?"

—Aaron Nimzovich, Chess Master

Losing can be frustrating, humbling, or humiliating. But it can also be a great learning experience. So often an athlete will underestimate the power of his opponent and simply not put forth 100 percent effort until it is too late. How often have you seen your favorite player or team come to the court with an incredible nonchalant attitude, like they already have this one in the bag, only to wind up scrambling, and losing, in the end? Of course the moral of this story is it's not over until it's over—never take a match for granted. Play each match as if it might be the last one you'll ever play, fight to the end. If you feel yourself getting frustrated, remember to use your changeover periods to refocus, readjust your attitude. The worst thing you can do is allow your opponent to see or hear your frustration. This only fuels him on. The way you walk off or back on the court, your facial expressions, and your racquet throwing tell your opponent (and the spectators) that you are accepting defeat. This gives your foe the psychological advantage. He did not earn it—you handed it over to him on a silver platter so he can throw it back in your face. Andres Pedroso had this to say about players showing their frustrations on the court: "I love it when I see my opponent losing it. It just makes me want to pound him all the more—it pumps me up."

If you fight hard and with dignity, even if you lose, you'll know you played your best and there is some satisfaction to be gained from that. You can then go back to the locker room, replay the match in your head, think about what you might have done better. Had you arranged for a friend to tape your match, you might even be able to watch it later when you are objective enough to see where you faltered and where you excelled. Reinforce the positive aspects and attempt to fix the negatives. Then forget about it. Don't go into the locker-room and punch out the wall or break your racquet. Just accept losing. You don't have to like it though, and in fact you shouldn't. Jimmy Connors once said, "I hate to lose more than I like to win. I hate to see the happiness on their faces when they beat me!" Losing is what motivates you to learn from it and play again. But losing happens, and when you are playing 20-30 tournaments a year, there's going to be plenty of losing time to go around. So you need to believe in yourself. Believe that you hit the ball exactly as you planned. Believe that you played well. But some of your shots simply didn't make it. It doesn't mean you're not fit to be a pro. Your opponent just played a great match against you that day. Period.

But what if you lose, then lose again, and again, and again? What's going on? According to Dr. Allen Fox, a world-renown sport psychologist and a former tennis coach for the Pepperdine tennis team, the dark side of achievement is the fear factor. In order to achieve your full potential, you have to learn to overcome the fear of failure. Fox readily admits that losing is painful and the choking that you might see from a player on the verge of winning is often misdiagnosed as a fear of winning. Winning is a happy occasion. Losing is not. Players want to feel happy. So they want to win, not lose. And the more important the tournament, the more they want to win.

What is it that players fear when choking? It's the responsibility for that failure to win. They fear what a loss might mean—to them, to their family, to their fans. They perceive it as some type of character flaw, an inability to succeed. The insecure player who is not confident in himself (either on a consistent basis or for a particular match) is most likely to choke. It hurts the most when the player has a lot of himself invested in the match. If he trained extra hard and lost, it hurt more than if he took a more casual approach to the whole thing. Naturally, most serious players on the circuit respond poorly to losing.

Of course you can't win them all, but you do need to get back on track and win again. Besides reviewing your tennis strategies and setting out to correct errors that may have crept into your game, you probably will also need to get your mind out of a really bad funk. Just as Fox suggested, some athletes will lose their confidence and begin seeing their losses as personal failures rather than just part of a difficult side-road to winning. They will begin to perceive themselves as being inadequate, worthless, losing their tennis groove. They lose their ability to focus. They begin to listen, really listen, to the point of believing, the often-worthless negative chatter of competitors and spectators. They lose the "I can do this" attitude. They relapse into bickering on court with opponents, the refs, even the hecklers. They are miserable and may even try to make everyone else miserable around them.

So what can be done about it, especially if there aren't any leftover bucks to go visit a sport psychologist? Take a bit of time off to refocus. Relax. Get away from tennis for a short bit. Get yourself back into a positive frame of mind. Remember all the stuff you do well, really well. Remember your successes and how you achieved them. Imagine achieving them again. Use mental imagery to correctly execute a play, to win. Visualize what it felt like to win. Then get back on the court. Develop routines to manage your rising stress level on the court. Use mental imagery distractions or pre-shot routines. Practice with some worthy opponents, but also with ones you know you can beat. When getting back to the circuit, you might want to schedule yourself into a relatively easy tournament at first to boost your self-confidence. Then go full speed ahead. Work hard. Keep positive. Don't let yourself get distracted. If a call is bad, accept it and move on. Realize you will be under stress, but practice stress-reduction techniques. Use positive self-talk, focus on rearranging your racquet strings, listen to music, whatever works.

Mardy refocusing.

At the end of the day, review all the positive things you did and relish in what worked. Don't dwell on what didn't go your way. Get a good night's sleep. Then be ready to start all over again fresh the next day.

Nick Bollettieri sums it up as follows: "Some people think failure is the end of the world. Failure should be a challenge. If you don't get knocked on your ass ten or fifteen times in life, you'll never reach your level of excellence."

Handling Personal Stress: The Match Marches On

"Adversity causes some men to break; others to break records."
—William Arthur Ward, Spiritualist

"There is always the possibility that some good will arise from an unfortunate situation."
—Arthur Ashe, Tennis Champion

Besides the physical-ness of it all, tennis is a mind game. When you first began to learn how to play tennis, you may remember having been distracted by everything, the wind, the sun, the birds, the planes, your friends watching, the pain in your big toe, the fight you had with your friend...you name it, you'd get out of focus in a heartbeat. But you learned how to block out intruding thoughts. Now you are in the big leagues where this is more important than ever. You could be playing in a dismal small community park with no one around, or you might be at a challenger in a country club where the atmosphere is festive with plenty of distractions. Surrounding the court will be noisy onlookers, people milling about, and even video cameras. The focusing lessons you learned will be key for keeping your mind on the match when you have internal noise from personal events as well as for motivating yourself during those no-fan days. But in case you need a refresher course in refocusing techniques, or need some technique other than just straightening out your racquet strings, I have included creative suggestions from three different experts.

Well-known college sport psychologist Dr. John Silva at UNC recommends you visualize that you have two pockets, one in front for important things at the moment and one in back for all those other extraneous random thoughts that creep into your head. One by one, visualize yourself placing each random thought into your back pocket to ponder later, keeping them out of your consciousness for the moment. Then visualize putting the really pertinent thoughts needed to hit that ball into your front pocket for easy quick access.

Dr. Elizabeth Hedgpeth, a sports psychologist for several college sports teams at UNC, suggests a two-step technique that begins with focusing on your breathing to get yourself centered. It helps both sides of your brain to communicate with each other. The analytical/critical left brain must schmooze with the intuitive "I just want to rip it" right brain. Your "thinking" and "feeling" have to merge into a oneness in order to execute your serves. Apparently, breathing is one way to accomplish this. It's called deep abdominal breathing. To practice, lie on your back, then progress to doing it in a sitting position, then finally, in the standing position. This way, you can do this effectively whether sitting courtside during breaks or while standing at the baseline preparing to serve. There are only three simple breathing steps to learn as listed in Table 4.1.

The second part to centering is recognizing that increased stress alters your breathing in that you go from relaxed and controlled breathing to quick and shallow breaths. Besides reducing oxygen availability to your brain, this stressed-out breathing also causes tension to build in your upper body and alters your stance. You go from being balanced, knees slightly bent, and secure footing to a less stable posture, tilting too far forward with more rigidity. This tightness will throw off your center of gravity. So "getting centered," according to Dr. Hedgpeth, means thinking about where your center of gravity is located (about two inches below your navel). When

Table 4.1
Steps for Abdominal Breathing

1. Pick a quiet space to lie down and put one hand on your chest and the other on your stomach.
2. Breathe in deeply through your nose so that your lungs are full and you feel your stomach expand, but try not to move your chest while doing this.
3. Breath out through your mouth slowly and evenly. You should feel your stomach go down. At the same time, be aware of the air movement in and out of your lungs.

stressed out, tightening up your upper body/chest region displaces your center of gravity upwards, thereby making you off-balance, not just mentally, but physically. So think about your belly-button—and breathe deep.

Once you have mastered this deep breathing at home, try it on the court during practice. Then use it during a match whenever you are beginning to feel pressured or distracted when serving. You want to feel "stable" on the court and "centered." When you step up to the baseline to serve, and you feel tired or anxious, take some deep abdominal breaths. Close your eyes momentarily and clear your head. Concentrate feeling the tennis ball bouncing between the ground and your hand, which is positioned, by the way, around your navel. Imagine inhaling red energy and exhaling purple tension, dispersing it into minute particles into the air. As you exhale, relax your muscles and prepare for your serve. Your muscle memory will take care of the rest. Does this really work? Several tennis players and golfers swear by it.

Semi-retired tennis teaching pro Howard Schroeder's "old school" advice for calming yourself is to use a rating scale that ranges from 1 to 10, with 10 being totally stressed out and 1 being near comatose. Use this first during practice. At the end of every shot, rate your level of stress. When hitting for warm-up, you should strive to be calm, around a 2-3. When on the run for a shot, your stress level should momentarily increase, but then promptly return to a 2-3. When caught off guard, naturally your stress level will rise to an 8 or maybe even a 9, but once you hit (or miss) your shot, your stress level should again promptly return to a 2-3. If you remain hyped up after the shot, you won't be relaxed enough to respond appropriately to the return shot. You must forget about the last shot. Always stay in the moment. Realize when you have time and when you don't by carefully observing the ball dynamics—how is the ball coming at you? Is it fast and furious or slow and lobbing?

By focusing on the ball, practicing controlled breathing, de-stressing yourself, and clearing your mind, you should be able to handle the numerous on-court stresses you will encounter most of the time.

Life being what it is, you are bound to encounter some gut-wrenching turmoil at some point in your career, therefore you must learn to deal with it. Several athletes who experienced personal tragedies with 9-11 during their competition actually professed that tennis was their medicine; it gave their life some order when things were chaotic all around them. However, no man is an island. When bad things happen, talk to someone close whom you trust. Even if you are not looking for advice, it's important to talk about the upsetting event, if for no other reason than to let someone else know what's up. Maybe your listener will actually have a bit of good advice and offer some moral support. If you're on the road and really have no one you trust at hand, if you've got a cell phone or a bunch of quarters, you've got the means to reach out and call someone. E-mail is another option. If nobody's listening, pick up that hotel phone notepad and pen and jot your thoughts down. Then tuck them away somewhere in your bag. If you have a laptop, keep an e-journal. No one has to see what you write. The point is, just vent privately somehow. Get it out before you have to take to the court so you don't bring these feelings on the court with you. If you don't deal with the situation, and you push these emotions to the back of your mind, as soon as the going gets tough on court, these issues could resurface and wreak havoc with your playing focus. Toughing it out advice, such as telling yourself to "get over it, put it behind you" may not work with major issues. Minor stuff, sure, maybe you will forget for a bit. But experts in traumatic events claim you must first feel the pain in order to get over it. Not only will this help you sort through your emotional nightmare, it will help your close friends and family understand your behavior better, give you some space, and help you if asked.

There are several stages that have been identified which you might progress through while dealing with a really bad event—they are denial, anger, bargaining, depression, and finally, acceptance. You might not experience each of these stages, but if you find yourself experiencing any of them, you'll at least understand that it is a totally normal response, and that in time, with good internal and external support, you will be back to your normal self.

Denial is exactly as it sounds, you refuse to believe this bad thing has happened or is happening to you. Anger follows shortly thereafter. You get mad that it has, or is happening. You might get mad at yourself if you feel you were somehow to blame, you may blame others, or you might simply lash out at the most available victim regardless of his role or lack of involvement. You could be exploding with anger on the court at the most trivial things.

Next, you might find yourself making promises to yourself or others, even God if you are religious. Once you realize that bargaining or making promises to "be good" won't work, that the "bad thing" was random, had no cause, no reason, no cure, no reversal, or it just happened and you had no control over it, then depression sets in.

Depression can take on a number of forms. You could be noticeably sad or unhappy, or it might be more subtle. Your appetite might change dramatically, you may experience increased fatigue from normal training routines, incur more sport injuries, or become uncharacteristically accident-prone. You may have drastic changes in your sleeping habits or lose your motivation to compete. A normally laid back guy may become irritable or short-tempered. You could even have difficulty thinking and concentrating. In short, you will not be able to remain focused. By the way, these depression symptoms are also the same warning signs for over-training and burnout. Be aware of them even if you have not experienced a traumatic event.

Finally, at some point, you enter the last stage, acceptance. This is when you are really able to get on with your life, do what you need to do, what you normally do, and do it to your past level of satisfaction. In the case of an extreme event, such as death of a loved one, experts claim it usually takes at least a year to get your emotions under control. There will still be moments when something triggers your memory and evokes depressed feelings. It can take up to 5 years to not become emotional when personal memories of special events crop up. If you find yourself taking longer than expected to get over an emotional ordeal, or backsliding, then it's time to seek professional help. Your kind, listening friend, unless a licensed therapist, probably won't be enough to get your emotions sorted out. Hopefully, you will not have many experiences like this, especially early on in your pro career development, but we all must learn how to deal with these types of situations and get on with the business of daily life.

PART 3
The Business of Going Pro

"If you can count your money, you don't have a billion dollars."

— J. Paul Getty, Oil Billionaire

Chapter 5
Develop Your Business Sense

"A friendship founded on business is better than a business founded on friendship."

—John D. Rockefeller, Industrialist & Philanthropist

After watching several college graduates flounder about the business aspects of their tennis careers during their first few years on the tour circuit, I began to think there must be a better way. At the very least, players should not continue to burden their parents as they try to establish themselves in the pro tennis world. Unfortunately, most are not prepared to take matters into their own hands. While some had the foresight to major (or minor) in business in college, others scramble for advice from buddies on the circuit. Of course, this type of consultation leads to mixed results. You need to view your time on the circuit akin to running your own business. In an interview with *Tennis* magazine, former player Al Parker put it best: "It's not a traditional business, but it's a business career in its own right. You're self-employed, you're managing your own schedule, you're arranging your own travel, and you're coordinating expenses, budgeting, sponsorships, and equipment."

Can You Fire Your Family?

"Money frees you from doing things you dislike. Since I dislike doing most everything, money is handy."

—Groucho Marx, Comedian

Managing your tennis business is a big undertaking and takes lots of time. When someone volunteers his time to help you, even if it's a parent who has an undying love for you, at some point it's going to get in the way of his regular life. Among other things, your travel schedule must be mapped out, travel arrangements made, and finances figured out. Your prize earnings won't be able to cover your expenses for quite a while. Further, you must find partners with whom to travel, room, practice, and play doubles. And last, but not least, you even have to figure out when you will have the time for the more mundane aspects of traveling—such as doing your laundry.

If you have to do this managerial stuff yourself, it will take a significant amount of time away from practicing, off-court training, and even sleeping.

At the very least, when you are between matches, you will always be scrambling trying to get personal stuff done. If out of necessity a family member becomes your manager, you will need to set up some important ground rules so each of you can live peacefully. If you don't, you may find yourself constantly embroiled in family battles. If you add business problems to this formula, it becomes an ugly mix. If you fire a manager, you may never have to deal with that person again, but your family is your family, and you are stuck with them for life. If you do make it in tennis, money matters can become real points of friction. Money makes some people do stupid things, and relatives can be some of the worst offenders. It might be hard to fire a family member, and maybe it won't be necessary, but you must give it some serious thought before you get too far into your pro career.

Whether it's your uncle or a college buddy volunteering his time to be your manager, make sure there are no unspoken strings attached. Lastly, put everything in writing, even for relatives and best friends. People have short memories, especially when it comes to money. Although verbal agreements are legally binding contracts, it is very difficult to enforce them. I will discuss more on the legal aspects later.

The Taxman Cometh

"Income tax returns are the most imaginative fiction being written today."

—Herman Wouk, Writer

The first and most important lesson about taxes is not to be oblivious about your finances, no matter how small you think your earnings are. The IRS does go after the little guy as well as the big guy.

Reporting Your Earnings

The second most important lesson is not to lie about your earnings. Ever. You might make honest mistakes, and there is a procedure for you to handle that, but deliberately not reporting income or engaging in illegal tax shelter schemes is what will land you in the IRS stew bucket. It's easy for the IRS to track your earnings, especially if you are playing in ATP events, as your earnings are posted in a public forum. Your player profile is posted on the Internet along with how much prize money you won for each event, for the year, and your career earnings. It's a very neat starting point for an audit. It's posted because it's public domain information. Every organization with public ties has this type of accountability. Of course, the ATP tennis profile does not track extra money you earn by giving tennis lessons for cash, nonsanctioned events, monetary gifts, and so on. But, if your accounting doesn't at least match up with what is posted on that website—watch out!

The IRS has ways of calculating your income based on your expenses, so report the cash payments you get from lessons. If you are caught under-reporting, it won't work pleading "you didn't know." And don't forget about those "cash tips" that well-meaning students may give you in addition to your tennis lesson fee. Tips are considered wages. You will be expected to pay Social Security and Medicare tax on your tips. If you think you screwed up your taxes, you can always file an amended report, and you have up to three years to do so.

Avoiding an Audit

The IRS pays attention to your itemized expenses, so be honest and keep detailed business records. That includes saving your receipts and keeping track of gas mileage. Set up a separate bank account for your business income and expenses. You don't need to establish a business account, as that will cost money. Just open a free personal account at another bank in your own name. Get a bank ATM card from that establishment and mark it for business use only. Then file this banking information separately from your personal banking statements. It is also advisable for you to charge everything on a designated credit card that itemizes all your transactions for you at the end of the year. MBNA does this, as do may other credit card companies. Don't use this card for personal use. Your accounting will be much simpler to do at the end of the year if you keep a clear distinction between personal and business expenses.

Retain your tax records in an organized fashion (including all of your supporting materials) for at least seven years. If you are audited and don't have your records, it does no good to tell the IRS that you lost, discarded, or never saved your receipts. In the absence of evidence to the contrary, the IRS will calculate your taxes based on what they think you should pay. You will need those receipts to challenge its assessment. While it is not impossible to fight the IRS and win, it's better to run your business as a business so you'll never be called upon to defend yourself.

If you get an audit request, don't blow it off. First, they could be wrong. Second, if you don't respond, you will start accumulating fines. But don't just automatically pay the additional money the IRS claims you owe. Quickly take a copy of your filed tax return back to the tax accountant who completed your return. If you did the return yourself, have a tax accountant or lawyer evaluate your return and respond to the IRS within the time frame set forth in the audit notice. The tax preparer or lawyer, if willing, can represent you at an audit if you are off in Timbuktu playing a match.

Preparing Your Taxes

Because you're running a business and have deductions, you can't just file the 1040 EZ form anymore. If you have the time and inclination, though, you still can do your taxes yourself, either using the traditional paper forms, by purchasing tax software, or by subscribing to a web-based service. With these last two options, you can do everything electronically, including submission. This will save you some money, and electronic filing allows you to get your refund (if any) as quickly as possible. It's up to you, though, to do everything correctly.

Naturally there are tax scams you need to be aware of and avoid. The best way to do that is to be knowledgeable about the tax system. Remember that a deal that sounds too good to be true is probably either a scam or illegal. Hire a reputable tax accountant to do your taxes. Generic tax preparation specialists such as H&R Block may not be as knowledgeable about your needs. Your tax filing will be more complicated due to your self-employment status and the nature of your income (foreign and domestic). You need a tax preparer trained to handle potentially complicated returns.

You will pay about $20 for an on-line service, about $40 for do-it-yourself software, and about $300 for an experienced tax preparer. The prices for on-line service or do-it-yourself software are for the Federal forms only, so depending on where you live, there may be additional costs for the state filings.

Late Filing

Don't wait until the last minute to file. While you may have gotten away with cramming for exams at the last minute in college, it doesn't work that way with taxes, even if you have hired a seasoned professional. Murphy's Law applies here—what can go wrong will go wrong and at the most inopportune time. You don't want to get caught at the last minute, spending every waking moment hunting down receipts to give to your tax preparer instead of playing in a tournament.

You can file for an IRS extension which will allow you to postpone submitting your taxes until August 15th. However, you must get permission to do so, and you will still have to pay your taxes by April 15th, whether or not you've filed for, or received, an extension. You can file for an extension electronically, so that part is simple. It's IRS Form 4868 which allows a four-month extension. If you don't owe taxes, no problem. However, if you do wind up owing taxes and you don't pay by April 15th, you will have to pay penalties and interest. If you can't pay by April 15th, you should contact the IRS to set up an installment plan. Of course there is another form you have to file, Form 9465 Installment Agreement Request. Attach this to the front of your tax return. But you're still not done. If approved (you have to justify each of these requests), the IRS will charge you a fee plus interest on any unpaid balance. Your installment payment plan is supposed to include payments that will be large enough to have you IRS-debt free by the time you have to file again the following year.

Doing It Right

As a tennis professional competing on the circuit, you are considered to be self-employed because you are in business for yourself. You are not employed by the ATP or USTA. Even if you give lessons for a tennis club to supplement your circuit earnings, you may still be considered self-employed as an independent contractor if the club only has the right to control or direct the result of your work, but not how you do it. If you do provide tennis lessons for a club, you need to check on your state and city laws requiring licenses or permits to operate your business, but the IRS does not require any such thing. What the IRS does require is a Tax Identification Number which is usually your Social Security number. But if you have employees, say you hired a business manager, then you would need an Employer Identification Number. At that point you will need to deal with recording Social Security numbers, withholding taxes, sending withheld taxes to the IRS on a timely basis, reporting employee income, benefits, and so on.

When and What To File

To recap briefly, because you are self-employed, you are responsible for filing your own forms. There will be multiple forms to complete. You just have to figure out which ones you need. Again, the IRS is ready to assist you in this area at their online website. All you have to do is read and understand the information. As soon as your net earnings (not gross) are more than $400, you must pay the government its due. You will pay the self-employment (SE) tax and use Form 1040, Schedule SE. You are also required to report income and expenses on another form called a Schedule C or C-EZ to calculate your earnings. This form is attached to your 1040 Individual Income Tax return. If you expect to owe at least $1,000 in taxes, including the self-employment tax, you will need to make estimated tax payments. If you underestimate your taxes to a large degree (by more than $1,000), you will be assessed a penalty fee. Payments are to be made quarterly: April 15th, June 15th, September 15th, and January 15th of the following year. The Form 1040-ES can be used to calculate and pay your estimated taxes. The following forms are the first three you will need if you netted at least 400 bucks and you have no employees, and Table 5.1 summarizes all the forms you might need.

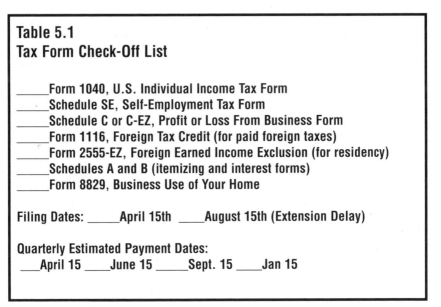

Table 5.1
Tax Form Check-Off List

_____Form 1040, U.S. Individual Income Tax Form
_____Schedule SE, Self-Employment Tax Form
_____Schedule C or C-EZ, Profit or Loss From Business Form
_____Form 1116, Foreign Tax Credit (for paid foreign taxes)
_____Form 2555-EZ, Foreign Earned Income Exclusion (for residency)
_____Schedules A and B (itemizing and interest forms)
_____Form 8829, Business Use of Your Home

Filing Dates: _____April 15th _____August 15th (Extension Delay)

Quarterly Estimated Payment Dates:
_____April 15 _____June 15 _____Sept. 15 _____Jan 15

You can download these forms, submit online, or pick them up at your bank or post office. Even if you don't owe any taxes, you are supposed to complete Form 1040 and Schedule SE to pay the self-employment Social Security Tax. If you expect to get Social Security benefits (that is assuming there are any to be had by the time you reach age 65), you need to have paid into the system for a certain period of time to claim the benefits. The minimum amount of time you need to put in is 10 years of work, and your claim is based upon how many "credits" you've accumulated. Theoretically, the more "credits" accumulated, the more you should get back (up to a point) when you retire. This tends to get complicated, and for those of you with inquiring minds, you can read up on this at the Social Security website, www.socialsecurity.gov.

If you don't file when you should have, the IRS claims that it will file for you. This is probably due to the growing number of Americans who are protesting the income tax in general for various legal and philosophical reasons. If this happens to you, it can actually be quite disadvantageous. They won't take the time to give you credit for deductions and exemptions to which you would otherwise be entitled, so you really over-pay, given the nature of your business. To add insult to injury, the IRS will top this off with a bill for taxes due, plus penalties and interest. Then there are eventually legal ramifications for the repeat offenders—like Al Capone, you could wind up in jail.

Foreign Money Rules

If you paid or accrued foreign income taxes during the year due to competitions outside of the U.S. (or conversely, if you are non-American and played matches in the U.S.), you usually can claim those taxes as a credit against your U.S. income. To do this, you need to use Form 1116. If you claim your main residence to be in a foreign country (you must meet certain qualifications for residency such as maintaining a "physical presence"), you can claim the foreign earned income exclusion by filing Form 2555-EZ. For more information on these two issues, you need to read two IRS publications: 54 and 514. Don't incur inaccurate-residency claims as did Boris Becker.

Your Car

If you use your car to drive to tournaments, it can be claimed as a business expense. You can deduct the mileage expense using either the standard mileage rate set by the government for any given year (for the last four months of 2005, that rate was 48.5 cents a mile while the preceding 8 months the rate was only 40.5 cents a mile [ref: www.selfemployed web.com/2005-mileage-rate-increase.htm]), or you can keep track of the actual expenses of maintaining your car. For actual expenses, you need to keep track of gas, oil, insurance, tires, licensing, repairs, and depreciation. If you choose the itemized route, you cannot take the standard deduction. Obviously, you'll want to choose the method that helps you out more.

Your "Home" Office

Even though you are traveling three-fourths of the year, you still have to sleep somewhere when you're not on the road. If you designate an area in your house (or apartment) for office work (planning trips, record keeping, computer use), you can deduct the cost of that area from your taxes if that area is used exclusively and regularly for your business, cannot be claimed to have dual use (like your bedroom), and you cannot conduct your business elsewhere in a "fixed" location. To make certain your home office qualifies as such, you simply set up shop in a closet, turn a spare room into an office, or creatively partition off an area of a larger room and claim it to be your office. Then you can deduct a certain amount of utilities (heat, electric) or usage space on your taxes (e.g., if 10 percent of your house is used for business and your house is 2,500 square feet, your "business use" constitutes 250 sq. feet of your house). These rules change from year to year, so you need to be current with those. However, if you are fortunate enough to be able to buy and sell your home every 5 years or so, you need to consult with a knowledgeable tax accountant regarding depreciation rules when claiming home office space.

You can also deduct business expenses such as furniture purchases (even if it is as simple as a table and a chair), business equipment (your computer, phone, and fax), supplies (writing pads, notebooks, file cabinets, stationary, and postage), computer software, telephone calling plan, and Internet services. Remember though, for anything that is used for personal matters as well as business, you must determine the percentage of business use and only itemize for that amount. Besides the regular itemization forms (Schedules A & B), there is a form you may also need for the business use of your home—Form 8829.

Equipment and Uniforms

Also part of your business is your "work uniform" and "work equipment." If you are not yet sponsored by a sporting apparel company or racquet manufacturer, all items you bought that are necessary for your competition are business expenses and are tax deductible. This includes your tennis supplies—tennis balls, grip tape, string and stringing, suntan lotion, sport drinks, and sport bars. You might even be able to claim coaching fees as an educational expense for self-improvement necessary for your continued successful job employment (i.e., winning matches). A word of caution to rein you in though, your business deductions cannot exceed your earned income. So for some of you first starting out, you might need to wait a year or so before you claim each of your deductions—you've got to win some prize money first. But hopefully you will do well in enough tournaments to at least write off your travel, laptop computer, and cell phone.

Depreciation

You can also depreciate items for tax credit—for instance, your car and your computer. If you bought your own ball machine, this can be itemized too, as well as depreciated over time. This is where it helps to have an experienced professional helping you with your taxes. Not only will he help you maximize your deductions and depreciation, but he will help you steer clear of the type of "creative" claims that generate audits. If you do depreciate your business equipment, just make certain you use "fair market values." If you do need to buy equipment that is considered a "fixed asset," such as a car, computer, or tennis ball machine, it has been suggested that you buy near the end of the year in order to minimize something known as the "half-year" rule, so you can claim at least half of the regular depreciation. Otherwise, you lose some of the depreciation benefit. Be on the lookout for new tax breaks too. For instance in 2002, the IRS allowed an additional 30 percent depreciation for business property and made it retroactive to 2001. On the other hand, breaks you once got might be voided out the very next year. So you need to stay on your toes about retractions as well as those welcomed additions. One last tip regarding depreciation. If you know that you will rise to a higher income tax bracket the year after you bought all your office equipment and such, you could defer filing depreciation claims until then, so as to offset the higher taxable income. Of course you would have to be playing very consistently and winning currently to have that much confidence in your following year's potential earnings. Also, as mentioned earlier, it is sticky business depreciating your home, so don't do so without a good tax accountant. And guess what—when your business equipment gets old, you can donate it as a charitable contribution and deduct for that, as long as you get a receipt!

That Outstanding Student Loan

There are other tax tips that could benefit you as well. For instance, if you have student loans, you might be able to claim a deduction up to $2,500 for interest paid on it. In the past, interest paid on qualified higher education expenses has been deductible for the first five years of the loan. However, student benefits (like scholarships, tax benefits) have been under fire recently due to competing national defense needs, so do be sure to check the most current tax deduction rules.

Love and Taxes

If you fall madly in love with your mixed doubles partner and want to wed, you should wait until after the new year to get married. You will save on some taxes. But if your lovely partner isn't such a great player, besides gently dumping her as your tennis partner (while trying to keep her as your intended), as long as she won't be earning an income, go ahead and take the wedding plunge before the first of January. Alternatively, you could just enjoy each other's company and not marry as single filers pay less in taxes than a married couple filing jointly. Bear in mind, if your significant other decides to retire and not work, married couples with only one income pay less in taxes than individuals with separate incomes.

Medical Expenses

As a pro athlete, you should be pretty healthy, which is good because you have to spend more than 7.5 percent of your adjusted gross income on medical bills before you can start deducting medical expenses. Even if you are healthy, you still need medical insurance to cover your sports injury treatment bills. If nothing else, having good medical insurance might save you from being wiped out financially in the event of a catastrophic injury or illness. Be careful if your parents help pay your insurance premiums as they then become co-responsible for your medical bills should you not be able to pay up. Medical debt escalates quickly in the hospital and the costs could roll over and threaten their financial stability as well as your own.

Being self-employed, you may deduct up to 70 percent of your medical insurance costs—this would include not only yourself, but also your spouse and dependents (if applicable). This is done as an "adjustment to income" on your 1040. The only stipulation here is that you (or your family) are not covered by some "other" employer health plan. So if your wife works and has a plan that carries you, you can't use this self-employed health insurance deduction. Similarly, if you are still being carried on your parents' health insurance, you can't claim this deduction either.

Medical Mileage

Besides business mileage, you can itemize mileage to and from your doctor or dentist, as well as to and from your pharmacy. You won't get rich, but every penny counts. You are allowed to deduct nonreimbursed medical and dental bills, so be sure to file the health insurance billing claims you get— they could help you out at tax time. There are some medical deductions people tend to forget about. Besides mileage, you can deduct payments for contact lenses, eyeglasses, physical therapy, lab tests, x-rays, even nursing care, should you need that. Anything that your health insurance denied payment for, or only paid partially, you might be able to get back from Uncle Sam at the end of the year. In addition, if you plan carefully, you could maximize the potential for a medical tax break for the year simply by scheduling (and paying for) your routine appointments (such as dental work, annual physical, eye care) by December 31st. For example, the off season for tennis tournaments runs from late November through mid-January. Rather than having some of your appointments in December 2004 and the rest in January 2005, it would be better to schedule these routine visits during the same year, say January 2005 and November/December 2005. Just make sure the bills are paid by December 31st of that same year (for this example, it would have been 2005). If you forgot and paid it on January 1, 2006, well, you just lost that potential itemization for year 2005.

Your Parents' Taxes

If your parents are claiming you as a dependent, then they will be the ones to reap many of these deduction benefits, not you (including use of their house for your business location, the second car that they let you drive, etc.). Take this quick "Dependency Test" to determine if your parents can still claim you on their tax return:

1. You did not file a joint return.

2. You live in your parents' household.
3. You are a citizen of the U.S.
4. You had a gross income of less than $3,000 (and you are not still in college).
5. Your parents provided more than 50 percent of your support.

Miscellaneous Job-Related Expenses

As for other job-related expenses, you can deduct union dues (such as your ATP union dues) and job-related magazines and books. Travel expenses are deductible (transportation costs other than your car—such as airfare, lodging, laundry while away). Meals are also deductible, but only at about 50 percent. Bank safety deposit box fees are also deductible. Travel deductions must exceed two percent of your adjusted gross income. Legal fees are also deductible. For instance, if you hired a lawyer to draft or review your sponsorship agreement(s), you could claim that on your tax return. I will save the "charitable contributions" discussion for the next section, because if you do succeed, you will be expected to take part in some charity events. Even if you don't strike it rich, you should participate when asked at least once in your tennis career.

The Gift Tax

The recipient of the gift (you) doesn't report the income because gifts aren't considered income. Only the giver needs to worry about the gift tax, and only if the amount is more than $11,000 (that was the law in 2004, it does change, so make sure you know the prevailing figure). Any gift you receive must be a "true" gift. That is, you can't call something a gift when it is given to you in exchange for services or some other consideration. Further, if you receive a gift that generates income, such as stocks, you must report dividends paid on that gift stock.

The tax liability of sponsorships depends upon the nature of the sponsorship. If you are being sponsored by a benevolent tennis supporter who just wants to help you get on your feet, as opposed to a corporate entity, then you can basically think of that sponsorship as a gift, because a gift can traditionally be defined as "helping someone else." Hence, no tax worries for you. Your "sponsorship" may or may not come with a contract of some sort, even if it is only for a couple thousand dollars, but we will get into the details of sponsorships later. If your sponsorship is one of equipment or clothing, generally there are no tax issues as long as the company doesn't expect something from you in return, such as giving lessons to the children of their executives, making commercials for them, and so on. Most companies who give you products just want you to use them so their products get seen.

However, receiving a financial sponsorship from a company or corporation is a whole different ballgame, as they will expect you to perform (win) and promote their products. These types of financial sponsorships do have tax implications as corporate sponsorships are usually for a lot of money, but you can deal with that tax issue when you come to it. For now, this probably isn't a problem for you. But if it is, it is a welcomed problem and you should take the sponsorship contract to your lawyer to go over the fine print.

State and Local Taxes

Don't forget about state and local taxes. As you can imagine, they are widely variable and you need to really research the situation in your state of residence. As an alternative, you can move to a state that doesn't have a state income tax. Just as New Hampshire doesn't have a sales tax, the following states currently don't have a state tax: Alaska, Florida, Nevada, New Hampshire, South Dakota, Tennessee, Texas, Washington, and Wyoming. Maybe that's why so many pro tennis players live in Florida—perfect weather year-round for tennis (except for when a hurricane floods your tennis court), bountiful beaches, and more money in your pocket at the end of the year.

Philanthropy

"From what we get, we can make a living; what we give however, makes a life."

—Arthur Ashe, Tennis Champion

Philanthropy is the desire to help others as shown by acts of charity via service or donations. Arthur Ashe gave his time and money to develop several charitable organizations devoted to encouraging the total development of young athletes. Arthur formed the ABC (Ashe-Bollettieri Cities) tennis program, the Athletes' Career Connection, and the Safe Passage Foundation—a program for kids designed to assist them with their transition into adulthood via tennis.

Fortunately, Arthur's philanthropic nature has rubbed off on several of today's tennis stars with many of the high-profile players following in his footsteps by "giving back" to the community. Some athletes have gone the extra mile and set up their own charitable organizations. Agassi has raised over $4 million for kids at risk in his Las Vegas hometown. Pete Sampras raised over a million dollars for his charity, Aces for Charity, by donating $100 bucks for every ace he hit. James Blake creatively raised $2300 for a

Connecticut inner-city girls basketball team by simply auctioning off his dreadlocks.

Having said all that, this doesn't mean you are expected to donate a third of your income to the church. But even you, early on in your career, can give back in terms of time or equipment donations to the tennis facility that helped you get to where you are now. Maybe a manufacturer gave you a racquet to try but you didn't particularly care for it. Rather than toss it in the corner of your garage, donate it. Or, maybe your racquets are old by your standards, but with some new string, they may be the perfect starter racquets for some needy community center program. When tournament organizers are seeking players to help with a community event by giving lessons to the kids, it wouldn't hurt you to volunteer a morning. When you get to the point where you have thousands or even millions to give away, and you want a charitable organization of your own, have your attorney and accountant set it up. There are a lot of rules and regulations you must observe.

Chapter 6
Financial Planning

"It's not easy for men to rise whose qualities are thwarted by poverty."
—Juvenal (55 AD-130 AD) Satires

I t is difficult to stay focused on your game when you have to worry about your next payday and whether your prize money will actually be enough to pay for anything. Even though there's no way of knowing how long you will be on the Futures and Challenger circuit, history shows that you would be very lucky to make it in one year. Many take more than two years to make the move to the ATP events where the real money is.

In any case, you will need to determine in advance approximately how much money you will need to compete and survive. You won't be living glamorously, but if you have a budget plan, at least you will be able to manage what you do have. Perhaps you will even impress somebody to donate toward your tennis development (see Chapter 7, "Your Sponsorship Plan"). You want donations rather than loans because you have to pay back loans, and the odds aren't in your favor that you'll make enough out of your tennis career to do so. Of the 1,500 or so players in the Futures ranks at any given moment, only a few actually make it out of the "tennis dungeon" and stay out long enough to turn a profit. If you do have to borrow money, my advice is that you don't borrow from your relatives. No matter whom you borrow money from, set up a repayment plan in advance, based upon realistic expectations.

Typically, the first year or two on the tour is going to be expensive. You'll have to pay for items such as travel, lodging, equipment, and tournament entry fees on top of your normal living expenses. If you have (or have access to) more money than you can spend, this won't be a problem. If not, it's going to take some planning.

Financial Wizardry: What's in Your Wallet?

"Finance is the art of passing money from hand to hand until it finally disappears."
—Robert W. Sarnoff, Chairman of RCA

Y ou need to start off by determining your "base," which is the amount of money you have or will be getting between now and the time when you start winning the bigger tournaments and earning enough prize money to support yourself. Your base will consist of two categories, assets and income. Assets include your savings account, checking account, CDs, money market funds, stocks, real estate, or anything valuable enough that it could be sold to raise money. Income includes wages you get from jobs, rental properties, the allowance from your parents, money you will inherit, trust fund payments, and income from sponsors (Chapter 7).

If you don't have many assets and you are not winning much prize money, then you will need to periodically generate income outside of tennis in order to stay on the circuit. Besides coaching part-time, some players have relied on other income sources. Johnny "Blazed" Valenti is a landlord, Jon Pastel is an actor, and Eric Matuszewski is both a paralegal and a musician in a rock band. These "not-famous" players represent the average Futures/Challenger player on the circuit. Not many have vast financial resources available, so most need to be realistic about paying for their tennis life.

Out of your base monies will come your expenses, called "fixed" and "variable." Fixed expenses are those you would have whether or not you were playing tennis. Variable expenses are those that change based on the business decisions you make related to your tennis career. Examples of fixed expenses include food, lodging, utilities, the minimum payment on your credit card, other loan and revolving credit payments, and student loan payments. Examples of variable expenses include travel, lodging, equipment, coaching, training, and purchases for business purposes. If your expenses exceed your income, you may need to tap into your assets to survive.

While you're looking at your expenses, examine each of your credit card statements and see how much you are paying in finance charges. If the monthly interest you are charged on your balance is half or more of your "minimum amount due," you have a bad credit deal, are carrying too much debt, or both. In any case, you should attempt to pay off all of your charges as quickly as possible so that you can start out on the tour with a fairly clean financial slate. If your balances aren't out of control, this should be relatively easy to do if you have any income at all (of if your parents help you out). You will need two charge cards, one for all of your business expenses and the other for personal use. This will make your life much simpler come tax time.

If you have several outstanding debts (not including your school loan, which is a different issue), you should talk to a banker about consolidating your debt into one credit card for easier management—and try to lower your interest rate as well. Once you do this, put that card away so you don't use it. Just pay off the debt regularly and quickly.

Regarding that school loan, if you are unemployed and have no income, there are deferment methods. Check with the repayment officer about your options. You won't get 100 percent deferment (unless you are back in school, e.g., grad school), but you should be able to get the principle deferred and only have to make payments on the interest.

Budget Planning

"I'm living so far beyond my income that we may almost be said to be living apart."

—E. E. Cummings, Poet & Painter

N ow that you know what your money base is, let's see how to manage it. At the end of this chapter is a budget worksheet (Tables 6.4 and 6.5) for you to use in your tennis sponsorship portfolio, which you will create in Chapter 7. It will also come in handy at tax time. For each expense listed in the "Estimated" column, fill in the amount you think you will be spending each month, then project it out for a full year. You may only be playing matches a total of ten months a year, but many of the expenses you will encounter will still be due, regardless of your tournament schedule. Therefore, you will need to know how much money you may need for the entire year, not just during the period of time you are competing. If an item doesn't apply to you (e.g., you have no rent because you are either living with your parents or freeloading off your friends), just write in "N/A" (not applicable). Alternatively, white it out and put in something that is missing from this list.

If you approach a sponsor, he can decide whether your sponsorship money will be allocated solely for tennis or if you can spend the money as you see fit. The arrangement you make will dictate what type of annual report you will eventually be submitting to your sponsor, and you would amend this budget report accordingly. At the end of the year, you will complete this form by filling in your actual expenses. This means you must keep good records, save receipts, and so on—you have to do this for taxes anyway. The final column will determine how well you estimated your budget, that is, if you are in the red or not. Obviously, if you are in the red (i.e., you have a negative number), you will need to downsize your spending habits and/or win more prize money to cover those additional expenses. If you grossly overestimated, your sponsor may think you padded your budget for a larger sponsorship promise. However, it may simply reflect the very likely possibility that you had to downsize due to lack of funds. You will need to explain either outcome to your sponsor in your annual report.

Budget Examples

Based upon some generic approximations from Brian Vahaly, *Tennis* magazine posted a "hypothetical" budget for a "hypothetical" player with a ranking of 100. The "hypothetical" income was $230,000 ($215,000 in winnings; $15,000 in endorsements). The "hypothetical" expenses of $183,000 are itemized in Table 6.1.

Table 6.1
Hypothetical Annual Expenses for 100th-Ranked Player

Taxes: $54,000 *(may as well take this right off the top!)*
Coach: $90,000 *(annual salary of $60K plus $30K in expenses)*
Travel: $25,000 *(on the Challenger circuit)*
Food: $6,000
Racquet Expenses: $5,000
Miscellaneous: $3,000 *(cell phone, laptop, etc)*
Total: $183,000

You can see that there is quite a hefty payout before this hypothetical player claims his $47,000 cut. Out of this, he must pay his general living expenses as detailed in Table 6.4 at the end of the chapter.

In 2000, when Paul Goldstein was at his peak with a singles ranking of 67, he figured that out of the approximately $200,000 he would earn, he'd spend close to $70,000 on items such as airfare and meals. Another $10,000 a year would go to racquet stringing, plus $6,000 for a personal trainer. Each of these items is considered a necessity, not a luxury.

When starting at the Futures level, you will have a long way to go before getting to these modest levels. When you start putting together your sponsorship plan, you must project your needs—and most often you will want to project the most favorable scenario, without losing all ties to reality. Then, if sufficient sponsorships don't materialize, you downsize accordingly. That is exactly what Tripp Phillips had to do his first year out. Like most players, much of his initial financing came from his parents or relatives. He wanted to try to ease their burden by getting "investors" in his future. But in order to do that, he had to develop a budget. He did so with the help from a former UNC teammate, David Caldwell, who attained a world ranking around 170 before calling it quits at about the same time Tripp was just embarking upon his journey.

Tripp created a $62,000 budget based on a 10-month playing plan. He diligently itemized within his sponsorship proposal so that potential investors would know exactly how he would spend their money. He projected becoming solvent within two years to let investors know when to expect a return on those investments. Table 6.2 shows that his tennis budget was only a third of what *Tennis* magazine suggested would be needed for successful play at the Challenger level.

Table 6.2
Comparison of Estimated Annual Expenses:
Tripp Phillips vs. "Hypothetical" 100th-ranked player

	Tripp's Plan	Hypothetical Player Plan
Travel	$ 24,000	$ 25,000
Coaching	$ 14,500	$ 90,000
Meals	$ 10,500	$ 6,000
Equipment	$ 6,200	$ 5,000
Car Rental	$ 5,250	----
Misc.	$ 750	$ 3,000
Clothing	$ 710	----
	$ 61,910	$129,000

You can see the largest disparity is in coaching expenses. You can also see that Tripp wasn't counting on manufacturer freebies at this stage of his career.

Although Tripp managed to get a little bit of money from various sources, it was not nearly enough to meet his budget. He also realized he needed to plan for 12 months even if he was only competing approximately 10 months out of the year. What he didn't have to worry about much were general living expenses as he either lived at home or with friends and extended family. But if you compare these two budgets with yours (Table 6.5 at the end of the chapter), you will see there are a lot of expenses unaccounted for—which could wreck your budget. Tripp's proposed annual budget plan and actual first year expenses are shown in Table 6.3.

From a projected need of $62,000, Tripp whittled down his first year expenses to around $22,000. He traveled not only across the U.S. but also ventured to South Africa, Spain, Mexico, and Canada. He made a little over $11,000 in prize money. You can see he was not making a profit at this point. Though he's close to $11,000 in the hole, that amount is before accounting for gifts and business tax write-offs. Although he didn't land any big sponsors, he did manage to receive a couple thousand dollars in gifts from friends and family (as do many other players). If you examine Tripp's budget list, you can also see that many of his business expenses were potentially tax-deductible. Taking these factors into account, he may have been able to reduce his profit-loss disparity with wise income tax filing. Thus, Tripp managed his first year on tour with smart planning—realizing

Table 6.3
Proposed vs. Actual First Year Expenses for Tripp Phillips

	Proposed Plan	First Year Expenses
Travel	$ 24,000	$ 10,000
Coaching	$ 14,500	$ 1,600
Meals	$ 10,500	$ 4,100
Equipment	$ 6,200	$ 1,800
Car	$ 5,250	$ 1,800
Misc.	$ 750	$ listed w/meals
Clothing	$ 710	----
Health/Business	-----	$ 2,600
		(health insurance, business-expenses
		cell, phone, computer, etc.)
Total	$61,910	$21,900

what he didn't have and adjusting his financial strategies accordingly. This is called tennis survival.

After competing in 25 tournaments, Tripp's first year-end (2001) ATP singles entry ranking was 616, and doubles was 335, although his rankings had been as high as 579 and 289. Early on, Tripp was showing a definite flair for doubles with a winning percentage of 66 percent versus a 48 percent winning record for his singles. This was a bit hard to take, given his winning percentage in college just the year before had been as high as 82 percent. Even though he was disappointed, he maintained a bravado and "I can do it" attitude, which is exactly the mindset any aspiring tennis pro needs in order to stick out the rough times. Tripp persisted and his winning percentages, rankings, and earnings improved each year, with his negative balance decreasing accordingly. As he became more accustomed to the circuit life, he began reinvesting his prize money in himself by going to more tournaments in more locations for more experience. That approach seemed to pay off. But the journey for Tripp, as with many others, has been an arduous one. He is now a top-100 doubles specialist with escalating career earnings of about $136,000 (as of April 2006). What's the take-home message? You must be up for the long haul, as only a limited few find success immediately.

Your Budget Worksheets

The time to prepare your budget is when you don't have other competing distractions, for instance, before you actually hit the tour. Or, if you are on tour, update it during one of your vacation down times. Table 6.4 shows what your completed budget might look like. You can see that in this example, the player actually over-estimated his car rental and equipment expenses but forgot about health insurance needs and underestimated his cell phone use. All told, he over-estimated his budget by $5,332. This is a better situation to be in, rather than under-estimating. Scaling back your spending is preferable to bouncing checks due to insufficient funds.

Table 6.5 provides you with your own blank budget worksheets. Make 13 copies of these worksheets (that's 13 copies of each page of the worksheet, then collate and staple together). Your first copy will be used not only to estimate your monthly and yearly needs, but it will also be the copy used for your taxes, as it will provide a good accounting summary. For your taxes, you may find that you need to consolidate your itemizations to match the tax deduction guidelines. Do remember to take the appropriate percentage-use deductions for items like your personal car and cell phone (i.e., percent of time used for business).

The remaining 12 copies will help you organize your monthly receipts. Label the 3-page worksheet packets with the 12 months of the year. Then all you'll have to do is tape or staple your receipts directly onto the monthly report page as you collect them. If you also put each worksheet packet in a separate envelope (labeled with the month), you'll be able to stick the

---

Table 6.4
Example of Budget Preparation

	ESTIMATED		ACTUAL		VARIANCE FROM ESTIMATED
ITEM	Monthly	Yearly	Monthly	Yearly	Yearly
Car Rental	$525	$5,250 (only 10 mo)	$127	$1,524	- $3,726
Equipment (racquet, balls, String, fees, etc)	$620	$6,200 (only 10 mo)	$146	$1,752	- $4,448
Health Insurance	n/a	n/a	$221	$2,652	+ $2,652
Cell phone	$35	$350	$45	$540	+ $190
Rent	n/a	n/a	n/a	n/a	n/a
TOTALS	$1,180	$11,800	$539	$6,468	- $ 5,332 (LESS THAN-ESTIMATED)

NOTES: Didn't play in as many tournaments as projected due to lack of funds and injuries, therefore overestimated car rental and equipment costs; Didn't think I needed health insurance, but my parents insisted I did; cell phone fee increased due to switching services for better coverage.

envelope(s) in your travel bag and stuff receipts in as you get them. This way, you will be less likely to find your receipts in shreds with your freshly laundered clothes. Come tax-time, you'll be relieved that you took this extra little bit of effort.

Finally, don't forget about keeping track of your income. You may have various sources and it can be easy to forget an item or two. Your monthly budget copy can be used for stapling your pay stubs. On page three of your budget worksheet, a space is provided for you to record your income sources. This will be a listing of every tournament where you won prize money, a record of tennis lesson payments, and so forth. Now you have a complete report for your tax accountant.

Completing your Worksheets. In the "Estimated" columns, record your anticipated monthly expense for each item. Then project it out for a full year. You may only be playing matches a total of 10 months during a year, but many of the expenses you will encounter will still be due, regardless of your tournament schedule. Therefore, you need to know how much money you may need for 12 months, not just during the period you are competing. If an item doesn't apply to you (e.g., you have no rent or utility payments), just write in "N/A" (not applicable). The final column ("Variance") will determine how well you estimated your budget. You are simply subtracting your actual yearly expenses from your estimated yearly expenses.

Table 6.5
Your Budget Worksheets – Page 1
Your Name:_____ Tax ID #:_____
Year:_____

ITEM	ESTIMATED		ACTUAL		VARIANCE
	Monthly	Yearly	Monthly	Yearly	Yearly

GENERAL LIVING EXPENSES

Rent

Food

Utilities
(electric, gas, water)

Phone
  Cell
  "Regular"

Laundry

Personal Car
  Car Insurance
  Repairs/Maintenance
  Gas

Insurance
  Health
  Dental
  Life Insurance
  (if you have dependents)
  Professional Liability
  (if you also coach)

Recreation/Misc.
  (clothing, gifts etc.)

Table 6.5 (continued)
Your Budget Worksheets – Page 2

Your Name:_____ Tax ID #:_____

Year:_____

ITEM	ESTIMATED		ACTUAL		VARIANCE
	Monthly	Yearly	Monthly	Yearly	Yearly

TENNIS-SPECIFIC EXPENSES

FEES
Tournament Entry Fees
ATP Union Fees
USTA Membership Fees
ITF Fees
Website Hosting Fees

EQUIPMENT
Computer & Printer
Racquets
Balls
String
Stringing
Grip Tape
Clothing
   Shirts
   Socks
   Shoes
   Hats
   Sweatbands
Work-out Towels
Water Bottles
Sun Tan Lotion
MP3/i-Tune Downloads
Sports Nutrition
  (drinks, snacks)
Other?

Table 6.5 (continued)
Your Budget Worksheets – Page 3
Your Name:_____ Tax ID #:_____
Year:_____

ITEM	ESTIMATED Monthly Yearly	ACTUAL Monthly Yearly	VARIANCE Yearly
TENNIS-SPECIFIC EXPENSES (Cont.)			
EDUCATION/SELF-DEVLOPMENT			
Personal Coaches			
Tennis			
Facility Fees			
Coaching Fees			
Videotaping Analysis			
Sport Conditioning			
Club Membership Fees			
Personal Trainer Fees			
Fitness Evaluations			
Nutritional Analysis & Counseling			
Training Self-Help Books			
Tennis Training Camp			
TRAVEL			
Rental Car			
Lodgings			
Meals			
Airfare, train, etc.			
OTHER			
TOTALS			

- -

INCOME			
Tournament Prize $			
Tennis Lessons			
Other			
TOTAL			

Chapter 7
Your Sponsorship Plan

"Money was never a big motivation for me, except as a way to keep score. The real excitement is playing the game."

—Donald Trump, Business Entrepreneur

Playing tennis all over the world takes lots of money. Even playing within a six-state radius can be costly. If you've checked out the Futures schedule on the USTA Pro Circuit website, you probably have had an anxiety attack trying to figure out to how get from tournament to tournament given the high cost of travel these days, even with frequent flyer miles and discount airlines. While driving may be cheaper, there often won't be enough time to drive from wherever you are to northern California, then head eastward to the Midwest, shoot down to Florida, then trek back to southern California via tournament stops in Mississippi, Louisiana, and Texas. It's even more difficult on the Challenger circuit as the tournament schedule is not in any particular geographical order.

In order to get sponsorship money to help you pay for all of that travel, you must package yourself carefully. You need to present your abilities and desires in a manner that will make someone else want to reach into his pockets to support you.

Types of Sponsorships

When most people think of sponsorships, colorful marketing images immediately pop into their heads. It's easy to imagine all athletes are rich from the megabucks they receive from corporate sponsors, who in turn reap financial rewards due to having a popular athlete associated with their product.

While this might be true for elite athletes, it isn't for thousands of other tennis players inching their way to the top. Most of you are going to be gunning for private sponsorships—your great, great Aunt from Hoboken, New Jersey, or that guy who owns that store down the street and always shows up at your college matches. A sponsorship is financial support from family, friends, or fans who just want to help you out without expecting a return on their dollar. This type of sponsorship is neither a loan nor an investment. The money they give you, while of a philanthropic nature, cannot be claimed by them as a tax-deduction by them. While you will probably not be making a profit, you are not a nonprofit organization. Sponsorship money of this sort is basically a gift with no financial benefit to the private sponsor. This needs to be made very, very clear to your private sponsor, especially if he is new to the tennis business. Do not lead anyone on, and do not misconstrue or exaggerate your abilities to deliver. If you ignore this advice in the hopes that you will better entice a private sponsor, you are setting the scene for some seriously unhappy encounters down the road.

By the same token, make sure you understand the sponsor's motives as well. Make certain there aren't any strings attached. There will be situations which arise that you can't predict—such as the case of the infatuated sponsor or the benevolent benefactor who decides he deserves a piece of the action when you start winning a little prize money. Or alternatively, a sponsor decides to back out of an agreement when—not if—you perform poorly.

Selling Yourself: Creating Your Tennis Sponsorship Packet

It's time to develop your sponsorship plan. Creating this packet is the easy part (Sponsorship packet templates are provided in Tables 7.1–7.7 at the end of this chapter). The hard part will come when you have to peddle it. If you're lucky, a sponsor will come to you. But more likely, you'll be soliciting them, often through cold calls. A cold call is a sales call to someone you don't know, or don't know well. The first hurdle is getting your foot in the door, which you can do with either a phone call or a letter of introduction. You have to be sincere and convincing when marketing yourself so that you can get this person to meet with you face to face. In order to do this successfully, you first must be convinced in your own abilities. If you have the ability, but don't feel you express yourself well enough, you might consider bringing along someone else to do the talking for you. Whomever you approach, whether it's the person next door whom you've known forever or the biggest businessman in town, take each and every meeting seriously and give your pitch with 100-percent effort.

Part of your pitch will be the sponsorship packet you put together. It should tell your potential sponsor all about your tennis career, your plans, and your potential. It could even educate your potential sponsor a bit, as not everyone knows the ins and outs of the tennis world. Your sponsorship packet should be impeccable. The effort you put into your packet will tell the sponsor a lot about you without you uttering a single word. If your packet is sloppy, contains typos, or is incoherent, you're dead in the water and no amount of schmoozing will get you one red cent. If you hire someone to put this material together for you, remember, the buck still stops with you. Any errors will be a bad reflection on you, not your assistant. You must proofread the document carefully before sending it out for final print.

When you do get that meeting, treat it as if it is a job interview. Groom yourself and polish your shoes. Wear a sports jacket, collared shirt, and nice pants, or a suit, if you have one. Obviously, if the meeting is more informal, or even a sports event, you can dress more casually—but no t-shirt and shorts unless you are meeting him to play tennis. First impressions are lasting impressions, and very crucial ones. Save the tennis G.Q. grunge look for when you're so rich and famous that others have to dress to impress you.

The most difficult part is getting started, so I have created a "Ten Step Plan" to guide you in creating your sponsorship packet.

Ten Step Plan

Step One. Create your cover page. It should contain your name and your image, preferably a good action shot. What is a good action shot? One that not only looks good (photo clarity, your tennis form is correct, it looks like you) but is also compelling. It makes you look aggressive and competitive. In other words, you look like a winner!

Step Two. Create a basic, more or less generic, cover letter template; you can adjust it to suit each potential sponsor. Because your target will only take a few minutes to read this letter, it should only be one page, 2–3 paragraphs, double-spaced—short, to the point, but compelling enough to get him to want look into your proposal. Be sure to address it to a person; do not use "To Whom It May Concern." If you are writing to a company, take the time to research the best person to whom to send your letter. If you are writing to a specific individual, learn a little bit about that person and tailor your pitch based upon what you know about him. This is your sales pitch. Make it convincing. Your future may depend on it.

Use an easy to read font such as Courier or Times. Don't use script or artsy fonts. Italicize, bold, or underline items that you want to stand out. Make sure you use a size 12 font, or one that has 10 characters per inch. Anything smaller is hard to read, and anything larger, unless your reader is legally blind, will look odd and may actually work to your disadvantage. Too much white space makes it look as though you are trying to fluff up your packet because you don't have any real accomplishments or information to disclose.

Step Three. Create a résumé highlighting your tennis career (one page, single spaced). Avoid any information that could be misconstrued or looked upon negatively, such as your age or marital status. Either might be viewed as potential roadblocks to success.

Step Four. ATP page. Explain how the professional tennis tour operates (1–2 pages, double spaced). Avoid jargon and speak in plain language so that even a non-tennis-savvy person could understand what is going on.

Step Five. Create an event listing, showing the schedule and prize money for various events. This will give your potential sponsor an identifiable goal.

Step Six. Create your detailed, itemized budget (two pages, single and double spaced).

Step Seven. Include some published news about yourself, highlighting your recent tennis-related achievements (2–3 pages). Clear photocopies of newspaper clippings will be fine here.

Step Eight. Have an attorney who is familiar with sports law draw up a short sponsorship contract agreement (about three pages). The simpler, the better for now—but you must make sure the right stuff is in there. Contracts are covered more fully in Chapter 8, including a sample contract.

Step Nine. Photocopy your packet onto good 20-lb. paper. Choose a professional color and avoid glitz. Have the copy center bind it. Don't use staples or paperclips—this looks tacky and cheap. If you want to have removable pages (for easier updating or for tear out sections, like sponsorship contracts), you can either choose perforated pages or have a less permanent type of binding—perhaps a clasp style. Even if you are almost broke, you've got to put a little money into this process. If you are using your image as the cover, be sure to include in the binding a clear-plastic front and back cover to protect your materials and to allow your photo to show through. Other types of covers could include opaque colors with a cut-out portion allowing your photo to show through. Browse an office supply store or sources such as PaperDirect on-line for ideas.

Step Ten. Create your potential sponsorship contact list and get 9 x 12 mailing envelopes. Go to the post office with a completed packet in an envelope and get the total mailing weight and postage cost. You can then prepurchase the correct amount of postage for your packets. The post office may also have prestamped envelopes, if you want to go that way, or you can use its slightly more expensive—but also more impressive—flat-rate Priority Mail envelopes. Foreign mailings will naturally cost you more. If you get the prestamped envelopes (or prestamp your own), you won't need to stand in line at the post office every time you want to mail one of your packets. You still will need to stand in line if you want to certify or register your mail. FedEx and UPS are usually quicker, but typically cost more. Whatever delivery method you choose, follow-up with a phone call to verify receipt.

Under no circumstances should you email or fax a potential sponsor unless invited to do so. Both are too impersonal and easy to ignore, plus your inquiry may just get tossed. When you do arrange a meeting, take another copy of your sponsorship packet with you, just in case.

Whom To Approach?

As tempting as this might be, you should not start by sending your materials out unsolicited, as this could be a real waste of your money. This is where a little homework will serve you well. First make sure you have an interested party. It's easiest to start with people you know or people you know who know people that might be receptive to your needs. Make up a list. With these people, it's preferable if you have the "personal touch"—that is, chat with them first about your goals, plans, and needs on an informal basis. Think of this as testing the waters to see if there is interest. If you get a favorable response, simply ask if they might be willing to discuss sponsoring you. Then you can arrange to mail them your sponsorship plan and follow up with setting a meeting date. This is not a time to be shy. Remember, the worst that can happen is they say no. You might feel stupid or embarrassed, but don't! This is also not the time to limit yourself; money can come from unexpected sources. Different things motivate different people. Maybe the person has a soft spot in his heart for struggling young athletes because he is mesmerized by the Olympic ideal. Maybe he just wants to live vicariously through you. Or maybe you will never know. Whatever the reason, you will never even have a chance for sponsorship if you don't ask.

Ideally, you already will be friendly with your potential sponsor—so all you have to do is introduce the idea of sponsorship and send him follow-up information. If you're lucky enough to jump right to the meeting, bring your information packet with you.

If not, follow up with a phone call after he's had your packet about a week. This should give enough time for him to at least realize he did in fact receive something from you and he will be less prone to forget about it. Longer than a week, he may misplace it, push it aside due to other priorities and interests, or wonder why it took you so long to follow up.

After you have contacted everyone you know well who might have had an interest (or ones who were referred to you to contact), make up another list of potential sponsors. This list should be the "acquaintance" list and "potential companies" list. With this list you are looking beyond your immediate comfortable circle of friends and family contacts. You can't be as "familiar" with them, as they aren't close friends; rather, these are more professional-type acquaintances. These are people you have met in various walks of life—business people from whom you bought your tennis equipment, a local businessperson whom is known to have supported the town's little league team, a health club that likes to advertise the athletes using its facility, a new sports-related company that needs exposure from testimonials, maybe even a former teacher. Brainstorm a bit—sometimes the most unlikely of prospects will surprise you. And, as a grammatical side note, don't discount people simply because of their gender. While this book uses the male pronoun almost exclusively, it is done so per "proper English grammar" rules in order to make the text flow smoother. It is in no way intended to exclude women from your potential sponsorship list.

Regardless of whom you contact, do make it clear to your potential sponsors how much money you need. That's where your written budget plan will be very useful. If your total sponsorship plan is rather high, and people seem to be balking at the cost, consider not hitting up just one person, but rather try to get smaller donations for the total amount. This is not ideal, but it can work. Let's say your plan requires $50,000 for you to compete successfully in any given year. This will be more than some are willing to fork out, but if you can rustle up 5 investors for $10,000 each, or 10 investors for $5,000 each, then you are in business. Perhaps one investor will donate money for your meals, another for your air travel, and yet another for your car expenses. Or perhaps each will just provide a lump sum for you to put toward the general fund and trust you to use the funds appropriately. Obviously, the more investors you have with lesser dollar amounts, the more difficult your financial accounting, so you should have some method (and another person) for handling this, as you should be focusing on playing tennis. For some, this can be a logistical nightmare, so weigh carefully the pros and cons of receiving small dollar amounts from several people.

Coming to Terms with the "No" Word

The worst that can happen when you ask someone for money is that they say no. I'm sure you've had the "no" experience many times during your growing up years when asking your parents for something. If your prospect declines to sponsor you, be gracious and say something like, "Well, it never hurts to ask, right?" This way, if they were feeling uncomfortable with you popping the question, you have given them the signal that you're okay with their decision not to sponsor you.

Not every "no" sounds like a "no," though. If, upon follow-up, your prospect puts you off, especially if he puts you off multiple times, the guy has a problem with saying "no" to you. If you mailed your packet in such a manner that you know he received it, you will be able to call his or his secretary's bluff if either denies ever setting eyes on the parcel. Be equally wary of those who "string you along" meeting after meeting unable to come to any type of decision. Again, they may want to help, but can't for some reason, and they are simply unable to tell you that. Alternatively, maybe they are curious, but with little desire to fund you, and thought they'd humor you with a meeting. However, if they are actually serious and able to fund you, consider the downside of this type of haggling and indecision. If they behave this way during discussions or negotiations, there is a strong likelihood that it will be equally painful to partner up with them for a sponsorship. Even though you desperately need funds, don't waste time on these types. Be polite, thank them for their time, and move on to another more promising, less aggravating prospect.

You will have to steel yourself for that "no" response—as you are likely to encounter that often. Even if you get as far as sitting down and actually reviewing your sponsorship plan line by line with them. It might seem as though some are leading you on or wasting your time. But try not to get overtly upset. They may be jerking you around or they simply may not have realized the extent of your needs or the limits of their own resources until they really reviewed your plan. Budgets are tight everywhere these days.

If there are no more prospects at the moment, bite the bullet, count your pennies, and devise a financing plan to get you through your first year. With any luck, you will do well enough to cover your expenses, win some matches, and maybe attract some attention later.

Don't Violate NCAA Gifting Rules

Be clear about whom you should NOT approach for sponsorships—namely, boosters of the school(s) you may be contemplating to attend or boosters for the college team that you play for while matriculated and playing competitively for that school. This also means, if you have been red-shirted and have a year of eligibility left, but you are not playing college tennis at the moment, you still can't accept a sponsorship from a booster club member. Further, NCAA Rule 16.1.1.4 prohibits enrolled student athletes from accepting awards of any kind, even if they have exhausted their collegiate athletic eligibility. What does this mean to a graduated student athlete? As a past student-athlete, are you bound by NCAA rules for life? The short answer is yes. Therefore, you must be very careful and check in with your college's NCAA compliance officer when accepting post-college sponsorships to prevent accidental NCAA infractions being levied against you, your college coach, and your college team. As long as you can provide evidence that you are in fact graduated, will not be playing college tennis anymore, and have no NCAA eligibility left, accepting a sponsorship from a booster in a legitimate business venture (via contracts) would probably be permissible. This is providing that (and this is a very important clause) the booster DID NOT approach you, your family, close friends, or significant other about sponsoring you at any time during your pre-college or actual college days. If the booster did so, then it could be construed that he somehow coerced you to go to a certain college or remain in that certain college for the benefit of that college team with promises of a reward upon graduation. And that's how to get into trouble with the NCAA.

The Progress Report

"The President has kept all of the promises he intended to keep."
—George Stephanopolous,
Presidential Aide for Bill Clinton, Larry King Live

Let's assume for a moment that you do a stellar job promoting yourself and line up a sponsor. Your writing days are not over. Besides the expectation that you will follow your mutually agreed-upon sponsorship plan relatively closely, you will need to touch base with your sponsor on a periodic basis. You may have formal or informal agreed-upon arrangements, or a combination. You don't just take the money and run. You will be held accountable for the funds disbursed to you and you need to take this responsibility seriously. Minimally you will need to prepare a year-end itemized report of your expenditures as well as your progress. The only exception to this is winning the national Van Nostrand award. The ITA gives out that financial award with no strings attached and no accountability as to how the winner actually uses the funds.

It is erroneous to believe that your sponsor is going to have the time (or desire) to follow your career progress on his own—regardless of how accessible the information is. Your sponsor might want to travel to a match just to watch what he is supporting and to reaffirm he made the right decision. If he doesn't know where you are likely to be competing, he can't do that. If you don't want your sponsor popping up at your matches, you should reconsider accepting money from him in the first place. If you don't feel comfortable with him, you shouldn't do business with him, regardless of how much you may need the money.

It will be easier for you to keep your sponsor informed about your travel and competition plans if you are organized. Obviously, if you are flying by the seat of your pants, you are not going to be able to provide information to your sponsor ahead of time. Depending on his personality, this may or may not suit his business style. Get your reporting requirements squared away in writing at the start of your sponsorship period and stick to the agreement. If you need to depart from the agreed-upon report schedule, you need to inform your sponsor in advance and have an excellent reason.

Blaming someone else for the inability to get your reports in on time is not acceptable. If you blow off an agreed-upon report date, if you constantly have excuses why your report is late, if it is put together poorly or sloppily, or if it is inaccurate (missing matches, missing prize money earnings or inaccurate prize money reporting, etc.), negative feelings will develop rather quickly and you risk losing a sponsorship renewal. Remember, these items are easily verified. If you screw up enough, your sponsor has every right to proclaim your sponsorship contract null and void and hold you accountable for returning whatever was disbursed to you. This and other legal issues will be covered in more detail in the next chapter. If your sponsor is someone with a vast network of connections, you risk losing other potential sponsors as word leaks out. On the other hand, if you upheld your agreements reasonably well, your sponsor will be one of your advocates.

About Corporate Support

Corporate sponsorships usually fall into one of three categories: philanthropy, grants, or a "true" sponsorship. The philanthropic route is where nothing is expected in return for the money, clothing, and equipment donations. All you need do is be a grateful recipient by sending a thank-you note and possibly acknowledging the corporate support at an event. Grants are another avenue; however, they aren't common for individual players. They are more for tennis organizations trying to get funding for programming and travel. The "true" corporate sponsorship is when a company supports you in return for defined, deliverable results of some

Corporate sponsor banners.

kind. For instance, at tennis matches, it is expected that the tournament host site displays advertising banners on fences, walls, and buildings in exchange for the sponsorship money that goes in part to pay, feed, and house you. As a private sport recipient of a corporate sponsor, similar expectations would be placed upon you. You would be expected to display its logo on your racquet or clothing and make certain that all photos of you display its logo in some manner.

Corporate sponsorships can be further broken down into hard and soft sponsorships. Hard sponsorships seek a direct improvement in sales as a result of sponsoring you. The sponsor will be asking itself how you will contribute to it making more money. Image consultants will determine if your image is the right one for its product. They are looking for sports figures with squeaky-clean images with whom kids and adults can identify. Players are expected to promote product sales and not embarrass the company.

Soft sponsorships are less specific and not directly dependent upon increased sales. They are more for building the image of the company. When a local company provides money for uniforms for the local little league team, the message the business wants to get across to the public is "we care." It's subliminal promotion of the business, creating empathy for it with the intent that the public will choose that business when in need of that particular service/product. This can work just as well for the local tennis club team, or you, as a struggling, aspiring pro player.

Companies who offer soft sponsorships might do so in the form of trusts. These trusts have charitable aims and can distribute money to projects or activities that fall under specific pre-defined categories. For instance, they might sponsor sports, fine arts, or those of a certain disability group, religious affiliation, or ethnic background. The trust can have an informal application process (meaning that all you might need to do is write a compelling letter) or a formal one (where there would be an application form). Obviously, cultivating this type of sponsorship takes time—time that you personally might not have but time that perhaps your manager might be able to spare. The way you do this type of search is through the Internet and your local library. Ask the librarian for assistance finding the necessary information. Keep in mind, you will have a lot of competition for this type of sponsorship. Although the odds are against you for being awarded one of these, if you are broke and have some time to do the necessary grant application research, it's still worth a shot.

In 1997, UNC-Charlotte's Professional Application MBA team did a survey of corporate sponsorship, and found:

- Although morality seems to be more of an issue these days, in 1997 the sponsorship survey reported that only 47 percent of corporate sport sponsors had moral clauses in their contracts, 40 percent had none, and 13 percent didn't know if they had a morality clause.

- 27.5 percent of corporate sport sponsors had no predefined goals for their sponsorship program, thereby lending credence to the "fact" that companies get involved in a particular sport due to a senior-decision maker.
- Only 25 percent of the sponsors tied an endorser's payment with market results.
- Contrary to popular opinion, there was not an overwhelming urge to sponsor major league professional athletes—52 percent favored pros while 47 percent favored Olympians, college athletes, and pro-minor leagues. (So there IS hope for tennis circuit players!)

The primary concerns for an endorser of products were:

- Name recognition (68 percent).
- Current popularity (56 percent).
- Overall image (53 percent).
- Character (51 percent).
- Speaking skills and general appearance (45 percent).

On the flip side, 64% reported that the least important attribute was education, and a little more than half were not concerned with a controversial image. So the old adage about all publicity being good, even if it's negative, appears to be true. Controversy is good, as long as it doesn't outrage the majority of people to whom the company is targeting sales.

Finally, while you may be desperate for funds, you need to be on your toes—don't get snookered. And don't be naïve. Be cautious when dealing with strangers or newfound friends.

Successful Sponsorship: Life of Brian

According to writer David Breslow, many players set up what is known as a limited liability corporation (LLC). At first, the sponsor(s) take most of the player's winnings. After an agreed-upon break-even point, the player keeps more of the money. He claims this works out great for the players as the investment for each sponsor is low and it takes the pressure off the player for the year. Supposedly the contracts often lead to larger contracts, up to $10,000 per player, if sponsors have the resources and like or believe in the player. They're not for everybody, though, including Brian Vahaly, who warns players to steer clear of plans that take too much of your prize earnings:

> "When I looked for a sponsor, I drafted up the expenses that I expected over the coming year and what my goals were with regards to ranking. I showed the income that someone of that ranking achieved and also where I saw myself over a 2-3 year horizon. From there, I came up

with a percentage of prize money that I would send to my sponsor, that would hopefully pay him back if I went according to my ranking goals and possibly even more if I achieved beyond my expectations. I submitted to him reports of my spending and signed an official document from his lawyer about the agreement. He has remained a pivotal part in my development, as I haven't had to worry about money, and he's been great with coming to some of my matches. With regards to tips, I'd say to make sure you do your research, have all the facts before you go into these meetings. There are many wealthy guys out there that are used to being asked for their money. However, they are used to making profits, so make sure you don't sign your career away, so that if you make it into the top 100, you're not basically giving all your prize money to the sponsor."

Brian's initial six-figure sponsorship was from a wealthy car dealer and UVA supporter, Allen Samuels, from Texas. After only two years on the circuit, Brian earned $288,002. Obviously this was one worthwhile investment for his sponsors, as they received a percentage of his earnings. Nowadays, his official website (www.brianvahaly.com) lists six sponsors—Texas Furniture Gallery, Adidas, Babolat, UBS, T-Mobile, and Turq Jewelry.

Your Sponsorship Packet Worksheets

Sample Cover Letter

You may spiff it up to your liking and relevance/situation, just keep it to one typed page on quality stationary. This letter should not be bound into your sponsorship packet as it will need to be adjusted according to the situation. It is sent with the packet, attached to the cover with a paperclip.

Table 7.1
Sample Cover Letter

Your Name
Your return address
Your phone
Your email address

Addressee (with appropriate title)
Dr., Mr., Mrs., Ms. Sponsor
Address

Current Date

Dear Dr., Mr. Mrs. Ms. _____, (if you know them well, you can be more familiar)

(Personalize your intro paragraph, about four sentences.)

I enjoyed chatting with you at {Jim's tailgate party} last week. It was great that we won the {game}. especially since it was homecoming. It also didn't hurt that it was {Duke} that we beat. Even though I am now a {UNC} alumni, old rivalries still hang on!

I am following up with your request for me to send to you my sponsorship materials for possible consideration. Ever since I started playing tennis, I have aspired to play on the professional tour. I have worked very hard to try to make that dream a reality, however, it takes considerable financial backing.

Your willingness to seriously consider my sponsorship proposal is greatly appreciated. After you have had an opportunity to review my plan, I will call you to further discuss our potential to work together to help further my tennis career. If you have any question regarding the enclosed materials, please do not hesitate to get in touch with me. My contact numbers are listed at the top of this letter. I have also enclosed my business card for your convenience.

Again, thank you for taking the time to read my materials.

Sincerely, (or "With Warm Regards", if you know the person)
Tommy Tennis Player

Your Business Card and Web Page

These two items are optional, but if you have time to create them, they are not a bad idea to have. You can get inexpensive cards made up at your local office supply store for as little as ten bucks, or you can design them yourself with business card stock purchased from that same supply store, as well as the computer software. Minimally, you need your name, address, phone number(s), your business (competitive tennis), and your website address (if you have one). You can develop a personal website for free or at a low cost from a service such as Yahoo. In it you can create your own PR about yourself that you wouldn't care if the whole world would see, because it will be available to the whole internet world. Make sure it is complimentary and will not harm your chances of obtaining sponsors. If you use an email address in your website, make sure it is separate from your personal email address to avoid cluttering it up with unwanted email solicitations from aggressive on-line marketers. Obviously, do not post any personal information that could pre-dispose you to privacy infringement or identity theft (e.g., do not post personal phone numbers, home address, ID numbers, full birthdate, or mother's maiden name).

Packet Introduction

This is a more generic message to tug at your potential sponsor's heart to entice him to sponsor you. Lay it on thick, but not so thick that it sickens them! You might notice that some of the wording is very similar to what was used in the letter to the potential sponsor. That's not a problem—in fact it is good to be a little redundant. It helps people to remember what you said, as long as you are consistent with what you say. Note also the double spacing and keeping the contents short and simple—one page. This will encourage the likelihood that they will read the entire page, and more. Table 7.2 is an example of what you might write (courtesy of Tripp Phillips).

Table 7.2
Packet Introduction

"The enclosed information consists of a proposal that may be unlike any you have ever seen. It is an opportunity for you to make a special kind of investment and, at the same time, to be a part of something very unique."

"I have been playing tennis my entire life and have competed at every possible level. Ever since I started playing tennis when I was four, it has always been my dream to play on the professional tour. I have just completed a very successful collegiate career at the University of North Carolina and am now focusing on the ultimate goal of my athletic career, professional tennis."

"What you are about to read is a brief synopsis of the professional tour as well as my tennis background and future plans and goals. I have included a proposal detailing specific investment and sponsorship opportunities. Currently, my financial position will not allow me to realistically pursue my dream of succeeding as a professional tennis player. I would greatly appreciate your serious consideration of this proposal. Any contribution or support you could offer would be greatly appreciated."

"If you have any further questions or comments, please do not hesitate to call me at _____, or email me at _____. Thank you for taking the time to review the enclosed material. I appreciate your consideration of a possible investment."

Your Tennis Resume

This should be standard business format, one page only. Highlight your best work. There is no need to write down all of your education as you stated that earlier. You need the space here for your compelling accomplishments. You can verbally discuss your education, along with other things that might be of interest to your sponsor, at your meeting.

Table 7.3
Tennis Resume

YOUR NAME IN BOLD, large typeface. Your address, phone, and email.

Objective	**Remember, this is your goal, it must be promising yet potentially realistic. You may choose it to be specific for singles, doubles, both.** "To successfully compete on the ATP professional tennis tour earning a professional ranking in the top ___ within ___ years of competing on the circuit."
Experience	**Junior Tennis:** list major highlights chronologically **College Tennis:** list your INDIVIDUAL, not team, highlights (avoid lowlights!). Again, list all in chronological order, starting with most recent. Be sure to list some significant wins against highly-ranked players. **Summer Circuits:** It will demonstrate your knowledge of the system. It would be especially helpful if you even won some of the matches, thereby demonstrating potential for the Futures circuit.
Awards	**List any award that reflects your ability to be successful**—this could even include non-tennis awards as it will reflect on your character, ability to manage yourself, etc.
Personal	Be careful here and only mention items that might help, not hinder you. Also, it would be better to use this space to highlight your accomplishments rather than to divulge fairly irrelevant personal information. Even if you are involved with a charitable cause, if your potential sponsor has negative feelings about that cause, it could hurt your sponsorship chances. This goes for extracurricular activities as well—for instance, not everyone is a supporter of the fraternity system, and they may even think you will be an irresponsible partier. You need to really know your target sponsor. If you still choose to include this section, tread lightly.
References	**Choose people whom you trust to give you an EXCELLENT reference.** Make sure these people are aware and willing to be contacted. Next to their name, provide their most accessible phone number and email address. Contrary to the standard business resume, do not say "References will be provided upon request." That will only slow you down. You need to project confidence that your references will provide good, accurate information about you. Good choices for references would include: coaches; college athletic director; an intelligent college teammate; a successful pro player who knows you well.

Explanation of How the Professional Tour Operates

This needs to be clear, concise, one page. In other words, SIMPLE. You can go to the ATP website and paraphrase the information they have on line. Do not plagiarize (i.e., direct copying without referencing or quoting). That is copyright infringement and is illegal. Put it in your own language—how you would explain it to your next door neighbor who doesn't follow tennis. If he (or she) can understand what you wrote, then you're golden. If not, rewrite it until the neighbor does understand. Again, borrowing from Tripp Phillips, I've included his explanation of the tour system. If you choose to borrow Tripp's words, please paraphrase (i.e., do not plagiarize) the information in Table 7.4.

Table 7.4
HOW THE PROFESSIONAL TOUR WORKS
(courtesy of Tripp Phillips)

The ATP tour and its working structure may appear very complicated to those unfamiliar with it. This is a brief synopsis to help make it clear.

The professional tour consists of three different overlapping tiers. The lowest level of professional tennis is where nearly every aspiring professional begins; these tournaments are known as Futures and Satellite tournaments. These tournaments are essential for attaining ATP points that are necessary to move to the next level of play, but the pay at this level is very inadequate. After attaining enough points, one can advance to the next level of the pro tour, which is known as the Challenger level.

This level is very tough and also much more rewarding in terms of the amount of ATP points one could possibly win as well as in terms of prize money. Players at the Challenger Level are on the verge of being full time ATP tour players and are also able to play the qualifying for almost all major tour events.

The top level of play is all of the tournaments that you see on television. The largest tournaments on this tour are the Grand Slams (Australian Open, French Open, Wimbledon, U.S. Open), but there are ATP tour stops all over the world virtually every week of the year.

Individual rankings are based upon the total amount of ATP points a person earns over the course of a year. The amount of points and prize money a person attains in any given tournament is dependent upon the level of the tournament and player performance. This is shown on the next page. A certain number of points does not guarantee entry into any tournament. After all entries are received, the applicants with the most points are placed into the main draw, and those who are just short of direct acceptance are placed in qualifying. Tournaments occur at the same time all over the world, so some tournaments will be easier to get into than others. For instance, it is likely that more people would rather play a series of Challenger's in the U.S. than in Malaysia, so it is possible to be accepted to these tournaments with fewer points. The goal is to try to work one's way through the Futures as fast as possible. The sooner a player has the opportunity to play Challengers and ATP events, the better. Therefore, it is imperative for an aspiring professional to have the means to travel to tournaments all over the world in order to have a realistic chance of succeeding.

As you will see, the Satellite and Futures tournaments do not provide enough prize money to support the expenses necessary to play on the tour. It generally takes an average of two years to move through the Satellite tours to the Challenger Level. At this point, the prize money improves, and frequent opportunities to qualify for ATP events allow for one good week to provide a great deal of points and large pay days.

Explanation of Tour Finances

This page is a continuation of how the tour works, listing points and pay-outs for various tournaments. Start with ones that will represent your initial level of play, then work up the tiers to provide an example of the various pay scales. You should also include doubles as well as singles for a well-rounded financial picture. Be sure to use current financial and point award figures. They change depending upon the amount of corporate funding available. This will take a few pages, but it is crucial to keep in so that your potential sponsor has a very clear idea of the prize money potential at the various levels, or tiers, of competition.

Table 7.5
THE FINANCIAL PICTURE OF THE TOUR

Please note that the payout schedule is the same for a given total sum of money, regardless of the location of the event. For instance, a $15,000 Futures event will pay out at the same rate regardless if it is held in California or Germany. Also remember that the doubles prize money listed below is per doubles TEAM. The pot is split between the two players equally. The figures below represent gross income, before taxes. Federal (or country) taxes are taken out at the tournament before the player receives his paycheck.

$10,000 Futures, Pittsburgh, PA, USA (2002)

Matches	Points	Singles Prize Money	Doubles Prize Money
Round of 32	0	$117.50	N/A
Round of 16	1 (0 doubles)	$200.00	$0
Quarterfinalist	2 (1 doubles)	$290.00	$180.00
Semifinalist	4	$480.00	$260.00
Finalist	8	$900.00	$330.00
Winner	12	$1,300.00	$630.00

$15,000 Futures, Kassel, Germany (2003)

Matches	Points	Singles Prize Money	Doubles Prize Money
Round of 32	0	$176.50	N/A
Round of 16	1 (0 doubles)	$300.00	$0
Quarterfinalist	2 (1 doubles)	$435.00	$270.00
Semifinalist	4	$720.00	$390.00
Finalist	8	$1,350.00	$495.00
Winner	12	$1,950.00	$945.00

Table 7.5 Continued

$25,000 Challenger, Sassuolo, Italy (2003)

Matches	Points	Singles Prize Money	Doubles Prize Money
Qualifiers	2	N/A	N/A
Round of 32	1 (0 doubles)	$260.00	N/A
Round of 16	5	$430.00	$180.00
Quarterfinalist	12	$730.00	$320.00
Semifinalist	22	$1,255.00	$540.00
Finalist	35	$2,120.00	$900.00
Winner	50	$3,600.00	$1,550.00

$50,000 Challenger, Dallas, Texas, USA (2003)

Matches	Points	Singles Prize Money	Doubles Prize Money
Qualifiers	2	N/A	N/A
Round of 32	1 (0 doubles)	$520.00	N/A
Round of 16	5	$860.00	$180.00
Quarterfinalist	12	$1,460.00	$320.00
Semifinalist	22	$2,510.00	$540.00
Finalist	35	$4,240.00	$900.00
Winner	50	$7,200.00	$1,550.00

Hall of Fame Tennis Championships, Newport, RI, USA (2004)

Matches	Points*	Singles Prize Money	Doubles Prize Money
Qualifiers	R = 1; E = 5	N/A	N/A
Round of 32	R = 1; E = 5	$3,650.00	N/A
Round of 16	R = 3; E = 15	$6,225.00	$2,000.00
Quarterfinalist	R = 8; E = 40	$10,600.00	$3,400.00
Semifinalist	R = 15; E = 75	$18,000.00	$5,650.00
Finalist	R = 24; E = 120	$30,600.00	$9,600.00
Winner	R = 35; E = 175	$52,000.00	$16,350.00

Legg Mason Tennis Classic, Washington, DC, USA (2004)

Matches	Points	Singles Prize Money	Doubles Prize Money
Qualifiers	R = 1; E = 5	N/A	N/A
Round of 32	R = 1; E = 5	$4,,870.00	N/A
Round of 16	R = 3; E = 5	$8,,300.00	$2,000.00
Quarterfinalist	R = 8; E = 40	$14,100.00	$4,915.00
Semifinalist	R = 15;E = 75	$23,900.00	$40,700.00
Finalist	R = 24; E = 120	$40,700.00	$13,850.00
Winner	R = 35; E = 175	$69,200.00	$23,570.00

*R = ATP Race Points and E = General Entry Points

7.5 (continued)

Wimbledon, London, England (2004)

Matches	Points	Singles Prize Money	Doubles Prize Money
Qualifiers	(Additional points)	N/A	N/A
Round of 128	R = 1; E = 5	$16,294.00	N/A
Round of 64	R = 7; E = 3	$26,604.00	$8,778.00
Round of 32	R = 15; E = 75	$43,,964.00	$14,961.00
Round of 16	R = 30; E = 150	$77,817.00	$27,394.00
Quarterfinalist	R = 50; E = 250	$141,178.00	$51,545.00
Semifinalist	R = 90; E = 450	$241,488.00	$99,305.00
Finalist	R = 140; E = 700	$542,959.00	$193,695.00
Winner	R = 200; E = 1000	$1,085,531.00	$387,389.00

U.S. Open, New York, New York, USA DC (2004)

Matches	Points	Singles Prize Money	Doubles Prize Money
Qualifiers	(Additional points)	N/A	N/A
Round of 128	R = 1; E = 5	$14,000.00	N/A
Round of 64	R = 7; E = 3	$25,000.00	$10,000.00
Round of 32	R = 15; E = 75	$40,000.00	$15,000.00
Round of 16	R = 30; E = 150	$70,000.00	$25,000.00
Quarterfinalist	R = 50; E = 250	$130,000.00	$50,000.00
Semifinalist	R = 90; E = 450	$260,000.00	$100,000.00
Finalist	R = 140; E = 700	$500,000.00	$200,000.00
Winner	R = 200; E = 1000	$1,000,000.00	$400,000.00

Itemization of Your Expenses

These two pages will be the most crucial pages that you develop. Spend time making them clear, concise, and easy to read. Include whatever items you need help with financially. You can follow your budget worksheet completed in Chapter 6. Below is an example of how you might present your direct tennis costs in your sponsorship packet.

The asterisk next to "hotels" is because you will need to allot some space to explain how "hospitality" figures into your budget—that is, you will be able to reduce your hotel costs when free private housing is available. This can occur when tournaments are in locations where you have contacts; or it may occur when the tournament director has identified host families willing to take in a player from the tournament. Your sponsorship agreement (e.g., the legal contract) will detail how your potential sponsor will allocate your funds. Depending upon the sum pledged, your sponsor may provide the entire amount all at once (for smaller pledges, not likely to cover all of your expenses) or he may dole it out at specified time periods, such as an upfront 6-month advance or quarterly installments. Usually you will need to provide a financial accounting of monies spent prior to additional disbursement of funds from the sponsor.

Table 7.6
ESTIMATED TENNIS-RELATED EXPENSES

MONTHLY EXPENSES

ITEM		COST
Travel		
Airfare	4 domestic flights @ $300 RT	$1,200
Rental Car	$17.50/day, shared expense	$525
Hotel*	$40/day, shared, when housing is not available	-
Meals	$35/day	$1,050
	Travel Subtotal	*$3,975*
Expendable Equipment		
Tennis Balls	$3/can x 15 cans	$45
Racquet String	$80/ reel x 1 reel	$80
Racquet Stringing	$10/racquet x 15 racquets	$150
Grip Tape	$5/pack x 5 packs	$25
	Expendables Subtotal	*$300*
Miscellaneous Recurring Fees		
Tournament Entries	$30 x 4 tournaments	$120
Guest Facilities	Conditioning room, court fees	$40
Postal Services	Forms, reports, etc	$10
Phone/Internet Services	Non-personal	$25
	Miscellaneous Subtotal	*$195*

MONTHLY TOTAL: **$4,470**

(continued next page)

Table 7.6 (continued)

ADDITIONAL ANNUAL EXPENSES

ITEM		COST
Clothing		
Tennis Shoes	$100 x 2 pairs	$200
Shirts, collared	$40 x 10 shirts	$400
Shorts	$30 x 7 shorts	$210
Socks	$10/pair x 10 pairs	$100
Sweat Bands / Hats	$10 each x 5	$50
Laundry (on the road)	$10/month x 10 months	$100
	Clothing Subtotal	*$1,060*
Professional Coaching		
Personal Coach	$100/day x 100 days	$10,000
Training Camp	(all expenses for 3 weeks)	$2,500
	Coaching Subtotal	*$12,500*

Estimated Monthly Total—$4,470 x 10 touring months   **$ 44,700**
Additional Annual Expenses Subtotal   **$ 13,560**

Grand Total $58,260/year

Your First-Year Travel Plan and Projected Performance

Your travel plan should be based upon your anticipated financial support, best case scenario. This is your "dream plan"—where you are able to travel to any tournament within your projected budget. For this, you need go to the USTA, ITF, and ATP websites for tournament schedules to determine where the best matches for you are being held, and when. You also need to determine your days off. Then you need to project a winning attitude and forecast, using realistic mathematical deductions, what your approximate ranking should be and when. This will let your potential sponsor know that you have given this a lot of forethought. An example of this task is listed below. Your exact course will depend upon your personal college ranking and your residence, or home-base. Some of this information will also be included in your sponsrship contract.

PR Pieces

List your significant newspaper/magazine articles on a separate page or photocopy neatly and attach samples, or cut and paste from websites.

Table 7.7
Short-Term (Seasonal) and Long-Term (One-Year) Plan

College Graduation, Major/Minor: _____

NCAA Championships (where, when, your results):

Current ATP Entry Ranking:

Summer Tournament Travel:

Fall Tournament Travel:

Winter Tournament Travel:

Spring Tournament Travel:

Vacation/Recuperation Days:

Year-End Expected (Goal) Ranking:

Chapter 8
Sponsorship Contracts

"The secret of life is honesty and fair dealing. If you can fake that then you got it made."

—Groucho Marx, Comedian

"Sponsorship" is a "cash and/or in-kind fee paid to a property (typically sports, arts, entertainment, or causes) in return for access to the exploitable commercial potential associated with that property" (Stotlar, 2001). As a sponsored player, you agree to be exploited for profit by your sponsor. That's why, when it comes to evaluating sponsorship contracts, the watchword is "trust no one." As harsh as this sounds, it should be your mantra when selecting a sponsor. Get a lawyer. Get a good contract. If you are dealing with a stranger, get a background check. It's simple to do, just go to Yahoo or Google and type in "People Search." From there, you will be directed to a firm that does criminal background checking. This will cost you about $50, but it will be worth it.

And lastly, if the deal sounds "too good to be true"—watch out! As desperate as you might feel about needing money, you don't need to sell your soul to the devil. You're better off competing with limited funds.

Evaluating Your Sponsorship Contract

A sponsorship contract is a legal agreement between you and an individual, a group of individuals, or a company, regarding financing your tennis career. The main intent of the contract is to protect you, but the sponsor will also be looking for protection. Each of you will be viewing the contract from a different perspective. The contract will detail each of the party's expectations and provide recourse if things don't go according to plan. Your agreement needs to be in writing; a handshake or verbal "I do" simply won't cut it. If you are providing the contract, it needs to be carefully worded. In the end, it will save you, as well as your sponsor, money. A poorly worded, vague, ambiguous, or blatantly one-sided contract could force you or your sponsor to shell out more dollars in legal fees for revisions or clarifications. Besides that, if a dispute should arise, vague contracts can be manipulated by either party, which can result in an ugly legal battle (and more legal costs). It is better for you to come up with a contract rather than having to modify a contract provided by your sponsor. So first and foremost, hire a lawyer with experience in sport sponsorships.

al (private) sponsorship contract will be fairly different from
result due to a huge corporate deal. However, there are
lities.

Unless you are a superstar, you won't be dealing with issues such as
"image use," copyrights, trademark/logo protections, and other promotional issues. Your first private funding contract will be more basic, concerned
with terms of the agreement, payment plans, what you will deliver, and
contract termination.

At some point, however, you might find yourself entering into formal or
informal endorsement agreements with clothing, beverage, and equipment
manufacturers. These types of agreements fall under the category of
endorsement contracts, which are generally divided into three areas:
Headgear and clothing, hard goods, and non-marketing sponsorships.

For the tennis player, "headgear" refers to hats, bandanas, and head-
bands worn during a match, practice, and even off the court. "Clothing"
includes shoes, socks, shorts, and shirts. Anything that is visible to the public could fall under the domain of your endorsement contract.

"Hard goods" for tennis would be your tennis equipment: Racquets,
balls, string, and ball machines. Your sponsor will set limits as to what you
can (and can't) wear, to prevent you from promoting products from another company that is viewed as a competitor in the same market. These limits can extend outside of the tennis arena. For instance, if you are asked to
endorse Ford vehicles, you can't be seen driving around town in a Toyota.
The last type of endorsement, the non-marketing sponsorship, does not
allow advertising on your clothing. The sponsor will have the right to use
your likeness, image, or appearance in speaking engagements, ads, and
autograph sessions.

But for now, let's get down to specifics with the most basic of private
sponsorship contracts, beginning with the first paragraph of the contract
and working our way to the end.

The Parties

This is the first paragraph of your contract and it should identify who
is entering into this agreement. It should at least contain full names,
and possibly, addresses. If you are entering into an agreement with a
small business, relevant company information needs to be included (princi-
pal place of business, state of incorporation, its officers). This first paragraph is going to set the tone of your contract—it is going to ensure that no
ambiguity exists as to who has entered into this agreement. Your first paragraph (or clause) should look something like this:

"This agreement is dated and entered into as of the ___ (number) day of ___ (month), ___ (year), by and between ___ (athlete name) and ___ (sponsor's name) (Gruen pp. 62)."

If your sponsor is Joe's Tennis Club, then a third phrase would need to be added after the sponsor's name:

"..., a corporation organized under the laws of the State of ___ ." (Gruen, pp. 62)

Definitions

You may or may not even need this section or it may not be a stand-alone section, but rather some terms will just be identified in the first paragraph. Its purpose is to clarify the use of terminology specific to your contract. Certain words or phrases in contracts may have an alternative meaning in context with your contract and may not retain their "everyday meaning." Furthermore, the terminology should be consistent throughout the contract. If the athlete is defined as "professional," then that term should not be used interchangeably with the word "athlete" nor substituted for other similar-meaning words such as "player" or even the abbreviated "pro." This can create confusion or ambiguity, and the smart lawyer could possibly use this to challenge the contract should a problem arise in the future. Therefore, pay particular attention to the "definition section" so you know what the contract is actually talking about.

For instance, three commonly used words in sponsorship contracts are: *use, payment,* and *event of default.* The word *use* may not refer to actual using, but rather, it may be referring to selling, licensing, or gifting a product, say, photographs of you taken at a Challenger match to be developed and sold to fans in the stands. To you, the term *payment* may only refer to how your sponsor is going to pay you his pledged amount. But this could also refer to administration deduction fees or royalties. Also within the payment category lies the issue of the currency used for payment. Contracts usually have a section explaining what could happen in the event of a default. A *default* is failure to follow through on an agreed upon issue, a failure to deliver, whether it be payment not rendered to the athlete (you) or a report you fail to provide to your sponsor. Maybe your contract stipulates that your sponsor won't have to pay you if he becomes "insolvent," or alternatively, if you promised to pay your sponsor a percentage of your earnings, maybe you are released from that promise if you become insolvent. Insolvency can be a gray area, which is easy to contest. Therefore, some lawyers counsel not to raise the issue in the contract since it is contestable in court and potentially hard to defend. However, if you feel safer with including the clause, put it in, just don't be disappointed if it doesn't hold up in court.

Promotional Rights and Exclusivity

Product endorsement will not be a concern of yours for a while—it probably will not even be in your basic private sponsorship contract. But once you are somewhat established or have proven that you have some market value, sponsors may require the right to exploit you—that is, to use you and/or your image for sales and marketing purposes. Furthermore, they will demand that no one else similarly be permitted to exploit you while you are under contract with them. So if Wilson promotes you, giving you shoes and racquets, you can't go out and use a Babolat racquet and wear Nike shoes, not even during a practice session.

You and your lawyer will need to evaluate this section carefully to ensure that you will still benefit, that you will be notified about any promotion utilizing you or your image in any format, and that you receive a financial percentage of any and all marketing ventures that might use you and/or your image/persona in any manner. Obviously, it's best not to relinquish "all rights in the universe" for any type of marketing that somehow involves you. Also, don't endorse a product that you know nothing about. The last thing you need is to be associated with a bad product. Finally, you will need to be careful about the exclusivity portion of a contract and its length of time—you may not want to be tied to that sponsor forever. Sponsors will be very aggressive, which is why you and your lawyer will need to be equally aggressive. You can't wing this on your own.

If you are still in college playing tennis and approached by a company to promote its product while playing non-collegiate events, it's up to you not to do anything that could violate your collegiate eligibility (Gruen, pp. 73).

Terms of the Contract

The first consideration will be whether you are just starting out, are about to explode into the main arena, or are pretty well established. If you are just starting out, go for shorter contracts (one year) with an option to renew. This allows for renegotiations as you prove yourself capable and also allows you to move on to greener pastures if your sponsor no longer meets your needs. Two-year contracts can be considered if the conditions are appealing and "safe" for you. But locking yourself in beyond two years is not wise unless it is an absolutely incredible deal. When you get nearer to the end of your career, shooting for longer-term contracts is desirable so that you are assured some sponsorship in your twilight years. By the same token, a shorter contract period is desirable for sponsors if you are an unproven commodity. If you perform well, they will be eager to continue supporting you, but if you fall flat on your face, they can back off from further sponsorship and save themselves money. Your contract can also be for an indefinite period of time, not stating a specific termination date. This can get dicey, however, so you need to be careful when considering an open-ended contract. The contract can't let your sponsor ditch you at a moment's notice, leaving you in a lurch. Likewise, if you have your contract written in such a way so as to promise a financial return to your sponsor, and you decide to terminate at the same time that your career begins to skyrocket, your sponsor might feel you are trying to avoid paying him back the promised financial incentive. That of course could land you in court.

Renewals

It is very important to consider dealing with renewals in your contract. Be aware that the wording can impact you dramatically, especially if you are considering sole sponsorship. You need to know the meanings of the phrases: "Right of first refusal," "an option to renew," and "a right to negotiate."

Under the *right of first refusal,* the sponsor must be given the option to match any other offer you receive from any potential new sponsor, within a given time frame. This time frame is generally eight months to a year before your contract is supposed to expire. So, after having Mr. X. as your sole sponsor for three months, if Mr. Y comes by dangling more money to hop on board to his sponsorship plan, Mr. X has the right to match that, thereby knocking Mr. Y out of contention. You, the "sports property," are entitled to seek a higher bidder to outmatch Mr. X, but at no time can you accept a lower bid from someone else and dump Mr. X in the process. In effect, you are "locked in" to Mr. X. Most potential sponsors, when they find out that you have a "right of first refusal" clause with your current sponsor, will not bother to approach you. This means that even if Mr. Y was prepared to offer you a better deal, or if the sponsorship of Mr. X. was going sour for some reason, you will have a very tough time trying to change sponsors.

Option to renew simply allows the existing sponsor to propose extending your sponsorship when the contract term expires. This option must be exercised within a specified time frame, for a defined period of time, and the conditions remain the same as the original agreement. If the sponsor does not exercise his option to renew within the specified time period, then you have the right to negotiate a new sponsorship with someone else. The downside is that you are stuck with the terms and conditions of your old contract. If you didn't do such a great job with your old contract, you are stuck with those flaws after you renew. By the same token, your sponsor can't suddenly decide to change the terms either. If you and your sponsor are each satisfied with the terms of your old contract, you are good to go. If either party is dissatisfied with some aspect of your old contract, but you think you might still like to continue the sponsorship under different terms, a new contract should be drafted. To avoid needing to draft a new contract (which will cost you more money), a futuristic option to renew clause could be stated as follows:

> "___ [Athlete] hereby grants to ___ [Sponsor] the right to renew its ___ [Type of Sponsorship] hereunder the same terms and conditions as contain within this agreement,
> "EXCEPT:
> "The new sponsorship fee shall be [$]. ___ [Sponsor] shall exercise said option, if at all, by giving ___ [Athlete] written notice thereof within ___ [Days] prior to the expiration of this Agreement." (Gruen, pp 63)

The last phrase, *right to negotiate,* simply gives either party the right to initiate discussions concerning the renewal/extension of the contract. Of course there is a pre-determined time frame set forth within the original contract wherein contract negotiations are to be conducted, and the underlying assumption is that negotiations will be carried out in good faith. If you and your sponsor fail to reach a mutual understanding within the time frame established, then your contract is ended and both you and the sponsor are free. As you might have suspected, this isn't a perfect catch-all clause. When negotiations fall apart, courts have often found that they cannot endorse the contract because the phrase "to negotiate in good faith" is vague.

Payment Options

As you might imagine, there is no set payment plan. It all depends upon your needs and what will work best for your particular situation. This is where your sponsorship budget plan comes in handy. You already know how much you need for a year, and your sponsor has seen your budget. Now you need to translate that information into something that is applicable to your sponsorship contract. You might need several private sponsors to cover the entire amount, or maybe you will get lucky and secure a sole sponsor. The payment could be made in one lump sum if the amount is considered small (this depends on the sponsor, not you), most probably at the beginning of the season or in anticipation of paying for certain line items (such as tennis training camp, clothing, and health club membership fees). If the sum is larger, installments might be planned to occur on certain dates. The amount of the installment should be defined and not left to the whim of the sponsor. You will need to know how much money you have at your disposal at any given time. If your sponsor is erratic in his payment method or amounts, you will become frazzled trying to determine if you have enough money to do what you need to do. The main consideration is to allow some flexibility in case you or your sponsor experience cash flow problems. While you might like to have your sponsor pay you up front, this may not be practical or possible. Try to spell out the dates when you would like to receive payment. If you underestimate costs, and if your payment plan is flexible, you might be able to approach your sponsor for disbursement of funds ahead of schedule.

Multiple Sponsors, Assignment, and Indemnity

If you find yourself with multiple sponsors, as stated in the "Promotions" section, you must be sure there are no conflicts among the different sponsors. If you set up different levels of support (say $1,000, $5,000, and $10,000 options), then you have to spell out the benefits of each level to the sponsors and how they potentially interact with each other. Clarity of purpose is especially important if you pitched yourself as an investment. If you have some type of percentage payback scheme, your plan must be equitable and clearly stated. Your sponsors should not be left in the dark wondering how many other sponsors you have and how that will impact their financial return, should one actually materialize.

You probably should also consider prohibiting an *assignment* clause and clearly express in your contract an unwillingness to permit assignment of your sponsorship. Put simply, "assignment" means that a sponsor can turn your sponsorship plan over to someone else without your consent. This happens with home mortgages and school loans all the time, usually without a negative outcome, but it's not one you want to happen to your sponsorship. This elevates the risk that you will be sponsored by someone with whom you don't want to be associated for whatever reason. It could jeopardize your personal integrity, conflict with your morals, or conflict with another sponsor.

Let's say that Mr. X originally sponsors you, and you like him, his ideals, and his business. But Mr. X. lands in some financial difficulties and has to bail on you. Let's say Mr. Z offers to pick up the tab and Mr. X quickly agrees without doing a background check on Mr. Z. Without an assignment clause, you will be told about this transaction only after it's done. If later you find out that Mr. Z's money comes from unscrupulous sources, you are left with a sponsorship funded by tainted money, which could be a potential embarrassment to you. Or you could find yourself accidentally involved with a conflict of interest problem. Perhaps new sponsor Mr. Z is a major stockholder for Head. Mr. X, not knowing that you had a small deal to endorse Babolat racquets, might think he's done you a favor, getting you a new sponsor connected to an established racquet manufacturing company. See the conflict?

Your contract should also have an *indemnification* statement of some type. When you indemnify someone, it protects that person from legal responsibility for his actions, or the actions of others, or compensates him in the event of harm or loss due to his actions or the actions of others. Being indemnified, you reduce your chances of being dragged into court to pay for damages incurred for something that you had nothing to do with. If you are dragged into court anyway, you can be compensated for your costs and expenses. Likewise, if you say or do something that someone finds actionable and they sue you, your sponsor, by being indemnified, will not be your co-defendant. It's important protection for you and your sponsor—so be sure it's in your contract.

Termination

Every contract should stipulate the grounds on which to end the sponsorship relationship before its agreed-upon termination date. Although difficult, you must attempt to forecast situations for which the best response is to terminate the contract. These conditions must be included in your contract before your agreement is finalized. Examples of possible causes for early termination may be due to circumstances that prevent you from completing your obligations, such as a serious injury or illness; an unexpected financial or personal hardship; rocky dealings that cannot be resolved between you and the sponsor; or a breach of contract. The first two situations, illness or injury on your part and unexpected hardship, while disappointing, are relatively easy to handle and accept. The latter two, disputes and breaches, are far more difficult to handle and can get ugly. This is why it is better to stipulate potential sponsorship-ending situations in your contract and have recourse readily available.

To help iron out disputes between you and your sponsor, you should include a clause in your contract about *Alternative Dispute Resolution* (ADR) that will facilitate mediation or arbitration (Gruen, pp 68). If after arbitration, the dispute still remains irresolvable, the best course of action is to terminate the contract. In such an instance, some type of financial remunerations will be in order—usually in the form of repayment of any unused funds by the athlete to the sponsor, assuming that the dispute was of some other nature and not due to the athlete or sponsor not upholding the agreed-upon professional responsibilities (breach of contract).

Breach of contract means that someone in the agreement failed to uphold some condition (or conditions) set forth in the contract. For instance, the sponsor may not make payments as agreed. Alternatively, you might not uphold your end of the deal even though you are healthy. That is, you do not attempt to play the number of matches you said you would play, you don't practice or train, you party to excess, you use illegal drugs, you are found guilty of a crime, you misuse the funds allocated to you, you don't meet with your sponsor, you don't provide adequate reporting of your tennis activities and winnings, or you simply quit. If accused of breach of contract, the first consideration is if the nature of the breach is major or minor. Minor breaches may be handled by giving the defaulting party a chance to rectify the problem. In other words, the offending party is given written notice to correct the situation within a certain time frame. If the problem is not corrected within that grace period, then the contract may be terminated. But you need to specify in your contract the course of action to be taken if a breach results in contract termination. For instance, if your sponsor is the offending party, you might demand the total sum of the sponsorship to be paid within a certain period of days or else you will sue in court; conversely, if you are the offending party, your sponsor can declare your contract null and void and demand you repay every cent he ever gave you— and not just any unspent funds. It is even possible that either party could tack on interest claims, because that money could have been in a bank account accruing interest. If you go to court and lose, you might wind up paying not only your own legal fees, but also those of your sponsor's, in addition to any monetary finding against you. Litigation should always be used as a last resort as it costs time and money, both of which will be in short supply as you are starting out.

In the pages that follow, you have a sample of an actual contract agreement. Review it critically, comparing it to what your legal advisor recommends. Remember, this contract is to protect you, but the sponsor is going to want some protection and assurances as well. In the case of this particular sponsorship, things did not go according to plan, as you will see.

Sample Sponsorship Agreement (Contract)
Original Contract

Table 8.1 is an example of an actual contract that was written and pitched by a "real" tennis athlete wanting to go pro a couple years ago. It was requested that he remain anonymous, as well as the exact amount of his sponsorship request, but the basics of his contract proposal is intact for you to learn from. The contract is specific for tennis and not unwieldy—it's only thee pages. Those are the pluses. The minuses include a variety of potential pitfalls. The contract, in its quest to be brief, seems to have ignored some of the more basic items recommended to be in a contract. Compare what was discussed earlier in this chapter and note which sections were included versus those that were omitted. Do you think this was wise? Also pay close attention to the inconsistencies in use of terms. First the athlete is identified as the "Professional," but midstream the contract begins to refer to the athlete as the "player." Similarly, at one point, the "Sponsors" are referred to as "investors." In fact, under item 1, there is clear reference to this sponsorship agreement being an "investment" which alludes to a potential financial gain for the Sponsor(s). Is a sponsorship for a player really an investment? Consider that later, as this very contract stipulates that this is a risky venture and that no financial gain may occur at all. If you recall, it is well known in tennis circles that it usually takes at least two years for a player to break even, let alone make enough prize money for "investors" to see a 50 percent return on their dollar. Do you think a tennis-savvy sponsor/investor would agree to this contract? Finally, did you detect any editorial or grammatical errors? Spacing and inconsistency with capitalizing "Professional" and "Sponsor" throughout the document is the doing of the athlete, not me, the author of this text. The same disclaimer goes for any misspellings or word misuse. A potential sponsor could have viewed all of these mistakes as careless errors and conclude that this plan is not very well thought out. Hence, the athlete unintentionally could have sabotaged his own efforts in procuring a sponsor. Nevertheless, this athlete did manage to secure a few funds, but not to the extent he desired. It's not known if that was because of the [poor] economic climate at the time, the presentation style of the athlete, or the contract itself. As you will see, this original boilerplate contract was revised by at least one of his sponsors. Let's follow along this tennis player's path to securing funds on the pages that follow.

Table 8.1
Original Sponsorship Proposal

[ATHLETE'S NAME]

"This agreement, made and entered into this as of the [calendar #] day of the year 19xx, by and between [Athlete Name] ("Professional") and ("Sponsor") as set forth below:"

"Whereas Professional is a professional tennis player and desires to secure sponsorship for a period of 24 months through [DATE] , 19xx."

"Whereas Sponsors are willing to provide such sponsorship as hereinafter set forth"

"Now, therefore, in consideration of the mutual promise and agreements hereinafter set forth the parties agree as follows:"

Table 8.1 - Continued

1. Sponsors' Investment

"Sponsor agrees to sponsor the Professional, and the Professional agrees to be sponsored, for a term of twenty-four (24) months commencing [Date, 19xx] and ending [Date, 19xx], or until the investor has received their initial investment plus 50%, whichever comes first."

2. Professional Duties

"Professional shall engage in the business of being a professional tennis player during the term hereof to the best of his ability. Professional shall exercise his best efforts in tournaments sponsored by the ATP or ITF Tour for the calendar year 19xx-19xx. If Professional is successful in such endeavor, Professional shall play or attempt to qualify to play in at least fifty (50) tournaments sanctioned by the ATP or ITF during the term. The Professional shall attempt to play both singles and doubles events. Scheduling of these events shall be at the Professional's discretion, but the Professional shall play in or attempt to qualify for at least fifty (50) such events during the term."

"Professional shall, to the best of his ability, keep physically fit and shall at all times conduct himself in such a way as to be a credit to himself, Sponsors, and the sport of tennis."

3. Expenses, Advances, and Division of Income

A. "A six (6) months advance will be required from sponsor to fund allocated expenses. The sum total of the advance will be $xx,xxx. The sponsor may however elect to use a credit card that allows expenses to be tracked and accounted for with a credit limit on the card.

B. Sponsor accepts the risk that he may not receive his initial investment back within the two (2) year period of this agreement.

C. Sponsor can only apply after tax prize money, exhibition money after fees, or endorsement income after fees as a source of revenue to repay sponsor."

D. "Sponsor may be released from this agreement with written notice received by player with a thirty (30) day notice. Notice must be sent via certified letter to the player. If sponsor wishes to terminate this agreement, the player has no obligations to repay any expenses incurred other than which is outlined in Item (C) up to the termination date but not beyond that date.

E. The player will pay back the sponsor from income outlined in Item (C) above on a 70% Sponsor, 30% Professional basis until Sponsor has received his initial investment plus 50%. Frequency of the pay back to be worked out between player and sponsor.

F. Should player become injured and unable to play for an extended period of time, all unspent monies will be returned to sponsor until player can continue to play.

G. Player and sponsor will meet every six (6) months to evaluate the past six (6) months income and expenses versus budget and to determine the estimated amount of the next six (6) months income which will not exceed the $xx,xxx , the maximum player expense.

H. Should there be more than one sponsor than income would be divided on a pro-rated basis."

Table 8.1 – Continued

4. Default

"In the event of default by either of the parties in the performance of any of the covenants hereunder, the other party shall notify, in writing, the party alleged to be at fault of the specific covenants not being complied with. If the party alleged to be at fault does not remedy the situation to the satisfaction of the complaining party within fourteen (14) days, the complaining party shall have the right to cancel this Agreement upon thirty (30) days written notice. And may exercise, separately or cumulatively, any one or more of the remedies provided at law or equity for such default. The waiver of any default shall not constitute a waiver of any subsequent default."

5. Relationship

"Professional shall act hereunder exclusively as an independent contractor. It is expressly agreed that the master servant relationship does not exist herein. Sponsors shall be liable to no one for any acts committed by the Professional."

Sponsor	Date
Professional	Date

Revised Original Contract

The original contract (Table 8.1) was slightly modified (see the arrows in Table 8.2) by a family friend (and his lawyer) who ended up agreeing to become a sponsor to the athlete for an undisclosed sum of money over the proposed 2-year period. What do you think of this version? Is anybody (athlete or sponsor) better "protected"? Do think it was specific enough? Are there still changes that you would make? Although not in this text, the actual revised contract also had both the "Professional" and the "Sponsor" initial each page at the bottom, providing written verification that they indeed read, understood, and agreed upon all items set forth on any given page.

Changes within the text lines were also initialed by both parties

Table 8.2
Revised Sponsorship Agreement

[ATHLETE'S NAME]

"This agreement, made and entered into this as of the [calendar #] day of the year 19xx, by and between [Athlete Name] ("Professional") and ("Sponsor") as set forth below:

Whereas Professional is a professional tennis player and desires to secure sponsorship for a period of 24 months through [DATE] , 19xx.

Whereas Sponsor is willing to provide such sponsorship as hereinafter set forth."

"Now, therefore, in consideration of the mutual promise and agreements hereinafter set forth the parties agree as follows:"

1. Sponsor Investment
"Sponsor agrees to sponsor the Professional, and the Professional agrees to be sponsored, for a term of twenty-four (24) months commencing [Date, 19xx and ending Date, 19xx], or until the Sponsor has received his initial investment plus 50%, whichever comes first."

2. Professional Duties
"The Professional shall engage in the business of being a professional tennis player during the term hereof to the best of his ability. The Professional shall exercise his best efforts in tournaments sponsored by the ATP or ITF Tour for the calendar years 19xx-19xx. If the Professional is successful in such endeavors, the Professional shall play or attempt to qualify to play in at least fifty (50) tournaments sanctioned by the ATP or ITF during the said 2-year term. The Professional shall attempt to play both singles and doubles events. Scheduling of these events shall be at the Professional's discretion, but the Professional shall play in or attempt to qualify for at least fifty (50) such events during this 2-year term. The Professional shall, to the best of his ability, keep physically fit and shall at all times conduct himself in such a way as to be a credit to himself, his Sponsor, and the sport of tennis."

3. Expenses, Advances, *Extensions*, and Division of Income
→ A. "Sponsor agrees to provide a total sum of [$] for the 2-year term, with 50% payable in advance as a lump sum payment of [$] on/about [Date], 19xx and the balance [$] payable on/about [Date], 19xx.

B. Sponsor accepts the risk that he may not receive his initial investment back within the two (2) year period of this agreement.

C. Sponsor can only apply after tax prize money, exhibition money after fees, or endorsement income after fees as a source of revenue to repay Sponsor.

Table 8.2 – Continued

D. Sponsor may be released from this agreement with a written notice received by the Professional with a thirty (30) day notice. Notice must be sent via certified letter to the Professional. If the Sponsor wishes to terminate this agreement, the Professional has no obligations to repay any expenses incurred other than which is outlined in Item (C) up to the termination date but not beyond that date."

E. "The Professional will pay back the Sponsor from income outlined in Item (C) above on a 70% Sponsor, 30% Professional basis until Sponsor has received his initial investment plus 50%.

→ The frequency of the pay back to the Sponsor by the Professional will be on a quarterly basis.

→ F. Sponsor retains the option to extend this agreement as outlined in Item (E) for a period not to exceed one additional year should performance of the Professional indicate success or ability to repay Sponsor will probably not occur until his third year on the professional circuit. The Sponsor must submit the extension request with a written notice via certified mail to the Professional thirty (30) days prior to the expiration of the original agreement term.

G. Should the Professional become injured and unable to play for an extended period of time, all unspent monies will be returned to the Sponsor until the Professional can continue to play.

→ H. Professional and Sponsor will meet a minimum of once each year during the agreement period to review sponsorship-related expenditures, actual income and expenses versus the projected budget.

I. Should there be more than one sponsor, income would be divided on a pro-rated basis."

4. Default
"In the event of default by either of the parties in the performance of any of the covenants hereunder, the other party shall notify, in writing, the party alleged to be at fault of the specific covenants not being complied with. If the party alleged to be at fault does not remedy the situation to the satisfaction of the complaining party within fourteen (14) days, the complaining party shall have the right to cancel this Agreement upon thirty (30) days written notice, and may exercise, separately or cumulatively, any one or more of the remedies provided at law or equity for such default. The waiver of any default shall not constitute a waiver of any subsequent default."

Table 8.2 – Continued

---

5. Relationship

"Professional shall act hereunder exclusively as an independent contractor. It is expressly agreed that the master servant relationship does not exist herein. The Sponsor shall be liable to no one for any acts committed by the Professional."

_____	_____
Sponsor	Date
_____	_____
Professional	Date

Renewal/Addendum to a Contract

Here they are, two years later, at the option to renew the contract. As you will see, based upon the revisions requested, the athlete and sponsor were apparently embroiled in conflicts. What started out as a rosy, feel-good sponsorship turned out to be quite the opposite. At the contract renewal, the sponsor tried (unsuccessfully) to incorporate some major revisions to the contract prior to renewal due to unsatisfactory interactions with the athlete over the first contract term (see Table 8.3). Note the strike-throughs. These were all the changes the sponsor desired to be included in the renewal contract due to his perceived inadequacies on the part of the athlete. Fortunately for the athlete, due to how the original contract was written, a change in the rules at this renewal stage was not appropriate and the athlete rightly refused to consider/negotiate any alterations.

Table 8.3
Sponsorship Agreement Addendum

[ATHLETE'S NAME]

"This one (1) year extension addendum, made and entered into on [Date] 19xx, by and between [""Professional""] and [""Sponsor""] outlines past, present, and projected conditions set forth from the original two (2) year agreement, [Date] 19xx [Date] 19xx, now nearing completion:

Per Section 1, ""Sponsor" Investment" and Section 3, Item A, "Expenses, Advances, Extensions, and Divisions of Income":

The "Sponsor" met his part of the agreement by providing a sum total of [$] for the said term of twenty-four (24) months, paid in two equal installments of [$] via bank transfers on or about [Date], 19xx and [Date], 19xx."

Per Section 2, "Professional" Duties:

"The "Professional" competed in both singles and doubles events. The "Professional" competed in [#] tournaments from [Month] through [Month] 19xx. For the year 19xx, the "Professional" reported participating in [#] tournaments, [#] of which appear to be non-sanctioned club/state events, resulting in a net participation of [#] acceptable tournaments. The "Professional" competed in [#] tournaments from [Month]—[Month] 19xx. The 19xx participation statistics were gathered from the Stevegtennis.com website postings as the "Professional" has not yet provided competition information regarding locations or results for that year to the "Sponsor". Hence, as of [Date] 19xx, the "Professional" has entered/competed in a total of [#] sanctioned ATP-ITF tournament events since [Date] 19xx, [#] of which he withdrew from due to personal circumstances. ~~Based on these statistics, the "Professional" did not meet the tournament competition requirements of entering and/or qualifying for "at least" fifty (50) ATP-ITF tournaments set forth by the "Professional" under the original contract agreement."~~

Per Section 3, Expenses, Advances, Extensions, and Divisions of Income:

"*Item H:* The "Professional" met with or was in communication with the "Sponsor" at least once each year during the agreement period. The "Professional" provided an accounting of income and expenses for the 19xx calendar year only. Expense information regarding tax prize fees and entry fees was not provided or detailed. Financial information from [Month]—[Month] 19xx was not provided. Information was not provided regarding additional sponsorships obtained during the two-year term. As of yet, information regarding the 19xx calendar year has not been provided but is expected to be received on or before [Date], 19xx."

"*Items E and F:* Whereas the performance record of the "Professional" during the course of the original two (2) year agreement suggests he will be unable to begin repayment to

Table 8.3 – Continued

"Sponsor", the "Sponsor" is enacting the option set forth to extend this agreement for a period not to exceed one (1) additional year, through [Date] 19xx. This extension ~~[does not require any additional financial investments on the part of the "Sponsor"~~. *Note: first draft of renewal crossed out by athlete]* may involve either a lump-sum payment or periodic deposits into the Professional's bank account throughout the one-year agreement term for a sum total of [$] *[Note: added back in by athlete per original contract]* [~~pending written disclosure by the "Professional" regarding how these additional funds may be spent and calendar year needs. Allowable expenditures are detailed below under "Addendum Conditions"~~. *Note: second draft of renewal crossed out by athlete]*. The exact amount(s) and date(s) for deposit will then be determined between the ""Sponsor"" and ""Professional" *[Note: added back in by athlete per original agreement]*."

"This extension does not require the commencement of any financial repayment obligation by the "Professional" to the "Sponsor" during this time period. The nature or manner of the deposit will be worked out with the "Professional" based upon the ~~following:~~ previously agreed upon contract."

~~Addendum Conditions:~~ *[Note: Entire addendum section crossed out by the athlete.]*

~~"1. Allowable Expenditures: tennis coaching (legitimate travel coach/recognized pro tennis clinic or camp/home tennis coach); personal conditioning fees at a club or billing from a certified personal trainer, certified massage therapist; dietary counseling from a trained/certified individual (RD, LRD, physiologist/ trainer with nutritional certification); sports/medical expenses for training/rehab; itemized travel to/from/within tournament events (hotel, air/ground transport modes) for "Professional" only; meals/nutritional supplies during tournament events only; expendable (ongoing) equipment needs (racquets, stringing, balls, tennis shoes). All of these expenditures must be verifiable via billing/agreement statements and/or receipts indicating payment and included with your end-of-year report."~~

~~"2. Non-Allowable Expenditures: any item/product/service that can have dual use (business/personal — computer upkeep, internet services, cell phone, office/postal supplies, personal car, clothing, etc) unless a percent use can be accounted for (e.g. X% of internet service fee for conducting tennis business, etc.); entertainment/recreational pursuits of any manner; meals/drinks not directly related to tournament competition for self-consumption (this includes exclusion of 'business' type meals for "Sponsor's", advisors, other contractual arrangements, as well as family/friends dining/drinking excursions); meal/travel expenses for friends/family/tennis partner(s) to/at tournaments. Any other expense(s) not specified under "allowable" expenditures."~~

~~"3. Following conclusion of this one-year extension period, the "Professional" will provide a full and final accounting to the "Sponsor" regarding tournament participation, incomes, and expenses (including all fees) for the term of the original agreement plus the one (1) year extension (Date, 19xx – Date, 19xx) on or before [Date] 19xx. The final report will include a~~

Table 8.3 – Continued

~~financial disclosure sufficient to determine ability to repay the "Sponsor's" investment as set forth by the original agreement under Section # 3, "Expenses, Advances, Extensions, and Division of Income", Items C and E. The final report must incorporate not only standard federal tax information for the year 19xx, but also income and expenses for 19xx [Months] as well as the year 19xx [Months]. Furthermore, the 19xx financial report will be amended to rectify any errors, omissions, or oversights. In addition, sponsorship information will be provided so as to determine rate of repayment in the event that additional sponsorships were attained.~~ Upon review of the financial disclosure, a repayment schedule will be set forth should it be determined that the "Professional" is in a position to assume repayment in some manner based upon his earnings."

"Sponsor" accepts the risk that he may not receive his initial investment back despite this one (1) year extension period. "Sponsor" agrees there will be no more extensions following the completion of this one-year extension [Date], 19xx."

"The "Professional" agrees to continue to engage in the business of being a "Professional" tennis player by playing in at least [#] ATP-ITF sanctioned events during this one (1) year extension period. The "Professional" shall, to the best of his ability, keep physically fit, engage in "Professional" training, and conduct himself in a "Professional" manner."

"All ~~other~~ aspects of the original agreement ~~and current addendum~~ conditions remain in effect unless mutually agreed upon changes are enacted upon in writing by both "Sponsor" and "Professional"."

"Sponsor"   Date

"Professional"   Date

Chapter 9
Do You Need a Sports Agent ?

"I told [GM] Roland Hemond to go out and get me a big-name pitcher. He said 'Dave Wehrmeister's got 11 letters. Is that a big enough name for you'?"

—Eddie Eichorn, White Sox Baseball Owner

You should now realize how much money you will need to become a pro player, and you'll probably need some financial help, maybe even a lot of help. You should also now realize that it will take considerable effort on your part to snag a sponsorship when you are first starting out. Someone who can help get you the sponsorship you need is a sports agent.

When You Are Good Enough, They Will Come

Most tennis players just venturing out into the professional ranks don't have a sports agent. But, as you begin to prove yourself and show promise, the offers may start coming your way and you might need one. First, by way of equipment and clothing offerings, and later, financial offers. *Tennis* magazine writer Dan Weil reported that after one year of being on the circuit, Brian Vahaly's record enabled his management company, SFX, to negotiate sponsorships worth thousands of dollars from Adidas and Babolat. Companies and corporations sponsor athletes because they realize the benefit of being able to advertise their wares in a less cluttered advertising arena. David K. Stotlar reports in his book *Developing Successful Sport Sponsorship Plans* that the average consumer is bombarded with more than 5,000 ads daily. As consumers, we learn to "tune out" some ads and "tune in" to particular ones that match our personal interests.

To reach tennis fans, companies target the audience with commercials featuring John McEnroe driving around in a certain car; Andy Roddick, using a certain charge card; and Andre Agassi and Stephanie Graf dueling it out on court to promote the idea of using a banking service.

A good sports agent should be able to negotiate with your potential or current sponsors a mutually-agreeable deal so that the sponsor benefits but doesn't treat you like an indentured servant, and you in turn respect and honor your sponsorship's terms of engagement. For doing this, your agent gets a percentage of the income you receive from each deal.

After the deal is signed, sealed, and delivered, a good agent will also be able to help when the demands placed on you by your sponsor become annoying, excessive, or even inconvenient. At the same time, he's trying to get you more money from other sponsors and help out with some of the chores you really don't have time to do, but have to get done. According to Bruce Schoenfeld's interview with Paul Goldstein in *Tennis Match* magazine, Goldstein's agent, Karen Piner of SFX, aided Paul by completing tournament entry forms, renewing his passport, and making travel arrangements. Having an agent do these tasks frees up time for you to practice, and it also frees your account manager to make your money work for you rather than having to also be your travel agent.

Where Are the Agents?

Tennis Week provides an annual listing of pro player representatives. Your best bet is to review that list and contact at least one player represented from each management organization. Find out how well he is being treated. Ask if he is happy with his agency's services. If you can talk to more than one player per agency, even better—you might get different opinions. If you see a routine exodus from a certain management company or agent, ask why. There's obviously some type of problem. If a player switched agencies, again, ask why. If you don't have the time to do this, assign it to someone you trust to do the research.

You also need to remember that the agent with which you first sign may not be your one and only agent for life. Players change agents for a variety of reasons but usually because the agency/agent just isn't suitable anymore. Maybe the deals aren't coming in the way the player feels they should be, maybe the agent is signing bad deals, or maybe there's a personality or moral/ethics clash. This is why you must be particularly diligent about any contract you sign—including the one signing yourself over to an agent or agency. Get a good sports-savvy lawyer to review any contract before you sign it.

Agents Listing

Below is a listing that appeared in *Tennis Week* in August 2005 for many of the top sports management firms and the male pro tennis players they manage (as of 2005).

- **ACE Group International**
  21 Quayside Lodge
  William Morris Way, London
  SW6 2UZ, UK
  Phone: 44-20-7384-4870
  E-Mail: info@acegrp.com

Touring Pros: Thomas Enquist, Gaston Gaudio, Nicolas Lapentti, Andreas Vinciguerra

- **AMI Promanagement**
  370 Felter Ave.

Hewlett, NY 11557
Phone: 516-569-8922
Touring Pros: Tomas Cibulec, Martin Damm, Leos Fried, Andrea Gaudenzi, Markus Hipfl, Donald Johnson, Petr Pala, Cyril Suk, Daniel Vacek, Pavel Vizner

- **Andre Agassi Enterprises**
  3960 Howard Hughes Pkwy, Suite 750
  Las Vegas, NV 89109
  Phone: 702-227-5700
  Fax: 702-866-2929
  Touring Pro: Andre Agassi

- **B & A Sports Mgmt. Consulting**
  Buckingham Court
  10 Church Rd., Northolt
  Middlesex UB5 5BA,UK
  Phone: 44-20-8842-4611
  E-Mail:
  mba@bethencourt.fsnet.co.uk
  Touring Pros: Emanuel Couto, Franco Squillari

- **Edgley Smylie Management PTY LTD**
  2 Chapel Street, Richmond 3121 Victoria, Australia
  Phone: 61-3-9428-7711
  E-Mail: info@smylietyzzer.com
  Touring Pro: Scott Draper, Tony Roche

- **Elite Management L'Estoril**
  31 Avenue Princesse Grace
  98000 Monaco
  Phone: 37-7-93-25-86-34
  E-Mail: elite@monaco.mc
  Touring Pros: Goran Ivanisevic, Marat Safin

- **Excel Sports Management**
  12100 Olympic Blvd., Suite 400
  Los Angeles, CA 90064
  Phone: 310-407-0517
  www.excelsm.com
  Touring Pro: Marcelo Rios

- **Global Sports**
  Holzgartenstrasse 9, 85221
  Dachau, Munich, Germany
  Phone: 49-8131-54023
  Address2: Ludwigstrasse 12, 61348 Bad Homburg, Frankfurt, (Ger.)
  Phone: 49-6172-121243
  E-Mail:GlobalSportsMan@aol.com
  Touring Pros: Lars Burgsmüller, Juan Ignacio Chela, Diego Cubas, Daniel Elsner, Andy Fahlke, Luis Horna, Pavel Ivanov, Jens Knippschild, Irakli Labadze, Hyung Talk Lee, Harel Levy, Jene-Rene Lisnard, Vasilis Mazarakis, Boris Pashanski, Azel Pretzsch, Sebastian Prieto, Martin Rodriguez, Ricardo Schlachter, Rainer Schuettler, Dmitri Sitak, Diego Veronelli, Christian Vinck, Mikhail Youzhny

- **Humarks S.A.**
  Darwin 1489 Capital Federal
  1414 Buenos Aires, Argentina
  OFfice: 005411-4772-7070
  Touring Pros: Agustin Calleri, Guillermo Cañas, Mariano Zabaleta, Jose Acasuso

- **IMG**
  1360 East 9th Street, Suite 100
  Cleveland, OH 44114
  Phone: 216-522-1200

www.imgworld.com
(They have 62 other international offices.)
<u>Touring Pros</u>: Mario Ancic, Boris Becker, Thomas Berdych, James Blake, Nick Bollettieri, Bjorn Borg, Sergi Bruguera, Pat Cash, Arnaud Clement, Cuillermo Coria, Taylor Dent, Thomas Enqvist, Nicolas Escude, Brendan Evans, Wayne Ferreira, Guy Forget, Richard Gasquet, Magnus Gustafsson, Tommy Haas, Tim Henman, Joachim Johansson, Thomas Johansson, Alex Kuznetsov, Feliciano Lopez, Nicolas Mahut, Zavier Malisse, Paul-Henri Mathieu, Shuzo Matsuoka, Max Mirnyi, Carlos Moya, John & Pat McEnroe, Rafael Nadal, David Nalbandian, Jarkko Nieminen, Magnus Norman, Mark Philippoussis, Marcelos Rios, Greg Rusedski, Pete Sampras, Fabrice Santoro, Robin Soderling, Jimmy Wang, Mats Wilander, Donald Young, Mariano Zabaleta.

- **InsideOut Sports & Entertainment**
  494 Broadway, Suite 200
  New York City, NY 10012
  Phone: 646-367-2770
  www.insideoutlive.com
  <u>Touring Pro</u>: Jim Courier

- **ITMS Sports**
  Frankfurter Landstr. 15 61231
  Bad Nauheim Frankfurt Germany
  Phone: 49-6032-34590
  E-Mail: info@tmssports.com

<u>Touring Pros</u>: Jao Cunha-Silva, Henrik Holm, Libor Pimek, Claudio Pistolesi, Simon Walsh

- **Robert Kaplan**
  9 Lewis Drive
  Maplewood, NJ 07040
  Phone: 973-761-8567
  E-Mail: jboys1902@comcast.net
  <u>Touring Pro</u>: Sargis Sargsian

- **Lleyton Hewitt Marketing**
  209 Toorak Road, Suite 35
  South Yarra, Victoria, 3141
  Australia
  Phone: 61-3-9824-2888
  <u>Touring Pro</u>: Lleyton Hewitt

- **Octagon**
  1751 Pinnacle Drive
  McLean, VA 22102
  Phone: 703-905-4495
  Address2: Ghiradelli Square, 900 N. Point St., Suite D405
  San Francisco, CA 94109
  Phone: 415-292-2355
  www.octagon.com
  (There are 11 other intl. offices.)
  <u>Touring Pros</u>: Jonas Bjorkman, Kenneth Carlsen, Michael Chang, Lee Childs, Francisco Clavet, Brian Dabul, Frank Dancevic, Robby Ginepri, Sebastien Grosjean, Chris Guccione, Dominik Hrbaty, Jerome Inzerillo, Scoville Jenkins, Andrew Kennaugh, Nicolas Kiefer, Richard Krajicek, Alexander Krasnoroutsky, Gustavo Kuerten, Mikael Llodra, Cecil Mamit, Todd Martin, Emiliano Massa, Leo Mayer,

Miloslav Mecir, Juan Monaco, Jeff Morrison, Gael Monfils, Andrew Murray, Jamie Murray, Ilie Nastase, Timothy Neilly, Patrick Nicolls, Josselin Ouanna, Aisam-Ul-Haq Qureshi, Tommy Robredo, Sjeng Schalken, Phillip Simmonds, Alex Simoni, Raemon Sluiter, Pavel Tchekhov, Mark Verryth, Vladimi Voltchkov,

- **Paul Theofanous**
  108 W. 75th St., First Floor
  New York, NY 10023
  Phone: 212-874-3043
  E-Mail: ptheofanous@att.net
  Touring Pros: Andrei Medvedev, Jeff Tarango

- **Perenterprises Inc.**
  370 Felter Avenue
  Hewlett, NY 11557
  Phone: 516-569-8922
  Touring Pros: Tomas Cibulec, Martin Damm, Leos Friedl, Markus Hipfl, Petr Pala, Cyril Suk, Pavel Vizner, Donald Johnson, Thomas Muster, Jim Pugh, Michiel Schapers, Daniel Vacek

- **SFX Sports Group, Inc.**
  2665 South Bayshore Drive, Suite 506
  Coconut Grove, FL 33133
  Address2: 5335 Wisconsin Ave., Suite 850, Washington DC 20015
  Phone (FL): 305- 285-3273
  Phone (DC): 202-686-2000
  E-Mail: contact@sfx.com
  www.sfxsports.com
  (Other offices in London and

North Carolina)
Touring Pros: Andre Agassi, Igor Andreev, Brian Baker, Mattias Boeker, Alex Bogomolov Jr., Bob Bryan, Mike Bryan, Ramon Delgado, Amer Delic, Younes El Aynaoui, Agustin Etcharte, Mardy Fish, Paul Goldstein, Fernando Gonzalez, Vladimir Ignatik, Robert Kendrick, Kevin Kim, Evgeniy Kirilov, Nicolas Massu, Scott Oudsema, Bobby Reynolds, Andy Roddick, Eduardo Schwank, Stan Smith, Paradorn Srichaphan, Michael Stich, Brian Vahaly, John Van Lottum, Martin Verkerk, Branden Wagner, Todd Widom, Wayne Bryan

- **StarPro Sports Mgmt. Inc.**
  1159 Oxford Circle
  Akron, OH 44312
  Phone: 30-628-8610
  E-Mail: brad@starprosports.net
  Touring Pros: Alex Calatrava, Lionel Noviski

- **Sunset Consulting**
  P.O. Box 1289
  Beverly Hills, CA 90213-1289
  Phone: 310-271-1852
  E-mail: mrstgsjr@2way.net
  Client List: confidential

- **William Morris Agency**
  One William Morris Place,
  Beverly Hills, CA 90212
  Phone: 310-859-4036
  www.wma.com
  Touring Pros: No men currently listed

PART 4
The Reality of Going Pro

"Half of my time is in Florida, half of my time is in L.A. When I'm at tournaments, that's the other half of my time."

—Maria Sharapova, Russian tennis player's comment during her first Wimbeldon Tournament 2003

Chapter 10
Matchmaking

"Matchmaker, matchmaker make me a match...."

—Broadway Musical, Fiddler on the Roof

A s you begin your professional tennis life, you'll need to decide which tournaments you will enter, which tournaments you will skip, where you will live while on the road, how you're going to get from tournament to tournament, who will be your traveling partner(s), and who will be your practice partner(s).

Choosing Your Matches

"You got to be very careful if you don't know where you're going, because you might not get there."

—Yogi Berra, NY Yankees Baseball

N ear the end of the year, each major professional tennis organization posts the next year's schedule of tournaments dates, locations, draw size, last year's required cut-off ranking, and prize money on its website. Each of these factors should be taken into consideration when creating your travel plans. The locations are fairly consistent year to year because requests to host tournaments must be made well in advance, and some sites are locked in for multiple years. That's not to say the schedules don't change, they do, and some events get cancelled at the last minute due to extenuating circumstances (hazardous weather, financial difficulties, etc.). Unannounced or late cancellations play havoc with your schedule and your wallet, but they do happen on occasion.

Beginning in 2007, your beginning option will only be Future tournaments as the ITF is discontinuing the Satellite tournaments at the end of 2006. Some players liked this circuit just to gain experience before hitting the Futures. Satellites are generally considered to be one rung lower and less competitive than Futures, making it easier to get into the main draw. While you do get points and playing experience, you have to commit to the entire series (4-5 weeks), the payouts are relatively low, and you can run into dismal living and playing conditions. All of these factors probably led to the ITF's decision to discontinue the Satellite Circuit. Many players feel more comfortable starting out in their own country competing on the Futures Circuit. Futures tournaments are fairly logical in their travel locations in that you might find yourself able to stay in a certain locale for up to three weeks, thereby economizing your time and your budget.

Let's use the 2006 Futures schedule as an example to see how scheduling works. Remember, this is only one possible scheduling plan—it all depends on where you'd like to visit (because some of these cities might be new adventures for you), who might be your tennis opposition, how much rest you need, and your finances.

The first three U.S. Futures tournaments in January 2004 were in Florida: Tampa (F1), Kissimmee (F2), and Boca Raton (F3). Tampa is located in central Florida, on the Gulf coast (west side). Orlando is a three-hour drive inland, and Boca is about four hours' drive south of that. From there, you might fly from Miami to Texas for F4, F5, and F6 (in Brownsville, Harlingen, and McAllen, respectively). You could then rest a week (no tournament, just practice), skip F7 (which is in Little Rock, AK), and head to Mobile, Alabama, for F8. Or, you could fly to Little Rock, AK for the F7, practice for a week in Florida (that is, skip F8), and then play in the Vero Beach F9, the Orange Park F10, and the Tampa F11 on clay. This would take you up to May.

Your summer schedule could take you to northern California for three weeks (F12 in Rocklin, F13 in Woodland, and F14 in Chico). To streamline your travel and also rest a bit after that, you could choose to skip F15 in Buffalo, New York and F16 in Pittsburgh, Pennsylvania. This way, you could unwind a bit, only have to travel to the Midwest (which by car would take a couple days), and cross just two time zones rather than three. Here you could compete in F17 (Peoria, Illinois), F18 (Joplin, Missouri–depending upon when you finished up in Peoria), F19 (Godfrey, Illinois), and F20 (Decatur, Illinois). You could skip Kenosha, Wisconsin (F21), taking the remainder of August off in order to rest/train to come back strong for the Fall leg of your tour.

You could complete your year by flying to southern California in September for tournaments in Claremont (F22), Costa Mesa (F23), Irvine (F24), and Laguna Niguel (F25), then head south to northern Texas (Arlington F26) and finish up the year at Baton Rouge, Louisiana (F27). If you had some extra travel cash, you could skip Baton Rouge, take in the last two tournaments in Hawaii (F28 in Waikoloa and F29 in Honolulu), and still be home in time for Thanksgiving.

Granted, this schedule is fairly rigorous, but it's pretty standard fare. You would get some additional time off any week you don't make it to the semis and final. If you have to qualify to get into the main draw, you may still be able to make it. On the otherhand, if you are lucky enough to get into the Sunday finals, you may have to bow out of the very next tournament if you can't get there in time to sign in. All you do is call the tournament director on your cell phone to keep him updated. This schedule is naturally more demanding than a college schedule, but by the same token, you don't have to go to classes, and you get to schedule your own practice times.

Now let's suppose that after completing this circuit (or even just a few weeks into it), you decide you want to see the world. The ITF website (www.itftennis.com) has the schedule for every Futures event worldwide. You can also check Steve G's Men's Tennis Results and Rankings website (www.stevegtennis.com), under the "Calendar and Results" link. There he lists every sanctioned ATP, Challenger, Futures, and Satellite tournament for the year in every locale. Details about each tournament are just a click away.

When you plan your global travel schedule, in addition to trying to live within your means and avoid overlapping tournament dates, you'll have different court surfaces, time zones, and environments to cope with. It can become very tricky, and if you don't plan well, you can miss out on some potentially good opportunities or, even worse, screw up your biological clock (and performance) royally, while rapidly depleting your finances.

This is when it is helpful to know someone with some tour experience to assist you in developing your competition plan. He can steer you away from pitiful places and maybe even set you up with good travel partners.

Tournament Resource Directory

The following list may come in handy when planning your global touring schedule.

- **ATP Tour:**
  www.atptennis.com
  United States:
  200 ATP Tour Boulevard
  Ponte Vedra Beach, FL 32082
  Phone: 904-285-8000
  Fax: 904-285-5966
  Europe:
  Monte Carlo Sun, 94 Boulevard
  D'Italie, 98000 Monaco
  Phone: +377-97-97-04-04
  Fax: +377-97-97-04-00

- **Austrian Tennis Federation:**
  oetv@asn.or.at
  Haeckelstraße 33, A-1235
  Wien, Austria
  Phone: 43-1-865-45-06
  Fax: 43-1-865-45-06

- **Brazil Tennis Federation:**
  cbt@zaz.com.br
  Confederação Brasileira de Tênis,
  Av. Paulista, 326 Cj. 23 a 29, CEI
  01310-902 São Paulo/SP Brasil
  Phone: 55-11-282-1788
  Fax: 55-11-283-0768

- **French Tennis Federation:**
  fft@fft.fr
  2, avenue Gordon Bennett
  Stade Roland Garros
  75016 Paris
  Phone: 01-47-43-48-00
  Fax: 01-47-43-04-94

- **German Tennis Federation:**
  dtb@dtb-tennis.de
  Hallerstrabe 89, 20149
  Hamburg, Germany
  Phone: 040-41-178-0
  Fax: 040-41-178-222

- **ITF (International Tennis Federation):**
  www.itftennis.com
  Palliser Rd., Baron's Court,
  London, W14 9EN, England.
  Phone: 44-171-381-8060
  Fax: 44-171-386-3989

- **International Tennis Hall of Fame:**
  tennisfame@aol.com
  Newport Casino,
  194 Belleveue Ave.
  Newport, RI 02840
  Phone: 401-849-3990
  Fax: 401-849-8780

- **Italian Tennis Federation:**
  www.federtennis.it
  Viale Tiziano 70
  00196 Rome, Italy
  Phone: 39-6-323-3799
  Fax: 39-6-368-58166

- **Lawn Tennis Association:**
  webmaster@lta.org.uk
  The Queen's Club,
  West Kensington, London
  W149EG, England
  Phone: 44-171-385-2366
  Fax: 44-171-381-5965

- **New Zealand Tennis Inc:**
  info@tennis.org.nz
  P.O. Box 11541, Manners Street,

  Wellington, New Zealand
  Sports House, Level 4, Central
  Library Building, 65 Vicotira
  Street, Wellington, New Zealand

- **South African Tennis Association:**
  satennis@mweb.co.za
  P.O. Box 15978, Doormfontein,
  2028, South Africa
  Phone: 27-11-402-3608
  Fax: 27-11-402-0242

- **Swedish Tennis Association:**
  ake@vaxjotennis.com
  Hagalundsv 10, 611 57
  Nykoping, Sweden
  Phone: 08-16-40-38
  Fax: 08-16-64-88

- **Tennis Australia:**
  www.tennisaustralia.com
  Batman Avenue, Melbourne VIC
  3001, Australia
  Phone: 61-3-9286-1177
  Fax: 61-3-9650-2743

- **Tennis Canada:**
  commnctn@tenniscanada.com
  3111 Steels Avenue West,
  Downsview, Ontario
  M3J 3H2, Canada
  Phone: 416-665-9777
  Fax: 416-665-9017

- **Tennis Europe:**
  www.etatennis.com
  Switzerland, Olli Maenpaa
  Phone: 41-61-331-7675
  Fax: 41-61-331-7263

- **USPTA (United States Professional Tennis Association):**
uspta@uspta.org
One USPTA Center, 3535 Briarpark Drive
Houston, TX 77042
Phone: 713-978-7782
Fax: 713-978-7780

- **USPTR (United States Professional Tennis Registry):**
www.ptrtennis.org
P.O. Box 4739
Hilton Head, SC 29938
Phone: 200-421-6289
Fax: 803-686-2033

- **USTA (United States Tennis Association):**
www.usta.com
National Headquarters:

70 West Red Oak Lane
White Plains, NY 10604
Phone: 914-696-7000
Fax: 914-696-7269
(You can access regional sections via the national site)

- **U.S. Racquet Stringers Association:**
usrsa@racquettech.com
330 Main Street
Vista, CA 92084
Phone: 760-536-1177
Fax: 760-536-1171

- **WTA Tour:**
www.wtatour.com
1266 East Main Street, 4th Floor, Stamford, CN 06902-3546
Phone: 203-978-1740
Fax: 203-978-1702

Hotels

"Your comfort is our concern."

—Pride of Super8 Motel, Salina, Kansas

The easiest place to stay is the recommended "player hotel," as the tournament director will have negotiated player discounts and transportation to and from the tournament site. Player hotel information is contained on the tournament application sheet and is usually posted on the website where you download the entry form. Of course you can choose to stay at another location should you know the region or have friends or family in the area. On occasion, especially for Futures, the tournament director may also have located a few host families that offer free lodging. All you need do is ask the tournament director if any are available.

If you can't even afford the discounted rates at the player's hotel, you should be able to rustle up three roommates and split the hotel cost of the room. In small towns where hotel costs are likely to be less expensive, it's very possible your share will only be $20 a night if you have three other roommates. You might be tempted to sneak in a couple more bodies, but

Valenti aka Johnnyblazed.

more than four in an average-size hotel room will be extremely cramped, and if the management catches on, all of you will be tossed out of the hotel room. You could also use Google Local to look for cheap motels and eats in advance, while planning your tour schedule. When motel-hunting on the internet, do look at the number of stars the hotel has garnered and read reviewer comments from others who stayed there. They might tip you off that the cheap motel is no deal at all.

Bunking up with others in a vehicle (that is, sleeping in a van or car) might be fun on occasion, but don't let it impact your tennis performance. If your goal is just to see the countryside and play a little tennis, you can be as adventuresome as you want. To see how one player does it, check out John Valenti's website, www.johnnyblazed.com.

But if you are serious about a pro tennis career, wait until you have enough bucks to pay for a decent hotel room and edible food. Otherwise, your tennis will suffer and you may never see an ATP point.

Train, Plane, or Automobile: Can You Get There from Here?

"We'd have had more luck playing pick-up sticks with our butt-cheeks than we will getting a flight out of here before daybreak."
—John Candy, Actor, quote from film "Planes, Trains, & Automobiles"

Whenever possible, make time in your travel plans to allow for unanticipated, unavoidable delays. If you're like most other players, this is one of the aspects of circuit life you'll find the most difficult to deal with. When you have a tight travel schedule, getting hung up at an airport due to weather or some other delay can result in a missed tournament, and sleeping on the floor in an airline terminal is simply no fun. If you do get delayed, tournament directors will try to accommodate extenuating circumstances, such as scheduling your first round match as late as possible in the first round schedule, but they can only do so much. After that, you will either be replaced or defaulted.

Airlines

If you know the airline you want to travel with, then it's as easy as calling or visiting its website. You can also use online discount travel services, searching for the best deals (see the section on travel agencies below). If you don't have a clue which airlines to use, here are a couple of links to assist you:

- Airline coverage map: www.kls2.com/airlines
- Airline toll-free numbers and websites:
  www.geocities.com/ Thavery2000/

Because you will quickly accumulate a large number of air miles, sign up for frequent flyer programs. Make sure though that the rules are such that you can exchange your mileage for cheaper/free flights and not just free magazines as in the "deal" I saw from one airline. Frequent flyer programs are designed to entice you to use one airline over another, but because different airlines fly to different locations, you may need to be a member of several different airline frequent flyer programs. They are free, so it's no big deal to sign up.

On the other hand, some charge cards give you bonus air miles upon signing up for their services. Don't be fooled by that 10,000 free flyer miles come-on. Deals like this usually have a catch, such as high annual fees, high APRs (annual percentage interest rates), and monthly finance charges. The fine print can kill you. Pass on these offers unless you can get the charge card company to eliminate the annual fee, reduce the monthly finance fee, and reduce the annual interest rate on your outstanding balance. Otherwise, you might find yourself basically only paying off the fees and interest while making very little headway on paying off your outstanding balance.

Round trip tickets are almost always cheaper than one-way fares on major U.S. airlines. Sometimes, if the penalty for changing your flight plan is greater than the savings you could have by simply buying two round trip fares, you are better off buying round trips to a couple of destinations and then simply throwing away the return flights. For instance, say you are in Pittsburgh and you want to go to LA and then on to Atlanta. Rather than buying single excursions, it could be cheaper to buy each of these as round trip flights—Pittsburgh to LA (and back); LA to Atlanta (and back). You use the Pittsburgh to LA, and the LA to Atlanta, and ditch the return flights. Under no circumstances do you tell the airline reservation person that you plan not to use the return flight at the time of purchase; call them a day in advance and tell them that you had an unanticipated delay and will not be returning on that flight as planned.

Most likely they will try to sell you another return flight, which you can either decline or purchase, depending on whether you can get a good deal on an "open ended" ticket. Make sure the "deal" doesn't cost you any more than what you saved originally by purchasing that round trip ticket in the first place. Who knows, you may actually be in a position to use that return flight in the future. Also, because of airline security, you can't give or sell your return flight to anybody else. Otherwise, when you buy those cheap advance, non-refundable, non-exchangeable tickets (sometimes with high penalties), you will be forced to enjoy the tournament location for the duration of the event. Obviously, this buy-and-ditch option should only be done when you can get really great rates and, you shouldn't use this too frequently with the same airlines. There are still a few airlines, most notably Asian-based, where changing your flight plans without a fee are possible. So do check out the policies of all the airlines with which you plan to travel. You might find a few welcomed surprises.

Bus

Bus travel is slower than air travel, and actually more expensive than car travel (you can split the car costs with other players). But if for some reason you can't rent a car (e.g., lack of a license or credit card), or you fancy the Hollywood romanticized depiction of bus travel, here's some basic bus information:

- Greyhound, USA: www.greyhound.com
- Greyhound, Canada: www.greyhound.ca
- Bus transportation worldwide: http://routesinternational.com/ buslines.htm

Car Rentals

You get more freedom and options when you travel by car, but you need to figure in your travel time, especially when entered in back-to-back tournaments that are some distance away. Once you find a good company, stick with it. Don't get suckered into buying the supplemental car insurance. If you are a licensed driver in the U.S. with car insurance, your personal car policy should still cover you if wind up in an accident (check with insurer to make sure).

Another tip when renting a car is to choose the option to return the car with an empty gas tank. This saves you time, and you don't have to drive around trying to find a gas station at the last minute.

Here are a few car rental websites to check out:

- www.alamo.com
- www.autoeurope.com
- www.foxrentacar.com
- www.thrifty.com
- www.rent-a-wreck.com

Don't rent a car in a foreign country unless you have the necessary qualifications (you speak and read the language, know the country's driving laws, and have proper insurance). Remember, in Britain they drive on the "wrong" side of the road, and in Europe, the speed is listed in kilometers per hour (km/h), not miles per hour (mph), so 80 km/h equals 50 mph. If you want to feel "oriented," just divide the km/h by 1.6 to get mph. Before getting into a car driven by one of your newfound tennis buddies, make certain he is a responsible, sober driver. If you're not sure, don't hop in. Some players drive everywhere in Europe, as the countries distances are shorter than in the U.S. Fuel is expensive, and you need to be particularly careful on autobahns where speeds can exceed 80 miles per hour (128 km/h). Stay out of the fast lane unless you're passing someone else.

Taxi Service

When this is your only option, don't let the driver rip you off, which tends to happen most in foreign locales or large U.S. cities. Official taxis have a customer service complaint phone number posted on the driver's seat back in good view of the passenger. When you get into the taxi, make sure to jot down not only that phone number, but also the driver's name, his taxi number, and his taxi license. All that should be posted on the driver's seat back, facing you if you are sitting in the back seat. Then, if you feel you've been "taken for a ride," call that number and lodge a complaint. Don't attempt to argue with the taxi driver—he'll just pretend he doesn't understand you. For this reason, don't take one of those personal unregulated jitney services unless you really know the city and you can outwit the driver.

If you need airport-hotel transportation, and the tournament doesn't have something set up, see if there are airport hotel shuttles. They usually are free or have a reasonable set fee, with a discount if you buy a round-trip ticket.

Trains (Rail Services)

The train may be your most reliable travel mode outside of the USA. Trains are generally safer than you driving yourself to foreign destinations and in many first-world countries the rail system is quite punctual and dependable. They are also kind of fun, especially for Americans because our AmTrak Rail system isn't a very common travel mode anymore. Below are a couple of websites to get you rolling:

Most Comprehensive Website:
- http://transweb.sjsu.edu/europe.htm Mineta Transportation Institute with transportation information for Africa, Asia, Australasia, Europe, North America, and South America.

In the U.S.:
- www.amtrack.com

In Europe:

- www.thetrainline.com (for the UK)
- www.virgintrains.com (for the UK, N.Wales, Scotland)
- www.raileurope.com (for multiple country passes, Europass, Eurorail, etc.)
- www.fs-on-line.com (Eurorail Information Travel Center)

Travel Agencies

Forget about agencies that charge you fees to make travel arrangements for you. In fact, you no longer need to go to a travel agent as long as you have access to a computer. You can book your own arrangements via any number of web-based travel agencies. The drawback is that many of these agencies book you into inflexible arrangements. If you need to change flights, hotels, leave early, stay late, you could be stuck. Make sure you read and understand their booking policies.

Remember, you may lose in the first round of qualifying, so you want to have the flexibility to get to the next tournament. Do use these websites for exploring your options, but my advice is, once you know where you need to go when, book everything yourself. Call the airline, hotel, and car rental place directly and arrange the best deal you can. If you have a travel club card (such as AAA), use it to save a couple bucks. But if you must actually book through one of the computer-based travel-cheap companies, here are a few websites to get you started:

- www.bestfares.com
- www.cheaptrips.com
- www.hotwire.com
- www.priceline.com
- www.sidestep.com
- www.travelocity.com
- www.cheaptickets.com
- www.eurotrip.com
- www.orbitz.com
- www.shopzilla.com
- www.smarterliving.com
- www.travelsecrets.com

Travel Advisories

By now, all travelers should be accustomed to increased security when traveling. Pay attention to alerts posted by your travel agencies, listed on your e-tickets, and posted at transportation terminals. Carry-on luggage is limited to a small personal bag plus one slightly larger piece that supposedly must fit into those rectangular metal boxes stationed in the ticketing line (roughly 24 inches x 9 inches). A standard tennis bag with 4-6 racquets is about 9 inches wide (OK) x 30 inches long (not so good). If you must, try to explain patiently to the airline attendant why you absolutely cannot check your racquets into the cargo hold in the belly of the plane. According to the top pros, they've never had a problem with taking their racquet bags on board as carry-on luggage, not ever, not even during the height of the 9/11 security crackdowns. But if by chance you are given a real hassle, you could try binding up your racquets together and carrying them on without their case. Just make sure nobody dumps a carry-on suitcase on top of your unprotected racquets in the overhead bin.

Currency Conversions

If you travel outside of the United States, you most likely will need to become familiar with a variety of money systems, and the dollar exchange rate changes daily. However, the widespread adoption of the Euro through much of Europe makes it easier—you don't have to deal with a different currency as you cross borders. The best purchasing advice for foreign markets is to use your credit card. You will be assured of getting the best, most accurate rate because your bank does not want to pay one cent more than it has to. Another advantage to using plastic is you can keep better track of your expenditures come tax time because the itemized billings are sent to your home address. Also, if you lose your card, you can quickly cancel it and suffer minimal (if any) monetary loss. Of course this means two things. First, somewhere you have to keep a record of the credit card number and bank phone number in case you do have to report a lost (or stolen) card. Second, you will need to have a back-up charge card or debit card. Debit cards are great as most places now have cash machines. Just as in the U.S., you have to be streetwise regarding where (and when) you chose to withdraw your cash to avoid becoming a crime victim.

If you are going to be paying cash for items, the easiest way to know what you owe is to have some type of portable electronic pocket converter—then you just have to know the daily exchange rate. Don't trust merchants to know the correct daily rate or to give it to you even if they do know it. If you have computer access, you can determine the cost in U.S. dollars or whatever currency you are using at the moment at the following website:

• The Universal Currency Converter: www.xe.com/ucc/

One final word of advice: Count your change. Make sure that the merchant is giving you back what is due to you. It's very easy to short-change foreigners—and it happens wherever there is tourism and unscrupulous merchants. Do take the time to familiarize yourself with the country's money, especially its coins, as they can be very confusing.

Weather and Other Stuff
That Will Mess with Your Mind and Your Game

There's not much you can do about the weather, but you can be mentally and physically prepared. You may even need to pack gloves and hooded sweats to enable you to play in snow flurries. Before you depart to your venue, check out the website, Weather Underground: www.wunderground.com. You will be able to get an idea of whether you need to pack extra suntan lotion or your long underwear.

In addition to the weather, you need to understand what type of air conditions you will be encountering—that is, will you be at sea level or at altitude? Will it be calm or will you be battling against gale-force winds? The thinner air at altitude will play havoc not only with your breathing but also with the delivery of your tennis ball. While thinner air (less dense due to less oxygen) will help you run a little bit faster, your ball dynamics will also change due to lack of air resistance. And of course, the wind can ruin your perfect shot.

Then there are those "little things" that wear on your nerves, like balls provided by the local sponsor that seem as if they are 10 years old (maybe they are) or court surfaces that can range from slick to sticky topped off with cracks and lumps. And don't forget about the most important tool of your trade, your racquet. There's nothing worse than debarking from your plane only to find that your newly strung racquet has lost half its stringing tension. You might be the one with the tension when you find out that you can't get your racquet restrung.

If you can get to the venue a few days early, you will be able to practice and get the feel for the local conditions. All of these potential mishaps make your tennis touring a bit of an adventure, so you need to learn to go with the flow or your touring life will be short indeed.

Looking for a Few Good Men—
Choosing Doubles Partners, Training Partners,
and Coaches

"The man who goes alone can start today; but he who travels with another must wait till that other is ready."

—Henry David Thoreau, Writer

Time and again, the problem most often cited by players early on in their pro career was loneliness on the road. As many discovered, you can be lonely even when surrounded by a lot of people. Perhaps another word for it is homesickness. Most guys team up with someone they knew from college. This way each of you has a built-in traveling practice partner, and perhaps a doubles partner, too. If you get along on and off the court, you even have a trusted drinking buddy when you each win (or crash and burn).

If you are focusing on a singles career, as most do when they first start out, then it's not necessary to worry about whom you choose for the required doubles matches. Anyone will do, but preferably it's a guy who complements your doubles game style so that you can actually win some matches. Some simply wait until arriving at a tournament to scramble for a doubles partner. Others pre-arrange partners for certain tournaments based upon playing style and the other guy's travel plans. The up side to this approach is you get experience playing with many different partners and becoming more versatile; the down side is you don't really get a good "team" strategy going and therefore may not achieve a decent doubles ranking. While this may not concern you at first, doubles may in fact become more important the longer you are on the circuit, especially if your singles performance eventually falls short of your expectations.

To help you objectively assess how well you are playing with certain partners, at various time points, or at the end of the year, tally up your wins/losses with your various partners. Determine which ones suited you better, and which ones you did poorly with. Objectively analyze the situations. When you lost, was it because you were simply outplayed? Maybe your two styles just didn't match up well—maybe you both play "the same way" and therefore didn't bring any different weapons to your game. Or, did you lose because you had zero communication or cooperation?

On the subject of picking a doubles partner, Wimbledon Doubles Champ Don Johnson said, "First, look for someone to complement your game." For instance, Don's a lefty and covers the ad court well, so he looks for a good right-hander for the deuce court. Second, he said, "It's not really necessary to like the guy or even be friends with him as long as you can play well on court together." He even gave an example of a "team" who actually hated each other, never spoke to one another off the court, and yet played terrifically well together. Third, he said it wasn't really necessary to practice together to be good, although he does advise getting together at matches to practice for a bit before the tournament.

Once you have determined your winning percentage with each partner and figured out primary pluses and minuses of your playing ability with each of them, you should be better prepared to recruit successful future doubles partners. Although not "necessary" and apparently rarely done, ideally, you should try to get some practice time in with some of your partners away from the stress of the tournament. As Don said, this isn't always possible, and may not even be practical, but it could be something to shoot for when a particularly important tournament arises. The Bryan brothers have had the rare opportunity to practice together as a team for years. Besides their "twin connection," they know from experience how each is going to handle the ball in any given situation, and they can practice winning strategies so that they become second nature.

The Coach Dilemma

Even if you can afford to pay a coach to travel with you, unlike in college, he cannot coach you during your matches. If he visually or verbally reacts to a shot in such a way that it might be construed as guiding you covertly, he could be accused of coaching you from the stands, and you can be penalized. By the way, the refs understand more than just English, even in the USA.

What a coach can do is work with you during practice and help with your pre-match routine, plus provide you with valuable objective feedback after your match, either verbally discussing certain critical aspects he picked up or, better yet, via videos he makes of your matches. According to Danielle Tin-Ung at the USTA national home office in New York, video-taping a match is perfectly okay to do as long as you are unobtrusive and it doesn't bother the players involved. A travel coach can provide a sense of security or "comfort" to you in locales where you don't know a soul. If he can't travel with you, remember your cell phone and his cell phone number. Assuming you have built up a good rapport with your coach over the years, he should be available to lend an ear when you need a sounding board on the road.

You should keep your college coach as your pro coach only if you have been happy with your transition from college to the pros and he continues to be helpful to your game. If, however, you start to notice that his advice isn't working for you anymore, despite your continued efforts, then it may be time to consider a change. He may be a great college (or junior) coach, but perhaps not such a good pro coach. But don't rush into changing this aspect of your career. Initially there will be many factors that may be negatively impacting your performance, so don't use your coach as an easy scapegoat.

Chapter 11
Travel Toughness
"I've had a wonderful time, but this wasn't it."

—Groucho Marx, Comedian

Y ou already know that travel comes with the territory when playing professional tennis. In fact, it's one of the perks. It is as Jim Courier stated in "The Journeymen" in regards to traveling for professional tennis: "It's like having a backstage pass to the world. You get to experience life in new cities not as a tourist, but as an entertainer of sorts, with real people from the town guiding you to the best places where the locals go, away from the tourist traps." But you also know that it is year-round, almost non-stop. When you are first starting out, the travel experiences are both exhilarating and exhausting. Sometimes it's fun, sometimes it's frustrating, but on rare occasions, sometimes it's frightening.

Futures Travel: The School of Hard Knocks

J ose Hanza, only on the circuit for a short time, stated: "A bad experience was the unpreparedness for extreme weather changes on tour. In Mexico, the temperature dropped from a high of 80 to 8 below."
Tripp Phillips recounted the initial terror he felt when competing in a South African satellite where the host family carried a gun at all times for protection when transporting the players to and from the tournament sites. While there, he wrote to a friend, "We live in constant fear. It really is amazing, you can't walk anywhere by yourself, you can't take a lot of taxi's, and everywhere you go there are gates and guards. The family we are staying with, the father carries a gun in his car at all times—crazy." He closed his correspondence with, "As long you are careful though it isn't too bad, and we are having fun and playing well."

Andres Pedroso said, "I'm glad that I have had the opportunity to travel abroad because it gives me a better understanding of the world and an appreciation for what I have here in the U.S. India was absolutely horrid. All the travel is not exotic—for Futures, the matches are in the worst cities imaginable. The goal is to move through them quickly and get to the Challengers where you are in better places."

One player, whose chat board name was "ex-satie," left his account of travel life on the Satellite tours overseas on Steveg's tennis message board:

> "I recently picked up a book written by an ex-journalist/photographer called, *World's Most Dangerous Places* which highlights the most danger-

ous countries in the world. I realized that I had played tennis in almost 50 percent of the countries on the list. Feel lucky to have made it through without ever being robbed or victim of any crime. Did outrun a robber with a knife in Caracas once and also saw a guy get shot there in the street right in front of me. Did see a dozen or so players that were robbed or scammed though. At one future I was at in Lithuania, half the tournament was robbed of their passports as criminals were breaking into hotel rooms in the tournament hotel where the courts were. A few things I used to do to avoid incident: Whenever possible I would try to travel with as many other players as possible. Probably actually isn't safer but definitely feels safer. Had locks on all my luggage, including my racquet bag. Try to bring clothes common to the area/country. Also dress like you have nothing (ragged sweatshirts, no logos, etc.) and try to fit in as much as possible and maintain a low profile. Leave all jewelry at home. Keep credit card and ATM card separate (i.e. one in your room and one on your person). That way if you lose one you still have the other hopefully. Either one is equally useful to you. Never bring travelers checks they are just a pain to cash in. If you're English speaking, never listen to any local that you run into that speaks English and is friendly to you. They are trying to scam you and rip you off. I have seen a few players who have fallen for this. VERY IMPORTANT—Read U.S. [State] Department advisories on places you are going. This will update you on current political situation as well as "some" dangers there. It will often let you know of current scams/crimes. If you're American, NEVER tell anyone you are American. I used to lie and say I was Canadian. People tend to be indifferent to them around the world."

But not all Futures travel is bad. While there are admittedly some rinky-dink U.S. Futures locations with limited social life, they are usually safe and sound places with good drinking water and clean beds. Other foreign places, such as Jamaica, have been wooing Futures players with luxury beachfront resort locales and lots of planned social activities. Clearly, when you are still a tennis nobody, you really need to do a little bit of sleuthing about a location on your own, before deciding to travel there. This knowledge will serve you well. Many issues are simple: Preparing for the weather, getting your shots, and having your passport and other papers in order. You also need to determine if the tournament is held at sea level or at altitude, the stability of the political situation, the availability of personal items, the safety of the water supply, and phone and internet access. Some locations will have a professional racquet stringer on site, but you should bring your own string. The labor cost for stringing can be high ($25 per frame), and the quality of the stringing is not consistent. Talk to other players to find out more about the guy stringing at each tournament.

Forearmed is forewarned. After you have the details worked out, matches played, you can try to take in the new surroundings for a bit. Just don't go crazy or get yourself in a jam. Be a "smart" tourist and avoid the need to visit the American Consulate. And last, but not least, remember, you will still have to shuffle off to the next tennis venue in top form.

Jet Lag

To help you with your travel preparedness, here are a few more "must do" things in order to make traveling a little easier on yourself. The first is to combat the unavoidable jet let as you globe trot from one tournament to another. Jet lag symptoms include sleeping problems, moodiness, stomach upset, change in bowel function, tiredness and slower reaction times, loss of concentration, and an overall reduction in your sports performance.

Racquet stringer.

The extent to which you experience these symptoms depends upon how many time zone changes you have for one trip and whether you are traveling east or west. Eastward travel causes more disruptions to your biological rhythms because it shortens your day. For example, you might feel worse traveling to Poland, from the U.S., when you "lose" time, than when you are returning to the U.S. from Poland when you gain hours, thereby allowing your body more time to adapt. There are a few things you can do to minimize jet lag such as departing well rested, avoiding dehydration during flight by drinking plenty of non-alcoholic and de-caffeinated beverages, resetting your watch upon arrival to the new time zone, and immediately adopting the local time for your sleeping, eating, and training schedule. If all these things aren't sufficient, you can talk to your doctor about the proper use of a mild sedative (as the pros do). You can also try to get non-stop night flights (or one with few changeovers) so that you can actually get uninterrupted sleep on the plane and arrive in the morning to your destination. But on long flights, be sure to also get up periodically and walk or stretch to promote better blood circulation. Sitting immobile for extensive periods of time on flights has been shown to contribute to blood clots, even in young healthy people. As for seat location, the aisle seats give you the most legroom, as do the emergency exit seats. The middle seat is the most cramped, and seats too close to the bathroom will be disruptive if you are intending to try to sleep as there will be passengers using the facilities all night long.

Less Is More

Travel light. Remember, you have to carry all that stuff that you pack into your bags. Over-packing will make you feel like a pack mule. You will be hopping from planes, to trains, to buses, hoofing it on foot, and walking up staircases. You'll get fatigued pretty quickly if you bring half of your worldly possessions with you. Use your racquet bag for your overnight carry-on must-haves. Pack enough necessities to get you through a couple of days. Bring whatever you can't risk not being able to find in your new locale—from meds to your favorite pre-match snack. Once you're familiar with your new surroundings, you might be able to go out and search for some edible snacks and forgotten items. But if you are planning to compete in really desolate locations, you will have to pack extra supplies. Take powdered versions of your sports drink and buy bottled water as needed once there. Choose small, nonperishable, prepackaged healthy snacks. Pack one week's worth of clothing, and plan on doing laundry during your travels rather than packing a month's worth of clothes. The goal here is not to need a crane to lift your bag. Backpacks are easy to carry and expand easily to accommodate food or souvenirs. Make certain you can lock each of your bags. Use one of those small to medium-sized wheeled suitcases that will be easy to maneuver around city streets as well as tight bus aisles.

Body-checking

Keep your personal identification (passport, hotel keycard, etc.) close to your body and in a place where you won't be able to have it picked off you unknowingly. Airports are the number one place where people feel the safest, yet they are one the biggest venues for this type of thievery. Crooks who specialize in picking pockets, bag snatching, and the like are real artists. They often tag-team you with a distraction to execute their craft. Always be alert. If someone "accidentally" bumps into you, you better check your personal belongings immediately and see where your clumsy but personable interloper slipped off to—he may be having a beer at your expense. There are anklebands, waistbands, and necklace-type pouches you can buy at any travel store that will serve you well when out and about. Just don't have them dangling in full view for someone to snatch and grab. Wear them inside your clothing. It's inconvenient to get at the ID or money when you need it, but at least you'll have it.

Don't Drink the Water

Diarrhea can get you anywhere the water supply is bad. Anyplace where the water table is below sea level, you need to be careful as toxins can lurk in the water basins. Anyplace where the plumbing and sanitation are in question, you should be wary. When in doubt, drink bottled beverages from verifiable safe places (don't drink locally bottled water—make sure it is imported) and remember that any food item that is washed in polluted water sources will also be bad news. Don't even brush your teeth in it!

When you can't find safe drinking water anywhere, all is not lost. If you thought ahead, you could use the "SteriPEN." It's a very portable battery-operated water purifier (7-inches long, 7-ounces in weight) that can treat 16 to 32 ounces of water. You can find it at electronic gadget shops like The Sharper Image or order online from www.HerringtonCatalog.com (phone orders: 800-622-5221). This nifty little device is supposed to destroy 99.99% of all dangerous water-born junk for $195.95 (plus shipping and handling). It requires four AA batteries. Alternatively, if you have kitchen facilities, you can try boiling the local water, or you can simply use disinfecting tablets like the ones used by natural disaster victims. You can buy a box of 50 tablets for $3.95 on line at www.quakekare.com. One tablet will disinfect one liter of water.

Medical Stuff

If you restrict your travel to just U.S. events, you probably won't have much trouble finding what you need either at the tournament (via trainers) or at the local supermarket. But, according to sports medicine Drs. Pluim and Safran, if you venture onto the ITF or Satellite circuits, there is a chance that you won't have adequate medical care available on site, nor be able to find what you need at the local market, especially in remote areas.

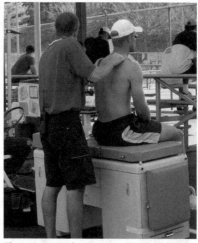

They suggest a travel kit including the following: thermometer, scissors, sterile blister puncture needles, contact lens supplies (including an extra pair, plus your eyeglasses), Steri-Strips for deep cuts, Betadine antiseptic solution, bandages, large gauze pads for

Therapist provides massage to an aching futures player.

larger wounds, sports tape, elastic compressive bandage (e.g., ACE bandage for sprains), oral pain meds, antidiarrheal and stomach upsets meds (Kaopectate, Pepto Bismol), antihistamines (Benadryl is good for all sorts of allergic reactions from bee stings to hay fever), short-acting sleep aids (for jet lag), motion-sickness pills, throat lozenges (sore throat), sunscreen, safety pins, tampons (for women, but also good for packing a nose bleed), spare shoelaces, plastic bags for ice, sterile latex gloves, medical passport if you use meds, vaccination card, and list of banned substances. Whenever possible, try to get the chewable pill form for meds as this will reduce the need for safe water to take the medication and also reduces cartage and spillage problems in your travel bags. Some meds are packaged specifically for travel, so choose those whenever you can.

Thomas Blake.

In the Players' Own Words: The Best and Worst Aspects of Circuit Life

Thomas Blake (USA): "Best is playing doubles in the U.S. Open with my brother; the worst are injuries. You have to stay positive."

Jack Brasington (USA): "The best is traveling and seeing places and experiencing the thrill of winning; the worst are the slum places you have to visit, losing, getting through the long travel days, waiting, and down time."

Marko Cerenko (USA): "The best part of circuit life is experiencing the outdoors most of the year and seeing new places. The worst part is traveling nonstop, being away from loved ones, and losing money."

Scott Draper (AUS): "The best was being on the Davis Cup Team; the worst was dealing with my late wife's health struggles while trying to play. My advice? Passion, discipline, no excuses."

Joan Jimenez-Guerra (AND): "The best aspect of circuit life is learning about life, getting to choose from many different options

Marko Cerenko (Duke '01 grad).

184

and maturing. But there are ups and downs. If you don't make a good living you always have doubts. Mentally it is a little difficult because you have to play many tournaments and that requires traveling a lot which I do not like."

Jose Hanza (USA): "Staying uninjured is the hardest but the worst experience was being taken by surprise with some of the dirty dealings or tricks. I didn't realize how cutthroat Futures was. One experience was with scoring. Occasionally out there you forget a score, but usually you come to some sort of agreement. After one tournament which I lost, I forgot to report the score to the officials. However, my opponent did report the score—the wrong one! He actually took more points away from an already losing score. I lost, but I didn't lose as badly as he reported. That ticked me off, but you learn."

Joan Jimenez-Guerra.

Bobby Hession (USA): "The constant grind of conditioning, travel, finances, and tournament scheduling was the worst."

Don Johnson (USA): "The best aspect was winning Wimbledon twice, playing Davis Cup, and representing my country. Most memorable is creating the dream and living it in the tennis world. The worst, or most difficult aspect is having to face the prospect of quitting, giving it all up, to work in the 'real world,' or business 9-5 world."

Cedric Kauffman (FRA): "Friendships and competition are the best circuit experiences, but the money and locations are bad."

Alex Kim (USA): " The best was beating a top 5 player; the worst was going to the hospital after cramping in a college match. My advice is to go to college for at least one year."

Ben Kronk: "The hardest experience is not being the best."

Peter Luczak (AUS): "The best experience was being on the Davis Cup Squad when we went to Argentina."

Nicolas Mahut (FRA): "The circuits are

Nicolas Mahut charging.

Mark Merklein and Eric Matuszewski receive doubles victory prize money at the Bellmont Challenger in Rocky Mount NC from tournament director, Albie Brice, 2002.

Bellmont Challenger, Huntley Montgomery, Rocky Mount, NC.

Frank Moser (Ger) after semifinal win over Jose Hanza, Elkin Futures.

steps toward bigger tournaments; the worst experiences are the locations."

Eric Matuszewski (USA): "The best part is meeting players from so many different places. I never played college tennis—the University of Baltimore didn't have athletics. The worst part is not being able to play fulltime, can't afford it."

Mark Merklein (BAH): "My best experience was reaching the quarterfinals in the 2000 Sidney Olympics. The worst was getting defaulted in the Aussie Open this year (2002). As for advice: Tennis is not an easy lifestyle. You need to have a selective memory and a great attitude to reach your goals."

Huntley Montgomery (USA): "My best experience is when I do well, obviously, doubles results mostly thus far; worst are the losing streaks, mentally draining. Advice? Travel with people you can work hard with on the court and enjoy yourself off the court."

Frank Moser (GER): "The best thing about the circuit experience is traveling and meeting new people, not working in an office, experiencing different cultures."

Ogidi Obi (USA): "Getting along with people is the best experience; the worst is lack of finances, loneliness, emotional stress, and staying in the moment."

Tom Oliver (AUS): "The expense is the worst. My best experience is practice."

Jonathan Pastel (USA): "Best aspect is doing something I love each day. Tennis is my true passion. But funding is the worst, plus traveling gets long and tiresome. I keep justifying to myself that playing tennis is the right thing for me to be doing."

Ogidi Obi survived the qualies and is battling in the first round of the Elkin, NC, 2002 Futures event.

Jon Pastel trying his hand in the qualifiers at Newport, RI, Miller Lite Hall of Fame Tournament, 2002.

Andres Pedroso, the 2002 Elkin Singles Winner.

Tripp Phillips.

Andres Pedroso (USA): "The competition is the best part, it's really fun. Guys fight so hard at the Futures level that makes you play your best—but the environment is not the best—public courts, bad hotels, bad food."

Matthew Rutherford (USA): The fact that I am giving it a shot and enjoying meeting new people all the time makes the circuit experience. I am seeing places I would never go otherwise. The experience is helping me mature emotionally and physically. The worst is the expense. It's a much higher level of play than college."

Tripp Phillips (USA): "I love tennis. I love to compete. But it's the little things that you have to learn to adjust to—the travel is tough but that didn't surprise me. The physical demands are a lot more than they were in college. It definitely took me a while to adapt to that. One thing that was a little tough from a mental standpoint is that in college I would lose only 3 or 4 times a year and losing to me was terrible, so I'd look at that loss like I failed. When you play professional tennis, you're going to lose almost every week. At first, if you're associating losing with playing tennis, you're going to be down on yourself pretty fast. It takes a while. You have to learn that

Rogier Wassen

Brian Vahaly serves at Bellmont Challenger in Rocky Mount, NC.

John Valenti and Paulo Francisco at Elkin, NC Futures.

Jack Waite and Jaime Fillol just win a round in doubles at the Belmont Challenger in Rocky Mount, Jack's last ATP tournament.

Louis Vosloo at Rocky Mount, NC.

losing is going to happen. You never have to be happy with it though. I still hate to lose."

Doug Root (USA): "The best, yet the worst, is the travel."

Eric Taino (USA): "The best is traveling to different places. My worst experience was playing in Salina, Equador. My advice is to practice hard and stay positive."

Marcio Torres (BRA): "The best experience is meeting great people and seeing great places."

Rogier Wassen (NED): "Winning a challenger event in Mexico in 1999 was the best; playing in Uzbekistan was the worst—terrible conditions!"

Brian Vahaly (USA): "So far my best experience was winning the challenger in New Zealand. My worst? Losing 6-0, 6-0 in the U.S. Open."

John Valenti (USA): "The best and the worst is traveling and meeting new people."

Louis Vosloo (RSA): "Seeing and traveling the world is the best. I can't think of any worst experience."

Jack Waite (USA): "My best experience was in Bastad, Sweden—tennis gets in the way of the social life that week though. My worst experience was in Cotia, Brazil—a destitute place, dangerous, eating mystery meat every night."

Do Blonds Have More Fun?

"God gave men both a penis and a brain, but unfortunately, not enough blood supply to run both at the same time"

—Robin Williams, Comedian

There's a lot of speculation about what really goes on off the tennis court. The myths versus the reality of life on the pro tour are quite intriguing to many fans.

When I tried to pry direct answers out of players during interviews, mostly what I got were sheepish grins, stuttering, or blank stares. But two players did finally come through. The blond South African, Louis Vosloo, confirmed he had a rip-roaring time during his teen years while living with his sponsor in Texas. He recalled being "home alone" on their huge Texas ranch and throwing pretty wild parties while the good-will sponsors were away traveling for weeks on end. He said he "grew up pretty fast" living in that kind of environment.

But for David Cheatwood, a former UNC college player, the tale was a bit different. He competed during the summers on the Missouri satellite leg. David said, "There weren't any girls there and there wasn't a lot of fun stuff to do. I think we went out a few nights—I mean, we would go see a movie. But it depends on the place too...Missouri wasn't the most exciting place." Still not 99 percent sure if this was truly an accurate picture of the Futures social life, I asked several photographers why they never had any "interesting" party pictures of these guys on the circuit. They said quite simply that the "important" guys hit the sack early during the tournaments—they are actually pretty boring, and pictures of the struggling partiers (the losing players) aren't of much interest to anyone.

As a Futures player, you will garner a small fan club of bored (not desperate) housewives and eager, impressionable junior players wanting to take a lesson or two from you and maybe even asking you for your autograph. Just remember two things: 1) Housewives have husbands and, 2) teenaged girls have fathers. In other words, stick to tennis and keep your nose clean.

As one moves up the tennis ladder and gets some success and recognition at the Challenger level and beyond, things change. Somehow even the toad prince of the Futures world turns into a Prince Charming on the ATP pro circuit. Girl groupies go gaga. And for some reason, you don't even have to be very good—just watch "The Journeymen" video. Of course, it is more helpful if you are winning prize money; after all, it takes some bucks to have fun. But remember, while these tennis groupies can bolster your ego, they can also spell disaster to your career (and your personal life) if you take to the partying lifestyle at inappropriate times. In fact, when I was interviewing players, I had the opportunity to have a chat with Rogier Wassen's (NED) mother. Now Rogier is a dashing fellow and his mother knew it. At the age of 24, Rogier's mother decided she had to accompany him on tour because, as she put it, "Rogier became 'too distracted' on his own and his performance fell." Hence, they made the decision she should manage his career and travel with him. At the time of my interview his singles ranking was 138, so I guess his mother's strategy was working.

When Good Players Go Bad

"If everything seems under control, you're just not going fast enough"
—Mario Andretti, Race Car Driver
"If you are going through hell, keep going"
—Sir Winston Churchill, Statesman

A recently released video, *The Journeymen*, depicts what can happen when you are living the fast life, perhaps too fast. If you are serious about being a top competitor, this video is most convincing in showing what not to do. The producers of the film, Mark Keil and Geoff Grant, are not to be emulated. Although they were promising young players, as they matured (and I use that term loosely) they became perhaps the worst possible role models you could follow, but for different reasons. If you view this video, treat it as entertainment. The one redeeming feature of this video is the interview with Jim Courier, which was cut from the main part of the film. It is listed under "deleted" scenes. It's not a flamboyant interview, just serious informal talk about circuit life. This is the part of the video where you should pay the most attention.

Mark and Geoff had early successes, but were derailed along the way, primarily due to their dislike for practice. The film, as promised, provides a candid look behind the scenes with a lot of the filming done in various locker rooms. There are some amusing as well as informative moments with famous pros including Agassi, Becker, and Rafter. It's difficult to feel sorry for either Mark or Geoff. In fact, at the outset, the two of them are whining about the life of a tennis player—for instance, bemoaning having to travel 26 hours to get to the Australian Open, only to lose in one hour in the first round. Apparently I was not the only one disgusted with this whining as in the locker room, upon hearing Mark complain about his travel plight, Goran Ivanisevic asks him incredulously, "What's the matter, didn't you realize it—this is tennis, this is what it's like." Upon which Keil retorted, "Yeah, but after 12 years…" At least he got into the first round. At the Australian Open that pays a tidy sum in and of itself. Later in the film, Mark has to beg to get a wild card into the Ericsson Open in Miami. But to his credit, his persistence paid off as he did manage to get one. The demise of Keil's tennis career is really a no-brainer though—his losses were to a large extent self-inflicted. Granted, aging players have to deal with younger, stronger, more eager upstarts, but Agassi rightly cautions about falling victim to partying and not being disciplined enough.

At one point, Keil had a doubles ranking of 109, but at the time of the film his ranking had dropped to around 250. Even so, he raked in 60 grand that year. But pay heed to a whispered comment by Marc Rosset about his doubles match against Keil and a young 21-year old partner whom Keil rustled up for the match: "C'mon—he's 15 pounds overweight…I'm not going to lose to him!" And he didn't. Keil's "kid partner" was devastated by the loss. Keil, on the other hand, either didn't get it or simply didn't care. He summed up the match loss as, "It's all in a day's work." Which is, of course, is true, you can't expect to win them all. But one has to seriously question Keil's standard mantra: "If I win, I'm gonna have a beer; If I lose, I'm gonna have a beer. Either way, I'm gonna have a beer." To prove this point, he displays his acquired beer belly proudly, like a show-n-tell scene, pointing to various regions of his belly and attributing it to a certain type of beer at a certain tournament. Mark point-blank states: "I love playing, but I don't like to practice that much." To demonstrate this lack of work ethic or discipline, he not only talks, but visually displays what a "great time" he's having when he visits various cities, getting out and enjoying the nightlife, the women, the alcohol—never mind that he is married during the time of the filming. He even got himself kicked out of the player's hotel with a police escort for being, as he put it, "a loud, drunken asshole." His justification was that he had just learned of some personal bad news regarding an old coach of his. Hence he was, in his mind, allowed to be a rude, loud, obnoxious drunk. It comes as no surprise that at the end of the film, the update on Mark states his wife divorced him and he enrolled in Alcoholics Anonymous.

Geoff Grant, on the other hand, is almost the opposite of Mark. He fretted before, during, and after his matches—to a fault. Geoff's self-talk did not reflect a positive "I can do it" attitude. He focused on the negative. To his credit, he tried to prepare his body with vitamins and hydrated with water. His words of wisdom were quite different from Mark's: "Treat your body like a Ferrari if you want it to perform like a Ferrari." Unfortunately, when he lost, he went back to his hotel room and sulked about not preparing his body enough—as if drinking insufficient water was the root of all his tennis problems. He didn't reflect much on his actual play or lack of practice and coaching. As with most promising pros, Geoff started playing tennis at age four when his dad realized that he had some talent. But it seems his dad was a taskmaster and was perhaps the driving factor behind Geoff's tennis. When dad was no longer available to fire Geoff up, Geoff's discipline and hard work went down the tubes. During an interview regarding how to be successful at tennis, Geoff's dad stated, "Perspiration is 80 percent of the formula. You have to be willing to play hard." Geoff felt that his dad thought he never put forth enough effort. Maybe he was right, maybe not, but the sheer thought of it left a permanent scar in Geoff's mind. Unfortunately, the pressure Geoff felt from his father led him to ordering that his father not be visible to him in the stands when he had matches. This extreme is not conducive to a healthy pro tennis career or, for that matter, family relations. Near the end of the film Geoff acknowledges that he was simply burned out and realized he just didn't want to practice any more. He then worried about what he would do if he didn't play tennis. Geoff's postscript states that upon retiring, he became a stockbroker but eventually realized he needed to be in the tennis world. He became a coach and commentator for The Tennis Channel.

Chapter 12
Knowing When to "Hang it Up"

"Be nice to people on the way up because you might meet them on your way down"

—Jimmy Durante, Comedian/Actor

Knowing when your competitive tennis days are over is as difficult, if not more so, than deciding to take the plunge and turn pro, or to focus only on doubles. When you make the decision to turn pro, you have your whole life ahead of you. Anything is possible. As you grow older and wiser, you understand your strengths and weaknesses better. You know the hardships of the road, as well as the rewards. At some point, playing tennis is no longer an adventure—It's simply a job. It might seem as though your body is turning against you. The aches and pains become tiresome to bear; the long periods on the road seem more like drudgery than fun. You are not winning enough matches to make the sacrifices worth it. You miss your girlfriend, your wife, your kids; or maybe you haven't even been home enough to make a family. The younger players are at the peak of their physical prowess, and you need to work out twice as hard just to keep up with them, let alone beat them. However, you take some comfort in the fact that you do have experience on your side.

There is no magic age when you should quit playing the circuit, but only a handful of players have been able to weather the physical storm into their 30s—Andre Agassi, Pete Sampras, Todd Martin, Don Johnson, and recent re-entry, "old man" John McEnroe. Most top pro players tend to retire when they realize their game is slipping, but they are not down and out. Pete Sampras was clearly annoyed when commentators and fans started debating when he would retire. In a 2002 *Tennis* magazine interview, Sampras was quoted to have said, "I'm sure a lot of people have written me off, but even if you've hit 30 or 31, it's a bunch of crap that you're done in tennis. It's a challenge to prove people wrong." He went on to win the 2002 US Open. One year later, Pete announced his official retirement when he was 32 years old. In 2003, Todd Martin asked *Tennis* magazine's readers a rhetorical question: "What's the rush?" He stated he tried semi-retiring in 2002 but couldn't stay away from the game. He felt something "still buzzing inside me." At the age of 34, Todd competed in four ATP doubles tournaments and 14 singles tournaments, only to bow out permanently after a first round loss at the 2004 U.S. Open.

The wisest thing to do is get out while you still have an impressive record (at least in your mind) and not getting your pants beat off you day in and day out. But now with the impending new doubles format, singles players may last longer, or choose to come out of retirement, like John McEnroe. At age 47, he teamed up with Jonas Bjorkman and won the doubles final at the SAP Open tournament in San Jose California in 2006. According to the ATP *Insider Newswire* (2/16/06), McEnroe claimed to be "way behind" other notable older athletes but that it's motivating him to work harder. There's even buzz about the possible return of Germans Boris Becker and Henri Leco.

If you have a college degree, you can use that to your advantage and get a meaningful job after you retire from tennis. If you are not ready to hang up your tennis racquet, there's always coaching and commentating. You have circuit tour experience, which makes you attractive to organized tennis programs as well as tennis newswires. You can also go back to school, if you've had an enlightening moment and discovered what you really want to do. In the "real" world, outside of the athletic arena, you are still young. So go for it, whatever your "it" may be.

The Decision

The decision to give up on tennis as a career comes at different times for different players. Only you will know when the time is right for you.

Consider the decision of David Cheatwood, a college UNC senior who was fancying trying out the tour in 2001, at least for the summer. After considerable thought, he decided to hang it up after college. He wasn't a college superstar, but he was a good, consistent player. He was ranked in the top 10 for juniors in the South and was recruited heavily by college teams. David played in the number one slot his senior year and was certainly as good as many on the Futures tour. But David had a serious girlfriend and he was planning to attend law school. In the end, he opted for law school,

The Thinker & me.

got married, passed the bar, and now resides in Charlotte employed as a lawyer with a good firm.

Albie Brice was a former circuit player and director of the Rocky Mount Challenger in North Carolina. Albie wasn't a tennis prodigy by any stretch of the imagination. He didn't start playing tennis until he was 15, but he did manage to attain a Southern tennis ranking of around 40 and was awarded a partial tennis scholarship to UNC at Wilmington. Due to financial constraints, he entered the USTA pro circuit rather late, at age 24. He endured for three years, earning a career ranking high of 1,200 in singles and 1,350 in doubles. When I asked him if he won many tournaments, he stated, "No, basically I was a second round, third round type of guy. A couple of wins in the qualies and situations like that. I had some wins in the juniors but not at the pro level." He realized he was not going to make it after a couple of years on the tour: "I realized that I definitely was already too old. One of the things that I had was, I was one of those late bloomers, so I had a lot mentally in the tank later on in life where some of these guys who started playing tennis when they were 10 were pretty much done, were toast, at 21. So what happened was at 27, I had a lot mentally in the tank but the body wasn't there. I just had a lot of things that were not as adequate for the tour."

In the *Tennis* magazine (2001) article, "Down But Not Out," Allen St. John reported on the reflections of Tyler Cleveland, a former member of the University of Iowa tennis team. At the time of the interview, Tyler was ranked 1,328. He reported spending $5,000 a month while attempting California's satellite circuit. He won one match and "got close" to winning another. His brief stint on the tour (he lasted one semester) made him realize that tennis, as a job, was real hard work. He knew he'd have to practice daily four or five hours. He lamented about not being able to take a day off like regular working stiffs. So he wasn't sold on the pro tour as a viable career option. After a career-high ranking of 1,297 and career earnings of $396, he became a day trader.

For a different perspective, everyone in the know said multiple All-America award-winner, college player, and former UNC standout, David Caldwell, had great pro potential. Yet after reaching a singles high ranking of 170 in the world within just three years on the pro circuit (1996-1999), he quit. Note that I used the word "quit" for David, not "retired." Accumulated debt and perhaps lack of commitment were David's deciding factors. While he may have been ranked in the top 200, and positioned to earn money, he wasn't earning enough to support both his lifestyle and his tennis travels—so he traveled and played less. After he turned pro in 1996, David played in only eight ATP singles and five doubles tournaments, but he earned $22,965 and showed much promise. The following year he put forth a bit less effort and not surprisingly, earned less, only $17,884. In 1998, it seemed like he finally got his act together and played in 28 singles tournaments plus a few doubles, racking up $33,483 in prize money. This was also the year he peaked at 170 in the ATP ratings. Unfortunately, in 1999 David competed in only 16 ATP-sanctioned events, earning him $19,184 from singles prize money. Considering himself to be a singles specialist, David only played a few doubles tournaments, meeting with marginal success. By the year 2000, he was basically out of it, playing in only two tournaments and winning $2,970. David is now a successful real estate developer.

Roland Thornqvist was another extremely talented UNC college player whose accumulation of accolades put him on a college tennis who's who list. Roland turned pro immediately after graduation. But much to the surprise, and dismay, of his coach Sam Paul, he quit the circuit life with only one year under his belt. Point-wise, Roland was doing very well. His highest ATP singles ranking high of 303 was attained just six months after graduating college; his doubles high of 422 was achieved shortly after being on tour for a full year. According to Coach Paul, Roland was just on the cusp of breaking into the big time. However, his prize earnings totaled only $2,960. It's no wonder that family life won out. He was newly married and the accruing debt was becoming problematic. Roland then applied his disciplined nature to becoming a highly successful women's college tennis coach. He began as an assistant men's tennis coach at his alma mater (UNC), then became a winning women's head coach at the University of Kansas. Two years later, he was back at UNC, this time as head coach of the women's team. Under his guidance, the UNC women turned into a top-10 team. In three more years he landed a lucrative head women's tennis coaching position at the University of Florida, leading that women's tennis team to an NCAA championship victory in 2003. But the transition to coaching wasn't an easy one for Roland. While a coach at UNC, Roland occasionally wondered if he had made the right choice. He will never know if he quit too soon, but he has learned to accept and enjoy the success he now has. Roland not only "made it" in the coaching world, but he also "made it" as a father and husband.

Last but not least, in the 1980s Al Parker was another tennis prodigy coming up the ranks alongside Jim Courier and Andre Agassi. Despite "expert advice," Parker decided to take a side trip to college while his peers stayed on the pro track. He excelled at the University of Georgia, majored in finance, and became a popular frat boy. Quitting college to turn pro wasn't even a thought. He felt college would give him a chance to hone his skills and give him options if the pro tour didn't work out. In the summer of 1991, Parker did give the pro tour a shot upon graduating college. He rejoined his buddies at Challengers and ATP events, but found himself losing against them and everyone else. He never climbed above 250. In his interview with *Tennis* magazine, Parker stated he didn't know if he really wanted it bad enough, plus he had a hard time adjusting to the pro tour life. On the circuit, there weren't friendly crowds cheering him on as there had been in college. There was no team camaraderie. And, it was a job; it wasn't fun anymore. That's when he knew it was time to quit. By then, he was

25 years old and still clueless about what to do with the rest of his life. Fortunately, he was a 4.0 college student and got into Harvard Business School. He also got engaged, married, and had children. The article quotes him as saying, "I enjoy my career, I enjoy my family, I enjoy the fact that I'm not still out there trying to grind through injury problems on the tour."

Many good college players try their hand in the pro arena, but only a few manage to work their way out of the tennis dungeon permanently. You can follow the course of any number of players and see a high dropout rate within the first two years; the better players hang in for three or four years before they move on. The best players, besides winning, know how to plan strategically for the long haul—physically, emotionally, and financially. That's what you must do to be among them.

Chapter 13
Looks Like You Made It

"First they ignore you, then they laugh at you, then they fight you, then you win."

—Mahatama Gandhi, Indian Pacifist

Knowing When You've "Made It"

"If a man does his best, what else is there?"

—George S. Patton, US Army General

Getting your first ATP point is a really big deal. Once you get over this hump, you know you have a shot at making a living playing tennis. This is the "maybe I can make it" phase. For those of you who graduated with an ITA ranking among the top 20 collegiate players, the points will come easily after that first one—going from a singles ranking of 1,200 to 600 will seem to fly by. For a few, doubles will be even easier. At some point, though, you'll realize you are in the same boat as the other tennis prodigies. This is when you really have to start clawing your way to the top, with each 100 ranking positions being harder to achieve than the previous 100. You also have to contend with the annual point drop-off factor: It's like running ahead five steps and falling back three. It hurts more the closer you get to the top 300. And just when you think you are about to crack into the top 200, wham! Your best matches fall off and you find yourself with a ranking down at 500 again. Anyone who is able to make it into the top 500 should feel quite proud of his accomplishments. In a moral sense, you made it.

Still, at this point, you are probably not making enough money to earn a living. So in the financial sense, you haven't really made it yet. Earning a living playing pro tennis tournaments happens after you get to the top 300 or so in singles or the top 100 in doubles. Once you reach these heights, you might be trying to decide whether to stick it out in the singles lane or concentrate on the faster, but less lucrative doubles lane (ascent in rankings is faster in doubles, but it, too, slows down once you get into the top 100). It's a very tough, and potentially precarious decision, especially in this anti-pro-doubles age. For most, the decision is a clear one, stick with singles.

It used to be that anyone who truly was more talented as a doubles player could make this transition quite successfully. Not anymore. If the new entry system for doubles remains, gone are the Bryan Brothers Specialist Days. Even though the Doubles Lawsuit against the ATP for anti-trust violations was "resolved," making a living at doubles-only will continue to be very difficult for aspiring doubles specialists. Yes, many of the scoring changes and high singles ranking requirements for doubles players proposed by the ATP were withdrawn; but in its place was a ruling allowing top singles players to enter doubles tournaments based on their singles ranking, rather than their doubles ranking (which is typically poor in comparison to a top doubles specialist). The end result is more top-ranked singles players (i.e., "well-known") filling slots that would have been available to top-ranked doubles players. So in effect, many doubles specialists are being squeezed out of their professional jobs—doubles tennis.

If this entry policy continues, the true doubles specialist will probably be extinct by the year 2010. Doubles will become a different type of match—it will be a battle of paired singles players hoping to communicate with each other effectively enough to win a few more prize bucks. If proposed promotional strategies go into effect, doubles will seem more like an exhibition match, with a lot of extraneous noise to liven it up for the fans and TV sponsors. Most of the current doubles specialists would need to go back to Futures and Challengers to regain a top 100 singles ranking in order to prevent being bumped by a top 100 singles player. Since that is unlikely to happen, the end result will probably be an onslaught of "early" retirements from the doubles professional ATP circuit. With or without the doubles lawsuit, the ATP corporate sponsors get what they wanted—the thinning out of the doubles-specialists so that more money is available to promote singles competition. The moral of this unfolding tennis history lesson is, don't abandon your singles ranking even if you want to be a doubles specialist.

Once you hit the top 100 in either singles (and maybe doubles), the money starts to roll in because you are now getting into the finals of Challengers and qualifying for pro events, even the majors. You don't have to win a major to make money—you make money just being in the qualifying. You also don't have to spend money on expensive hotels, as once in the main draw the tournament host picks up the tab. At this point you can probably safely say that "you made it," even though you are by no means a millionaire tennis celebrity, and your 100 ranking is certainly not secure. You have equally eager players nipping at your heels just waiting to pounce so that they can move up into your ranking position.

If you have set your sights on grabbing the golden ring in tennis, a lot of work still lies ahead of you. Dogged determination plus greater discipline and sacrifices are required. A high quality coach is now a must, not a luxury. If you are a cut above the rest, you will find yourself in the top 50, maybe top 30, and in time, perhaps even the top 10. For a select few, these are reasonable expectations. For the rest of the tennis gladiators, the probability is low. But, in tennis, nothing is really impossible given the right set of circumstances.

Looks Like He Made It

On the following pages are tables showing three years during Don Johnson's career, courtesy of the ATP website. The first table shows when he turned pro after completing college (1992), the second table is four years into his pro career (1996), and the last includes the year in which he won the Gentlemen's Doubles title at Wimbledon (2001). This will give you an idea of what it might be like for you: travel schedule, types of matches, types of courts, points accumulation, and prize money. Where there are gaps in the tournament dates, Don was playing Futures (early on), participating in non-sanctioned ATP events, or taking a break. These charts do not include mixed double events, in

Don Johnson.

which he was also successful; nor do they include his singles career (he attained a career ranking high of 185). Reviewing these tables, you will come to realize that you don't have to win every match to "make it" financially, even at the height of your career. In Don's case, he only won seven of his 23 tournament events in 2001, posting a 30 percent tournament finals win record. Yet, he made as much money as a physician and was ranked #1 in the world. He also had endorsements and sponsorships. Think he "made it"? Or more importantly, does HE think he "made it"? Let's allow Don to answer that: "I am retired now. I'll still play a little bit, but not on the tour—just exhibition matches. I'm enjoying my time at home. After traveling for almost 15 years, it's nice to spend some time in one place. Garland [his baby daughter] is now my first priority." His final advice to all of you reading this book? "Work hard. You will never be able to work hard yesterday."

Did They "Make It"?

If you are still wondering about what might be in store for you, how long you might last on tour, how much money you might make, take a look at Table 13.4, "What's in THEIR Wallets." Listed there are 30 real-life examples of players' cumulative incomes over the course of their pro tennis career, how long they lasted on tour, and whether or not they went to college. Go to the ATP website (ATPtour.com) and check out their player profiles. You don't have to enter the tour with your eyes wide shut. All you need is LOVE—love to work hard, love to compete, love to meet new people and see new places, and of course, you absolutely must love tennis. If you do what you love, according to the saying, the money will follow.

"Nothing on earth can stop a man with the right mental attitude from achieving his goal; nothing on earth can help the man with the wrong mental attitude."

—Thomas Jefferson, Third President of the United States

Table 13.1
Don Johnson, 1992 ATP Player Activity Profile (Doubles)

Tournament Type: CH = Challengers
Results:
Q = Qualifiers; R = Round; QF = Quarterfinals; S = Semi-finals; F = Finals; W = Winner

Event	Type	Surface	Date	Result	Points	Pay-Out (US$)
Santiago, Chile	CH	Clay	03/09	S	20	270
Gramoydo, Brazil	CH	Hard	07/16	R16	1	90
Campos, Brazil	CH	Hard	07/13	F	39	450
Belo Horizonte, Brazil	CH	Clay	07/20	R16	1	90
Lins, Brazil	CH	Clay	07/27	R16	1	185
Ribeiro, Brazil	CH	Clay	08/03	Q	15	160
Fortaleza, Brazil	CH	Clay	08/10	Q	13	160
Sao Paulo-2, Brazil	CH	Clay	08/17	R16	1	185
Ponte Vedra, FL, USA	CH	Hard	10/12	R16	1	365
Manila, Philippines	CH	Hard	11/02	S	27	270
Brunei, Brunei	**CH**	**Hard**	**11/09**	**W**	**52**	**775**
Kaula Lumpur, Malaysia	CH	Hard	11/16	F	39	450
Launceston, Australia	CH	Hard	11/23	S	20	270
Perth, Australia	CH	Hard	11/30	Q	10	160
Guangzhou, Chile	CH	Hard	12/07	S	25	270
Hong Kong, China	**CH**	**Hard**	**12/14**	**W**	**52**	**775**

Total Tournaments: 16   Total Wins: 2   Win Record: 13%   Total Earnings: $4,925

Table 13.2
Don Johnson, 1996 ATP Player Activity Profile (Doubles)

Tournament Type: CH = Challenger, GP = Grand Prix; TM = Tennis Masters;
IS = International Series; GS = Grand Slam
Results: Q = Qualifiers; R = Round; QF = Quarterfinals; S = Semi-finals; F = Finals;
W = Winner

Event	Type	Surface	Date	Result	Points	Pay-Out (US$)
Auckalnd, NZ	GP	Hard	01/08	R16	1	550
Australian Open	GS	Hard	01/15	R64	1	1,825
Shang Hai, China	GP	Carpet	01/29	R16	1	550
Punta Del Este, Uruguay	CH	Clay	02/19	Q	13	160
Salina, Ecuador	CH	Hard	02/26	R16	1	90
Mexico City, Mexico	**GP**	**Clay**	**03/04**	**W**	**172**	**10,750**
Key Biscayne, FL, USA	TM	Hard	03/18	R32	23	2,750
Barcelona, Spain	GP	Clay	04/15	R32	1	1,000
Prague, Czech Republic	**CH**	**Clay**	**04/22**	**W**	**63**	**755**
Prague, Czech Republic	GP	Clay	04/29	Q	35	2,450
Pinehurst, NC, USA	GP	Clay	05/06	Q	36	1,850
Coral Springs, FL, USA	GP	Clay	05/13	R16	1	550
Roland Garros	GS	Clay	05/27	Q	235	17,261
Zagreb, Croatia	**CH**	**Clay**	**06/10**	**W**	**72**	**1,550**
Eisenach, Germany	**CH**	**Clay**	**06/17**	**W**	**60**	**755**
Wimbeldon	GS	Grass	06/24	R64	1	2,809
Tampere, Finland	**CH**	**Clay**	**07/15**	**W**	**72**	**1,550**
Kitzbuhel, Austria	GP	Clay	07/22	R16	1	1,325
Amsterdam, Netherlands	**GP**	**Clay**	**07/29**	**W**	**190**	**17,500**
Cincinnati, OH, USA	TM	Hard	08/05	R32	1	1,000
Indianapolis, IN, USA	GP	Hard	08/12	S	145	8,500
Montreal, Canada	TM	Hard	08/19	Q	94	9,050
US Open	GS	Hard	08/26	R64	1	3,000
Palermo, Italy	GP	Clay	09/23	Q	35	2,155
Marbella, Spain	GP	Clay	09/30	R16	1	550
Barcelona, Spain	CH	Clay	10/07	Q	23	800
Toulouse, France	GP	Hard	10/14	S	72	4,660
Brest, France	**CH**	**Hard**	**10/21**	**W**	**104**	**3,100**
Reunion Island	CH	Hard	11/11	F	52	910
Mauritis Island, France	CH	Grass	11/18	S	26	270

Total Tournaments: 30   Total Wins: 7   Win Record: 23%   Total Earnings: $100,025

Table 13.3
Don Johnson, 2001 ATP Player Activity Profile (Doubles)

Tournament Type: CH = Challenger, GP = Grand Prix; TM = Tennis Masters;
IS = International Series; GS = Grand Slam; DC = Davis Cup
Results: Q = Qualifiers; R = Round; QF = Quarterfinals; S = Semi-finals; F = Finals;
W = Winner RR = Round Robin

Event	Type	Surface	Date	Result	Points	Pay-Out (US$)
Australian Open	GS	Hard	01/15	R64	1	2,069
Buenos Aires, Brazil	IS	Clay	02/19	QF	10	4,175
Acapulco, Mexico	**IS**	**Clay**	**02/26**	**W**	**50**	**28,850**
Scotsdale, Arizona	**IS**	**Hard**	**03/05**	**W**	**35**	**13,275**
Indian Wells, CA, USA	TM	Hard	03/12	R32	1	1,500
Miami Ericsson Open	TM	Hard	03/19	QF	25	10,600
Estoril, Portugal	IS	Clay	04/09	F	28	12,950
Monte Carlo	TM	Clay	04/16	QF	25	11,100
Barcelona, Spain	**IS**	**Clay**	**04/23**	**W**	**60**	**29, 650**
Mallorca, Spain	**IS**	**Clay**	**04/30**	**W**	**35**	**17,200**
Rome, Italy	TM	Clay	05/07	QF	25	11,100
Roland Garros	GS	Clay	05/28	R64	1	2,637
London Queens Club	IS	Grass	06/11	S	20	7,450
Nottingham, Gr. Britain	**IS**	**Grass**	**06/18**	**W**	**35**	**13,275**
Wimbeldon	**GS**	**Grass**	**06/26**	**W**	**200**	**144,772**
Montreal, Canada	TM	Hard	07/30	F	70	40,320
Cincinnati, OH, USA	TM	Hard	08/06	R16	15	5,000
US Open	GS	Hard	08/27	F	140	87,850
Moscow, Russia	IS	Carpet	10/01	S	22	12,850
IND v USA WGPO	DC	Hard	10/12	RR	no points	no pay
Stuttgart, Germany	TM	Hard	10/15	R16	1	5,650
Stockholm, Sweden	**IS**	**Hard**	**10/22**	**W**	**45**	**28,950**
Paris, France	TM	Carpet	10/29	QF	25	11,500

Total Tournaments: 23   Total Wins: 7   Win Record: 30%   Total Earnings: $229,530

Table 13.4
What's in THEIR Wallets? "Cumulative" ATP Earnings

Player (Country)	Born	Turned Pro	College	6/2002	Total Bucks 4/2006	
Thomas Blake (USA)	1976	1999	yes-Harvard	$64.2 K	$139.4 K	(retired)
Jack Brasington (USA)	1976	2000	some-UT	$92.7 K	$173.7 K	(retired)
Marko Cerenko (USA)	1979	2001	yes-Duke	$0.9 K	$0.9 K	(retired)
Ben Kronk (AUS)	1983	2002	no	$.3 K	$2.2 K	(retired)
Mardy Fish (USA)	1981	2000	no	$245.9 K	$1.5 M	
Joan Jimenez-Guerra (AND)	1978	1995	no	$40.0 K	$41.0 K	(retired)
Ivo Karlovic (CRO)	1979	2000	no	$134.3 K	$ 1.1 M	
Cedric Kauffman (FRA)	1976	1998	yes	$111.8 K	$118.8 K	(retired)
Robert Kendrick (USA)	1979	2000	some-Pepperdine	$66.6 K	$363 K	
Alex Kim (USA)	1978	2000	yes-Stanford	$102.2 K	$281.0 K	(retired)
Peter Luczak (AUS)	1979	2000	some-Fresno State	$80.3 K	$453 K	
Nicolas Mahut (FRA)	1982	2000	no	$111.0 K	$773 K	
Mark Merklein (BAH)	1972	1994	some-UF	$310.7 K	$502.9 K	(retired)
Huntley Montgomery (USA)	1978	2001	yes-UVA	$10.6 K	$71.9 K	(retired)
Frank Moser (GER)	1976	2001	yes-VCU	$13.1 K	$61.5 K	
Donny Opici (USA)	1979	2001	yes-Columbia	$0.9 K	$0.9 K	(retired)
Ogidi Obi (USA)	1975	2002	yes	$0.0 K	$0.7 K	(retired)
Jonathan Pastel (USA)	1976	2000	yes	$4.9 K	$4.9 K	(retired)
Andres Pedroso (USA)	1979	2001	yes-Duke	$12.6 K	$69.9 K	(retired)
Tripp Phillips (USA)	1977	2000	yes-UNC-CH	$12.9 K	$136 K	
Doug Root (USA)	1977	2000	yes-Duke	$14.6 K	$14.6 K	(retired)
Ryan Sachire (USA)	1978	2000	yes-Notre Dame	$17.6 K	$49.3 K	(retired)
Eric Taino (USA)	1975	1997	some	$313.4 K	$753 K	
Marcio Torres (BRA)	1981	2002	yes-UNC-G	$1.9 K	$17 K	(retired)
Brian Vahaly (USA)	1979	2001	yes-UVA	$48.0 K	$585 K	
John Valenti (USA)	1977	2001	yes-UNC-C	$0.1 K	$0.5 K	
Louis Vosloo (RSA)	1978	1997	no	$92.2 K	$133.7 K	(retired)
Jack Waite (USA)	1969	1993	yes	$589.1 K	$589.1 K	(retired)
Rogier Wassen (NED)	1976	1994	no	$227.3 K	$445 K	
Glenn Weiner (USA)	1976	1994	no	$250.3 K	$460 K	

Reference Sources and Additional Reading

Chapter 1: The College Debate

Blundel, N. 1995. *So You Want To Be A Tennis Pro?* A Lothian Book.

Coffey, W. 2005. Family Style. *USTA Magazine,* March/April.

Hackett, T. 2003. That Championship Season. *Tennis,* September.

Kodl, K. 2002. Wanted: Forehands or Forebrains. Is the Education of College Tennis Players on a String and a Prayer? *Tennis Week,* June 27.

McNulty, M. 2002. The Winds of Change. *USTA Magazine,* May/June.

Markowitz, D. 2004. When the Teacher is a Student. *Tennis Week,* October 23.

Chapter 2: Physical Toughness

ACSM Website. www.acsm.org.

Bloomer, R.J., Goldfarb, A.H. 2003. Can Nutritional Supplements Reduce Exercise-Induced Skeletal Muscle Damage? *Strength and Conditioning Journal* 25(5): 30-37.

Braden, V. 2002. What It Takes To Make A Champion: My Side Of The Court. *Tennis Week,* June 27, p 30.

DeVries, H. 1962. Evaluation of Static Stretching Procedures for Improvement of Flexibility. *Research Quarterly* 33: 222-29.

Gatorade Sports Science Institute. 2001. Genes and Sport: Are Your Parents Responsible For Your Wins and Loses? *Sports Science Exchange Supplement #83* 14:4.

Jones, Charlie and Doren, Kim. 2002. *Game, Set, Match. A Tennis Book for the Mind.* Andrews McNeel Publishing.

Keteyian, S.J. ACSM's Personal Trainer Certification Hits the Ground Running. ACSM's *Health & Fitness Journal* 9(2): 29.

Knudson, D.V., Noffal G.J., Bahamonde R.E. et al. 2004. Stretching Has No Effect on Tennis Serve Performance. *Journal of Strength and Conditioning Research* 18: 654-656.

Kovacs, M. 2004. A Comparison of Work/Rest Intervals in Men's Professional Tennis. *Medicine & Science in Tennis* 9(3): 10-11.

Kovacs, M. 2004. Energy System-Specific Training for Tennis. *Strength and Conditioning Journal* 26(5): 10-13.

Marks, B.L., Moore, T., Angelopoulos T.J., Galleher E., Katz L.M. 2003. Nutrition and Hydration Profile of Male Competitive Tennis Athletes. In *Tennis Science and Technology 2,* S. Miller (Ed). London: ITF, 263.

Marks, B.L., Galleher, E.W., Senga, M., Katz, L.M. 2004. U.S. College Tennis Athletes versus Australian International Scholarship Athlete. *Medicine and Science in Tennis* Volume 9, NR 1, April, 8.

McArdle, W.D., and Katch, F.L. 2001. *Exercise Physiology: Energy, Nutrition, and Human Performance*, 5th Edition. Lippincott, Williams, and Wilkins Publishers.

Moran, G.T., McGlynn, G.H. 1994. *Cross-Training for Sports*. Human Kinetics.

NSCA Website. Certification. www.nsca-lift.org.

NASM Website. Certification. www.nasm.org.

Nelson, A.G. and Kokkonen, J. 2001. Acute Balistic Muscle Stretching Inhibits Maximal Strength Performance. *Research Quarterly In Exercise and Sport* 72: 415-419.

Per Renstrom, A.F.H., ed. 2002. *Handbook of Sports Medicine and Science: Tennis*. Blackwell Science Publishers.

Pluim, S. and Safran, M. 2004. *From Breakpoint to Advantage: A Practical Guide to Optimal Tennis Health and Performance*. Racquet Tech Publishing.

Powers, S. and Howley, E. 2004. *Exercise Physiology: Theory and Application to Fitness and Performance*, 5th Edition. McGraw Hill Publishers.

Price, Robert G. 2004. *The Ultimate Guide to Weight Training for Tennis*, 3rd Edition. Cleveland: Price World Enterprises.

Shrier, I. 1999. Stretching Before Exercise Does Not Reduce the Risk of Local Muscle Injury: A Critical Review of the Clinical and Basic Science Literature. *Clinical Journal of Sports Medicine* 9: 221-227.

Sorace, P. and Lafontaine, T. 2005. Resistance Training Muscle Power: Design Programs that Work! *ACSM's Health & Fitness Journal* 9(2): 6-12.

USTA. *Complete Conditioning for Tennis*. 1998. Human Kinetics.

Chapter 3: Nutritional Toughness

Clark, N. 1990. *Nancy Clark's Sports Nutrition Guidebook*. Leisure Press.

Corley, G., Demarest-Litchford, M.I., Bazarre, T.L. 1990. Nutrition Knowledge and Dietary Practices of College Coaches. *Journal of the American Dietetic Association* 90(5): 705-709.

Craig, Jenny. 2003. Should You Count Those "Net Carbs" or "Low Impact" Carbs? www.geocities.com/Jenny_the_bean/products.htm (accessed April 24, 2006).

Groppel, J. 2003. The High Performance Plan: Nutrition. *Tennis*, March, 64.

Jacobson, B.H., Sobonya, C., and Ranson, R. 2001. Nutrition Practices and Knowledge of College Varsity Athletes: A Follow-Up. *Journal of Strength and Conditioning Research* 15(1): 63-68.

Katlan, Michelle. 2001. In the Balance. *Tennis,* August, 79-82.

Kleiner, S. M. 1998. *Power Eating*. Human Kinetics.

Marks, B.L., Moore, T., Angelopoulos, T.J., Galleher, E., Katz, L.M. 2003. Nutrition and Hydration Profile of Male Competitive Tennis Athletes. In *Tennis Science and Technology 2*, Edited by S. Miller. London: ITF, 261-270.

Marks, B.L., Angelopoulos, T.J., Shields, E., Katz, L.M., Moore, T., Hylton, S., Larson, R., and Wingo, J. 2004. The Effects of a New Sports Drink on Fatigue Factors in Competitive Tennis Athletes. In *Science and Racquet Sports III*. Edited by A Lees, J.F. Kahn, I.W. Maynard. London: Routledge Press, 9-14.

Maughan, R.J. and Murray, R. 2001. *Sports Drinks: Basic Science and Practical Aspects*. Boca Raton: CRC Press.

Mendosa, D. 2004. Can You Really Exclude Sugar, Alcohols, Glycerin, Polydextrose, and Fiber? www.mendosa.com/netcarbs.htm (accessed April 24, 2006).

Nelson, T.F. and Wechsler, H. 2001. Alcohol and College Athletes. *Medicine and Science in Sports and Exercise* 33 (1): 43-47.

Parsonage, S.R. 2000. Nutritional Status of Performance-Level Junior Players. In *Tennis Science and Technology*. Edited by S.J. Haake and A.O. Coe. London: ITF, 341-346.

Per Renstrom, A.F.H. Ed. 2002. *Handbook of Sports Medicine and Science: Tennis*. Blackwell Science Publishers.

Pierson, V.R. 2005. How Many Calories Does Your Body Need? The Fitness Jumpsite™ 1995-2005
http://www.primusweb.com/fitnesspartner/library/weight/calsburned.htm (accessed April 24, 2006).

Pluim, B. and Safran, M. 2004. *From Breakpoint to Advantage: A Practical Guide to Optimal Tennis Health and Performance*. Vista: Racquet Tech Publishing.

Shaffer, S. Filling the Tank. 2001. *Tennis*, October, 37.

Shifflet, B., Timm, C., and Kahanov, L. 2002. Understanding of Athletes Nutritional Needs Among Athletes, Coaches, and Athletic Trainers. *Research Quarterly for Exercise and Sport* 73(3): 357-362.

Chapter 4: Mental Toughness

Blundel, N. 1995. *So You Want To Be A Tennis Pro?* Lothian Book.

Bohling, C. 2002. Temper Your Temper. *Tennis*, April, 66.

Brawley, S. 2005. Game Plan: Mind Game. *Tennis,* July, ,36.

Brown, J. 2001. *Sports Talent*. Human Kinetics.

de la Torre, C. 2002. The Healing Power of Tennis. *Belmont Farms-USTA Challenger Program Guide*. Rocky Mount, NC., 39.

Fox, A. 2005. *The Winner's Mind. A Competitor's Guide to Sports and Business Success*. Racquet Tech Publishing.

Goldberg, A. 1997. *Sports Slump Busting*. Human Kinetics.

Greenwald, J. 2003. Solving the Riddle, Jeff Greenwald, *Tennis*, July, 62.

Hedgpeth, E. 2004. *It's a Matter of Mind*. UNC Printing Services.

Jones, C. and Doren, K. 2002. *Game, Set, Match. A Tennis Book for the Mind*. Andrews McMeel Publishing.

Kubler-Ross, E. 1969. *Death and Dying*. Simon & Schuster.

Markowitz, D. 2003. Saved By The Bell. The ATP Sends Its Players To Charm School. *Tennis*, December/January.

Murray, J.F. 2001. Get Smart. *Tennis*, December-January, 44-45.

Murray, J.F. 2002. Rebound Ace. *Tennis,* July-August, 62.

Orlick, T. 2000. *In Pursuit of Excellence*, 3rd Edition. Human Kinetics.

Orlick, T. 1998. *Embracing Your Potential*. Human Kinetics.

Smith, D. 2004. *The Carolina Way*. The Paragon Press.

St. John, A. 2001. The Throws of Passion. *Tennis,* September, 145-46.

Chapter 5: Develop Your Business Sense

Amalfi, A. 2004. Grateful Dead: Blake's Shorn Dreadlocks Raise Cash For Good. *Tennis Week*, February 23.

Ashe, A. and Rampersad, A. 1993. *Days of Grace: A Memoir*. New York: Knopf.

Avoiding Tax Audits. http://abclocal.go.com/kabc/features/Consumer/020304_fs_tax_avoid_audit.html (accessed Sept 25, 2004).

Bischoff, B. Avoiding an Audit. www.smartmoney.com/taxmatters/index.cfm?story=20030327 (accessed April 24, 2006).

Boris Becker faces fresh tax problems. Tues. Aug 5, 2003. *Daily Times*.

Broad-Based Income Taxes. http://www.ctj.org/html/spit.htm (accessed April 24, 2006).

Dodd, M. 2001. Athletes' Charities Tend To Be Small But Effective. *USA Today* July 20.

Evert, C. 2002. Charity Cases. Chrissy's page. *Tennis,* March.

Foreign Tax Credits. http://faculty.uncfsu.edu/jbalogun/foreigntaxcredits.doc.

Harwitt, S. Roddick, Courier Donate Time to Charities. www.tennisreporters.net (accessed April 24, 2006).

Internal Revenue Service. Small Bus/Self Employed. www.irs.gov (accessed April 24, 2006).

IRS Increases Mileage Rate Until Dec. 31, 2005. www.selfemployedweb.com/2005-mileage-rate-increase.htm (accessed March 3, 2006).

Quick Hits. *Tennis*, January, March, August, 2002.

Schick Xtreme III Tennis Challenge. *TennisRoundup*, Sept. 17, 2004. www.tennis-roundup.com/ofInterest/AgassiCancer.htm (accessed April 24, 2006).

Social Security Online. If You Are Self-Employed. www.ssa.gov (accessed April 24, 2006).

Tax Tips. www.accountingtechnologist.com/print_tips.htm (accessed April 24, 2006).

Tax Information for the Self-Employed. Jackson Hewitt Tax Service. www.jackson-hewitt.com/resources_library_topics_self.asp (accessed Arpil 24, 2006).

The Summons Power of the IRS. www.anti-irs.com/conklin/wc0118.htm (accessed April 24, 2006).

The Rules for Gifts. *Tax Gude for Investors.* Fairmark Press:
www.fairmark.com/begin/gifts.htm.

Toure. 2001. The Boy Who Fell to Earth, The Al Parker Story. *Tennis,* July/August.

Valenti, C. 2002. Famous Tax Slackers. Some Celebrities Who Fought the Losing Battle
with the Taxman. ABC News, April 15. http://abcnews.go.com/sections/business
(accessed April 24, 2006).

Chapter 6: Financial Planning

12 Players Names to 2001 USA Tennis Collegiate Team.
www.southerntennis.com/news_2001_usa_tennis_collegiate_team.shtml (accessed
Oct 10, 2004).

Becker, R. 2000. The Hard Road to Professional Tennis. *Tennis Match,* December.

Bureau of Internal Revenue, Republic of the Phillipines. www.bir.gov.ph/(accessed April
24, 2006).

Calendar/Results. 2006. www.stevegtennis.com. (accessed April 25, 2006).

Curry, T. 2003. Pro Circuit Celebrates 25 Years. *USTA Magazine,* May/June.

Intercollegiate Tennis Association (ITA). 2003. John Van Nostrand Memorial Award
Application Form. www.itatennis.com (accessed April 24, 2006).

IRS-U.S. Embassy Paris. www.amb-usa.fr/irs/taxtips10.htm (accessed April 24, 2006).

Lewis & Clark. Average Salaries of Head Coaches.
www.lclark.edu/~sports/misc/eada04public.htm (accessed April 24, 2006).

Martin, J. 2002. How Much Do Coaches On The Pro Tours Get Paid? Need To Know.
Tennis, November.

McNulty, M. 2004. The Winds of Change. *USTA Magazine,* May/June.

Quick Hits, *Tennis*, Aug. 2001, Sept. 2001, Nov. 2001, April 2003, Sept. 2003.

Schoenfeld, B. 2000. Rolling in Dough? *Tennis Match*, December.

University of South Carolina. USC releases salaries. Posted Wed., Apr 9, 2003.
http://www.thestate.com/sports/colleges/university_of_south_carolina/5591192.htm
(accessed April 24, 2006).

USC Releases Salaries.
www.thestate.com/mld/thestate/sports/colleges/university_of_south_caroli-
na/5591192.htm (accessed June 15, 2003).

USTA All-American Summer Team. www.collegeandjuniortennis.com/ustasm98.html,
www.collegeandjuniortennis.com/ustasum99.htm, and
www.collegeandjuniortennis.com/ustasum00.htm (accessed April 25, 2006).

Weil, D. 2004. The Bottom Line. *Tennis*, June.

Chapter 7: Your Sponsorship Plan

Brian Vahaly Official Website. www.brianvahaly.com.

Epstein, A. 2002. Marketing the Triathlete. www.thesportjournal.org/2002Journal/vol5-
no2/triathlete.htm (accessed April 24, 2006).

Finding a Sponsor. 2003.
www.tothenextlevel.org/old_site/docs/feature/finding_a_sponsor.html (accessed April 25, 2006).

Gallo, L. UNC Senior Associate Athletic Director and staff minutes review of NCAA By Law 16.12.1, extra benefit rule. Personal communication April 8, 2005.

Holcomb, T. 2003. Two for the Show. *Tennis Week,* July 22. www.tennisweek.com and www.brianvahaly.com/articles/twofortheshow.htm (accessed April 25, 2006)

Lainson, S. 1998. What is Sponsorship? The Creative Athlete, Issue 35. *SportsTrust.* www.onlinesports.com/sportstrust/creativeList.html. (accessed April 25, 2006).

Looking for three tour players to travel with this summer and will sponsor everything!!!! Carl B., May 11, 2002. www.stevegtennis.com.

Markowitz, D. 2000. The Fan: When You Got Nothin' You Got Nothin' To Lou's. *Tennis,* September, 92.

Promote-a-Pro Program. 2004. www.tennis.info.

Player Sponsorships, reply by book author, David Breslow, May 23, 2002, Tennis Business Discussion Forum, tennisbiz@tennisserver.com (accessed April 24, 2006).

Quick Hits. *Tennis,* June 2005, 23.

Sport England. Funding. www.sportengland.org/index/get_funding.htm (accessed April 25, 2006).

The 1997 Sports Sponsorship Survey. Sports Media Challenge. www.sportsmediachallenge.com/survey/CSsurvey.html (accessed April 24, 2006).

U.S. Figure Skating Association. 2000. Sponsorship Information and Suggestions for Figure Skating Athletes.

Chapter 8: Sponsorship Contract

Bloomquist & Halper. Sponsorship Deals Should Be Sealed With More Than A Handshake. http://library.lpfindlaw.com/articles/file/00668/004773/title/subjecty/topic/agriculture%20law.htm (accessed Nov 8, 2003).

Augustine-Schlossinger, Leigh. 2003. Endorsement Contracts for Professional Athletes.

Business Law Newsletter. *The Colorado Lawyer*, May 5.

Lech, D.W. 1999. *Doing Business With The Private Sector: A Commercial Handbook.* Ottawa, ON Canada: Centre for Sport and Law.

Gruen, D.T. 2002. *Legal Issues in Sports Sponsorship.* Team Marketing Report, Inc.

Hunter, R. 2000. *Sponsorship Agreements.* Matheson Ormsby Prentice.

Stotlar, D.K. 2001. *Developing Successful Sport Sponsorship Plans.* Fitness Information Technology.

Chapter 9: Do You Need A Sports Agent?

Leand, A. 2000. The Agent Game. *Tennis Match*, December.

Levey, J. 2005. Shooting Star. *Tennis,* August.

O'Keefe, K. 2003. Baseline: Popular Opinion. *Tennis,* April.

Pinter, E. Agents 2005. *Tennis Week,* August 29, 2005.

Quick Hits. *Tennis* July/August 2001, April 2003.

Schoenfeld, Bruce. 2000. Rolling in Dough? *Tennis Match.*

Stotlar, D. K. 2001. *Developing Successful Sport Sponsorship Plans.* Fitness Information Technology.

Weil, D. 2004. The Bottom Line. *Tennis.*

Weil, D. 2005. Baseline: The It Factor. Who's Getting Paid. *Tennis,* June.

Chapter 10: Matchmaking

Calendar and Results link. 2006. www.stevegtennis.com (accessed April 24, 2006).

Forums. www.stevegtennis.com.

Men's Professional Circuit Calendar. 2006. www.usta.com/schedule/custom.sps?itype=944&icustompageid=15910 (accessed April 25, 2006).

Tetley, J. 2006. India Satellite. www.itftennis.com/mens/news/newsarticle.asp?id=16304 (accessed April 24, 2006).

Chapter 11: Travel Toughness

ATP Men's Tour Website. www.atptennis.com.

Blundel, N. 1995. *So You Want To Be A Tennis Pro?* A Lothian Book.

Forums. www.stevegtennis.com.

Keil, M. and Grant, G. 2003. *The Journeymen.* Grant Associates (DVD). www.the-journeymen.com.

Pluim, B. and Safran, M. 2004. *From Breakpoint to Advantage: A Practical Guide to Optimal Tennis Health and Performance.* Racquet Tech Publishing.

Reese, D. 2003. Overseas Travel, Part I. www.tothenextlevel.org/old_site/docs/feature/overseas_travel.html 2006 (accessed April 25, 2006).

Chapter 12: Knowing When to Hang it Up

Arkush, M. 2002. The Remains of the Day. *Tennis,* July/August, 32.

ATP Men's Tour Website. www.atptennis.com.

Martin, T. 2003. What's the Rush? *Tennis,* 108.

McEnroe Inspired and Inspires. ATP insider. Feb 16, 2006 www.atptennis.com/en/newsandscores/news/2006/insider_0216.asp (accessed April 25, 2006).

St. John, A. 2001. Down, But Not Out. *Tennis,* June.

Toure. 2001. The Al Parker Story, The Boy Who Fell to Earth. *Tennis,* July/August.

Chapter 13: Looks Like You Made It

Holcomb, Todd 2006. ATP's Doubles Devotees Dwindling. The Atlanta Journal Constitutuion www.ajc.com/sports/content/sports/stories/0318tennis.html (accessed April 8, 2006)

ATP Men's Tour Website.Player Profiles, Donald Johnson. www.atptennis.com.

ATP Unveils Doubles Enhancements, June 30, 2005. http://www.atptennis.com/en/newsandscores/news/2005/doubles_changes.asp (accessed April 25, 2006).

Men's Tennis Website: www.stevegtennis.com. (accessed April 25, 2006).

Chapter (Lead-In) Quotes

Famous Yogi Berra Quotes. http://rinkworks.com/said/yogiberra.shtml. (accessed April 25, 2006).

Freeman, C. 1997. *The Tennis Lover's Book of Wisdom*. Walnut Grove Press.

Jones, C. and Doren, K. 2002. *Game, Set, Match. A Tennis Book for the Mind*. Andrews McNeel Publishing.

Professor Gabriel Robins' website, www.cs.virginia.edu/-robins/quotes.html (accessed April 25, 2006).

The Dumbest Sports Quotes of All Time. Comedy on Top. www.sportshollywood.com/dumbquotes.html (accessed April 26, 2006).

Wine, S. 2003. Maria Sharapova. *News and Observer Newspaper*, Durham, NC, June 2003.

Index

Index

Index